LONDON AND THE

London and the Civil War

Edited by

Stephen Porter
Assistant Editor
Royal Commission on the Historical Monuments of England

First published in Great Britain 1996 by
MACMILLAN PRESS LTD
Houndmills, Basingstoke, Hampshire RG21 6XS
and London
Companies and representatives
throughout the world

A catalogue record for this book is available
from the British Library.

ISBN 0–333–62279–0 hardcover
ISBN 0–333–65754–3 paperback

First published in the United States of America 1996 by
ST. MARTIN'S PRESS, INC.,
Scholarly and Reference Division,
175 Fifth Avenue,
New York, N.Y. 10010

ISBN 0–312–15844–0

Library of Congress Cataloging-in-Publication Data
London and the Civil War / edited by Stephen Porter.
p.   cm.
Includes bibliographical references and index.
ISBN 0–312–15844–0
1. Great Britain—History—Civil War, 1642–1649.   2. London
(England)—History—17th century.   I. Porter, S. (Stephen)
DA415.L66   1996
941.06'2—dc20
96–11521
CIP

---

10   9   8   7   6   5   4   3   2   1
05   04   03   02   01   00   99   98   97   96

Printed in Great Britain by
The Ipswich Book Company Ltd
Ipswich, Suffolk

Contents

List of Figures

Acknowledgements

In 1992 the Museum of London marked the 350th anniversary of the outbreak of the Civil War by presenting a series of lectures on London's involvement in the war. Revised versions of three of those lectures have been contributed to this collection of essays. I am very grateful to Geoffrey Toms, then Head of Education at the Museum, for inviting me to contribute to the lectures, which prompted me to focus my views on London in the 1640s and subsequently to contact others pursuing related interests. I have incurred numerous debts during the preparation of this book: to my contributors for their co-operation and for responding positively to my many queries, to Giovanna Davitti of Macmillan for her patience and help, to my colleagues at the Survey of London for bearing with me as the book developed, to Ian Roy for his support and generous assistance with my research into the Civil War over many years, to Joan Thirsk for her wise counsel and encouragement, and above all to my wife, Carolyn, not only for her help and advice, but also for maintaining her usual cheerful humour when it must at times have seemed that she was indeed living in a city at war.

STEPHEN PORTER

List of Abbreviations

A & O	*Acts and Ordinances of the Interregnum*, ed. C. H. Firth and R. S. Rait (London, 1911)
BL	British Library
CJ	*Commons' Journals*
CLRO	Corporation of London Record Office
CSPD	*Calendar of State Papers, Domestic*
CSPVen	*Calendar of State Papers, Venetian*
DNB	*Dictionary of National Biography*
GL	Guildhall Library
GLRO	Greater London Record Office
HMC	Historical Manuscripts Commission
LJ	*Lords' Journals*
PRO	Public Record Office
VCH	Victoria County History

Notes on the Contributors

Robert Ashton is Professor Emeritus and formerly Professor of English History, University of East Anglia. One of the leading historians of the Civil War period, his books include: *The Crown and the Money Market, 1603–1640* (1960), *The English Civil War: Conservatism and Revolution, 1603–1649* (1978 and 1989), *The City and the Court, 1603–1643* (1979) and *Counter-Revolution. The Second Civil War and its Origins, 1646–1648* (1994).

Ian Gentles is Associate Professor of History, Glendon College, York University, Toronto. He has written numerous articles on various aspects of the Civil War and the New Model Army, and *The New Model Army in England, Ireland and Scotland, 1645–1653* (1992).

Peter Kelsey is a chartered structural engineer whose principal field of activity is forensic work. His publications include a paper on the Civil War defences of London in *Veritas* (1991) and articles in journals related to the construction industry.

Lawson Nagel is a graduate of the University of Michigan, Ann Arbor. He was awarded a Ph.D. at King's College, University of London, in 1982 for his thesis on 'The Militia of London, 1641–1649'. After a career in publishing, he is now vicar of a parish near Chichester.

Stephen Porter is an Assistant Editor with the Survey of London, Royal Commission on the Historical Monuments of England. Author of a number of articles on urban history and the Civil War, his books include *A Gazetteer of English Urban Fire Disasters, 1500–1900* (1984, with E. L. Jones and M. Turner), *Exploring Urban History: Sources for Local Historians* (1990) and *Destruction in the English Civil Wars* (1994).

Keith Roberts graduated from the University of Leicester in 1977 and is now pursuing a career in banking. He is a military analyst and lecturer on the theory and practice of war between 1600 and 1660. His published work includes *London and Liberty* (1987), *Barriffe, A Civil War Drill Book* (1988), *Soldiers of the English Civil War 1: Infantry* (1989, 1991 and 1992) and several articles on the development of English military theory and practice.

Ian Roy has recently retired from the Department of History, King's College, University of London. He has written a number of articles and edited texts concerning the English Civil War, including the *Royalist Ordnance Papers*, in two volumes (1964, 1973), and has contributed chapters on the city and the University of Oxford in the same period, part of an ongoing study of three provincial cities in the seventeenth century.

Victor Smith is an historian of artillery fortifications and has a special interest in the conservation of defence heritage sites. He has worked on the research and restoration of fortifications in Britain and abroad and has published extensively. He is currently Conservation Officer of the Fortress Study Group and is Director of the New Tavern Fort Project at Gravesend.

Rosemary Weinstein is curator of the sixteenth- and seventeenth-century collections in the Museum of London. She is currently researching a unique regimental set of royalist cavalry colours from the Civil War, acquired by the Museum. Her recent publications include *Tudor London* (1994), 'The Tyssens, Lords of the Manor of Hackney: From Strangers to English Landowners', in *The Strangers' Progress*, Huguenot Society Proceedings (1994), and 'Women Pewterers in London, 1500–1800' in a forthcoming collection of conference proceedings on women's studies.

Introduction

Stephen Porter

When Thomas Hobbes wrote that 'But for the city the Parliament never could have made the war, nor the Rump ever have murdered the king' he was expressing the widely, indeed universally, held view that London had been of crucial importance to the parliamentarian cause during the Civil War. This was the opinion of contemporaries on both sides. In 1647 John Lightfoot told the House of Commons that it was 'London, that under a Parliament hath preserved a Nation; and London, that under God hath preserved a Parliament'.[1] Historians have seen little reason to dispute such judgements, for London was undoubtedly England's greatest single asset. The metropolis that consisted of London, Westminster and Southwark was by far the largest and richest city and its sheer size and wealth gave it a predominant position in the country's economic, social, legal and cultural life. Furthermore, it was the national capital, for Westminster contained the principal royal palace, the court and the meeting place of parliament, with all the trappings of government, the administrative machinery, the courts of law and the residences of foreign diplomats.

The climax of the political crisis of 1640–2 saw London and its resources lost to the king, before the war had even begun. On 10 January 1642, alarmed by the behaviour of the London crowds, he hastily left Whitehall Palace and did not return to the capital until he was brought in as a prisoner awaiting trial almost exactly seven years later. In leaving London so precipitously, Charles not only lost the use of its resources but also dramatically revealed the fragility of his own political position. A monarch who had lost control of his capital to the extent that he felt that he could no longer remain in it with safety was clearly in desperate straits. Such a manifestation of his weakness undoubtedly reduced his own prestige and credibility, among both his own subjects and foreign governments, deterring potential support. At the same time parliament benefited from the symbolic and diplomatic importance that attached to the national capital. More obviously and

1

fatally, the king had also resigned London's practical assets to his opponents: money, materials and the two immediate prizes contended for in the winter of 1641–2, the Tower, which contained the armoury and the mint, and the militia.

It may be an exaggeration to suggest that when the king relinquished control of London he effectively lost the war, for there were many other factors which helped to determine the outcome. Indeed, the king's cause revived remarkably during 1642, to the extent that he not only raised an effective army but in November posed a military threat to London that was checked only six miles from Westminster, at Turnham Green. This threat was sustained throughout the first half of 1643, which saw a rising tide of successes by the royalist armies, culminating in July in the capture of Bristol, the third city of the kingdom and second only to London as a port. In fact, many of the practical problems caused by his exclusion from the metropolis were overcome. In the autumn of 1642 a rival capital was established at Oxford, where the court reassembled, and which became the centre of royalist administration, a military headquarters and the meeting place of the royalist parliament summoned in 1644. On the other hand, the loss of the Navy's allegiance at the outset, the intervention of the Scots in 1644, inferior resources, organisational shortcomings, diplomatic blunders and, not least, errors of military judgement such as those that contributed to the crushing royalist defeats at Marston Moor and Naseby were all elements which ultimately produced the disintegration of the king's cause. Yet even when all of the many factors which influenced the outcome of the first Civil War are considered, the denial of the resources of London to the king and their successful mobilisation by parliament remains a crucial one.

I

The alienation of the majority of Londoners from the court was apparently complete by January 1642, when it was the threatening behaviour of the crowds that thronged Whitehall which caused Charles, concerned not only for the queen's safety but also for his own, to leave for Hampton Court. Although 'multitudes of gentry and soldiers' had made a show of strength in support of the king at the end of December, they were counted in hundreds rather than thousands and were unable to sustain effective resistance to the demonstrators, let alone restore order. Meanwhile, the growing *rapprochement* between leading figures in the City and the court was halted when those members of the governing élite of the City sympathetic to the king's cause were outflanked by the radicals following the elections to the common council on 21 December. During the next few weeks a series of measures, endorsed by parliament, shifted the balance of power on the corporation away from the lord mayor and aldermen to the common council, marginalising the king's supporters. Londoners were active participants in the political crisis, not merely observers of it.[2]

Hostile crowds attacked Lambeth Palace in May 1640, demonstrated in large numbers during the earl of Strafford's trial in the following spring, when already there were fears for the queen's security, and took to the streets in the winter months of 1641–2. The coincidence of the riots with Pym's offensives in the House of Commons was such that royalists, alarmed by the behaviour of the demonstrators and uncomfortably aware of their political potential, alleged that the crowds were manipulated and controlled by the radical leaders for their own ends. In truth, given the level of popular fears of a royalist coup or an attack by the increasing numbers of catholics who seemed to be lurking in the capital, together with the strong sense of community that existed in the City, little prompting was needed.[3] A climate had been created in which the king's political misjudgements quickly produced hostile reactions from the citizens. This is evident from the scale and speed of their response to his appointment of the manifestly unsuitable Colonel Thomas Lunsford as Lieutenant of the Tower on 23 December, at the height of the crisis, and his rash and bungled attempt to arrest the five MPs on 4 January. Given the partiality of observers who recorded their impressions of the demonstrations and the difficulty of estimating the size of crowds, it is impossible to know how many protestors were involved, but it is clear that on many occasions several thousand Londoners took to the streets.

The numbers signing the various petitions presented to parliament during this period were also counted in thousands: perhaps 15 000 signed the Root and Branch petition tendered in December 1640, at least 20 000 Londoners put their names to a petition against Strafford and 15 000 'Poor Labouring Men' supported a petition submitted on 31 January 1642 complaining about the effects of the economic recession. The demonstrators were often described as apprentices, and as many as 30 000 apprentices and those who had recently completed apprenticeships signed each of two petitions presented in December 1641, which implies that almost all the City's apprentices were subscribers.[4] Indeed, it is the scale of the opposition to the court which is significant, for the events of December and January 1641–2 demonstrated that effectively, if not unanimously, London's populace was behind the parliamentarian leadership.

Despite the large numbers involved and the highly charged atmosphere, which produced a panic in the City on the night of 6 January 1642, there was comparatively little violence. Dr Valerie Pearl has drawn attention to the comment of the French ambassador, M. La Ferté Imbaut, that had such events occurred in Paris blood would have been shed and his amazement that these dangerous days passed with so little bloodshed.[5] There were casualties none the less, especially during three days of fighting after Christmas 1641. Among those killed was Sir Richard Wiseman, who died as a result of injuries sustained during a clash at Westminster Abbey between demonstrators and the king's supporters. The apprentices took a collection to pay for his funeral,[6] the first, but by no means the most elaborate or significant, of the political funerals of the 1640s.

The French ambassador attributed the comparative calm which characterised the demonstrations to the orderly and disciplined conduct of the crowds, which contained citizens of the 'middling sort' as well as the apprentices, who came from a wide range of social backgrounds. Descriptions of the composition of the crowds during the crisis are no more reliable than the estimates of their size, however, and their identity was very much in the eye of the beholder; what one regarded as an uncontrollable rabble another saw as an orderly gathering of respectable citizens.[7] Nevertheless, it is clear that there was some variety in their character, depending on the nature of the protest and the area from which the demonstrators were drawn.[8] Those demonstrations in which the inhabitants of the eastern suburbs and Southwark were well represented were likely to have a different makeup from those in which the citizens of the City itself predominated. Some of the protestors operated as more or less coherent groups, such as the sailors who, demonstrating in January 1642, did not confine their protests to the immediate political concerns but also vented their wrath on traditional targets such as supposed bawdy houses.[9]

The apprentices, a much larger and more disparate group, were in greater evidence during the traditional holiday periods, such as May Day 1641, during Strafford's trial, and the twelve days of festivities following Christmas 1641.

The limited amount of violence, and the failure of the court to control the crowds, was also attributable to the unwillingness of the members of the trained bands, who were called out to restore order, to use force against their fellow citizens, as well as to the lack of organised support for the king.[10] Those who offered their support in December 1641 were soldiers, gentlemen, and students from the Inns of Court, rather than citizens. If there was a strong feeling in the capital in favour of the king, it was too disorganised and diffused to make an impact. Those elements among the mercantile élite who were still loyal to the crown, wished to resist the radicals, or were alarmed at the apparent breakdown in public order found their authority eroded during the early months of 1642 and failed to provide a focus for their fellow citizens who held similar views.

Nor had the clergy been able to sway Londoners in favour of the king and episcopacy, despite their personal allegiance, or even secure their own position. Indeed, London featured prominently among complaints about the clergy made during the early stages of the Long Parliament.[11] By 1648 perhaps as many as 132 London clergy had been sequestered or had resigned, including the incumbents of 96 of the 124 London benefices. This is hardly surprising, for the church and the crown held the advowsons of 80 of the 111 City parishes, in contrast to the rest of the country, where over 80 per cent were in lay hands. But this potentially powerful influence had not worked in favour of the established church. Many of the livings were poor and so were held in plurality, but more importantly the laity had bypassed the church through their control over the appointment of parish lecturers, the majority of whom were puritans. Under pressure from Laud the number of parish and other lecturers in the capital fell steadily in the years before the Civil War, from 121 in 1628 to 73 by 1640, but despite such pressure puritans still held over a half of the remaining posts.[12] Furthermore, those parishes beyond the control of the church and the crown also saw the appointment of puritan clergy. Indeed, St Stephen's Coleman Street developed a reputation as a strongly puritan parish and it was there that the five Members were said to have found refuge in January 1642.[13]

Any movement in favour of the court would have had to overcome the resentments against Laudian liturgical practices and the
persecutions of the 1630s, as well as the discontent caused by the
economic problems of the early 1640s, which were seen to be
bound up with the political crisis. Indeed, the religious and
economic issues were closely linked in the grievances of the
petitioners. Immediate solutions to the economic problems were
beyond them, but they were able to tackle some of the offending
religious practices. From 1640 onwards, congregations interrupted services, altered the liturgy, removed altars, altar rails and
organs, and destroyed or defaced popish images. In many cases
this was done with the consent of the vestries, in others without
it.[14] Yet despite the undoubted ascendancy of puritanism in the
capital and the power of the preachers, as the purveyors of both
news and opinions, there was a degree of popular opposition to
the prevailing mood. Some attempts to change the liturgical
arrangements were resisted, for example, and the bishops received
encouraging support. Petitions in their favour were circulated in
Southwark and in the City, where one supporting episcopacy
was 'much laboured' in early 1641, and was only abandoned
because it was thought that the argument had been won.[15] At the
other end of the religious spectrum, the members of the separatist
congregations – who probably numbered no more than about 1000
in 1642 – were the target for threatening crowds, which broke up
their meetings and laid violent hands on their leaders.[16]

The much-studied divisions among the mercantile élite and the
differing outlook and interests of the members of the various
trading companies were related in part to areas of trade. Those
merchants in the new, predominantly import-led, trades with the
Levant, East Indies and America were more likely to be pro-
parliamentarian than their counterparts in the older, cloth-based
and export-led, ones represented by the Merchant Adventurers,
although the distinction was by no means general or rigid. Similar
divisions were presumably repeated at the other, less easily
penetrated, levels of metropolitan society.[17] Indeed, it was inevitable
that the inhabitants of a city the size of London should hold a wide
range of opinions and it should be no surprise that it contained
many royalist sympathisers and Anglicans in 1641, or indeed
throughout the war. Its population was sustained by immigration from outside the capital. Rather over a half of apprentices
were drawn from beyond London and its neighbourhood,[18] and

the city also attracted the ambitious, those anxious to make or repair a fortune, aspiring members of the professions and those whose poverty drove them there more in desperation than hope. Immigrants brought with them their own political and religious assumptions and allegiances, derived from their families and communities, and doubtless retained many of these even after several years in the melting pot of the metropolis.

Whatever the complexity of the loyalties of the population, the tensions within the civic leadership, and indeed the events of 1641–2, the king lost control of London within a few weeks. With the elections to the common council and the steps which the new leaders of the City took to consolidate their power, the command of the militia and control of the Tower, London was secured for the parliamentarian cause in 1642.

II

Parliament retained the capital's allegiance throughout the first Civil War, despite fears of a royalist victory that would be followed by harsh retribution, and discontent at the high levels of taxation and the disruptive economic effects of the conflict. Some gloom and despondency was unavoidable, especially during the dark days in the spring and summer of 1643, with the string of royalist victories and parliament's increasingly burdensome financial demands as it struggled to pay for the war. Yet some saw London in the early 1640s as a refuge and others were immensely encouraged by what they found to be a city of opportunity, with its new-found intellectual freedom.

Fear of a brutal sack came partly from an awareness of the outcome of sieges during the Thirty Years' War, especially the looting and burning of Magdeburg by the Imperialists in 1631, and of the more recent and well-publicised horrors of the rebellion in Ireland. Propagandists whipped up such fears with gory tales of the atrocities in Ireland in order to draw parallels between what was happening there and what would inevitably happen in England should the court unleash a catholic army. The effect was to raise the level of foreboding in London and increase anxiety about its security. The problem for the parliamentarian writers was to keep popular apprehension at such a level that the citizens would continue to support the war effort, if only out of self-interest, but not to allow it to develop into widespread defeatism.

Apprehension there certainly was. The royalist successes in the early part of the war and the failure of the parliamentarian army under the earl of Essex to achieve the expected swift victory shook the resolve of some citizens. Inevitably, the first campaigns produced a degree of revulsion, when some soldiers failed to return, others were brought home wounded and maimed, and refugees from the towns sacked by the royalists began to arrive in London. The periodic influxes of demoralised troops and displaced persons during the next few years can have done nothing to raise morale or hopes of ultimate victory. The complaints of the apprentices who demonstrated in favour of peace in the winter of 1642–3 included the fact that some of their fellows had been killed. Unlike the protests of the previous winter, these demonstrations produced a reaction and counter-demonstrations by other groups of apprentices who were vociferously in favour of continuing the war.[19] Peace protests rumbled on intermittently during 1643, culminating in three days of demonstrations in the Palace Yard in early August 1643. The reluctance to take decisive action to prevent intimidation, particularly of the bishops, at the time of the tumults of 1641–2 had been replaced by a more brutally realistic attitude in these very different conditions and eventually the guards, reinforced by a detachment of Waller's horse, fired on the crowds and dispersed them, killing several protestors.

The sluggishness of the recovery from the recession of the early 1640s helped to fuel discontent. Although the war had brought some benefits to the capital's economy, it had also produced problems and an economic revival was impaired by many factors, even by such measures as the discontinuation of the annual lord mayor's show after 1639 and the closure of the theatres in September 1642. Both had provided not only pageantry and entertainment but also, directly and indirectly, a significant amount of employment.[20] One consideration behind the decision to close the theatres may have been an awareness of the need to prevent the exploitation of this potentially subversive medium as a channel for opposition views. It was justified on the grounds that 'Public Sports do not well agree with Public Calamities, nor Public Stageplays with the Seasons of Humiliation'. Clearly, puritan convictions were a strong motivation for taking that step as well as for the subsequent pressure to end the celebration of the religious festivals and to maintain strict observance of the sabbath. Even so, it was difficult to persuade Londoners to accept these changes in their entirety. For example, the churches remained closed on Christmas Day, but so did the shops. Those few shopkeepers who attempted to treat Christmas as just another weekday by opening for trade found themselves visited by groups of disapproving apprentices determined to enforce a complete closure. In 1647 and 1648 it even became necessary to call out the militia on Christmas Day to maintain order, and a riot in April 1648, provoked by an attempt to suppress sabbath breaking, required the attention of both the militia and the army.[21]

The image evoked by the closure of the theatres, the loss of the traditional holidays and the capital's economic problems is of a sombre citizenry deprived of its traditional pleasures. A pleasing corrective to this impression is provided by the example of Nehemiah Wallington and his family, who were not so depressed by events that they could not find the time to take an outing across the fields to Peckham on Easter Monday 1643. They cannot be accused of either indifference to the prevailing religious mood or unworldliness, for Nehemiah was an earnest puritan and an assiduous attender at sermons and lectures who maintained a close interest in affairs and the progress of the war. Even in the dark days of the spring and summer of 1643, as royalist victories mounted and fears grew of an attack on London, he still found grounds for hope, that 'God was preparing us for deliverance', although even his optimism was shaken by the news of Prince Rupert's capture of Bristol.[22]

Wallington's positive outlook was reflected in the scale of the response to the need for labour to construct the new fortifications encircling London. The various, overlapping, units of parish, ward, precinct and livery company within the City provided the sense of community and the organisational framework required for such a large-scale undertaking, as well as the basis for the social and political cohesiveness that characterised seventeenth-century London.[23] The suburbs had a much less elaborate administrative structure, but Southwark, at least, shared many of the characteristics that have been identified in the City.[24] Support for the construction of the works was not restricted to the City, for the volunteers also included the inhabitants of the suburbs, as well as the militia from all parts of the capital. This was only a small part of the contribution which the militia made to the parliamentarian war effort, for it was also a significant military force in its own right.

Nor did the militia regiments exhaust the manpower available from the capital, for large numbers were also recruited into the field armies.

Of even greater importance was the financial contribution which London made to the parliamentary cause. Its size and wealth ensured that it was the greatest contributor to the parliamentarian finances, a feature that was strengthened by the inability or unwillingness of county committees to pass on to the central treasury revenue which they had raised. London provided between a quarter and a third of the sums levied on the assessments, it probably maintained its share of the customs revenues, which before the war had been approximately 80 per cent of the national total,[25] and the excise was successfully imposed there (three of the eight commissioners appointed to administer it were City aldermen). Its importance to the economics of the parliamentarian war effort was not limited to the scale of the sums raised from it through taxation. Also crucial were the ability and willingness of the members of the corporation and livery companies to advance loans in anticipation of revenue, enabling the treasurers to bridge the gap between income and expenditure.[26] The practice ensured, for example, the provision of the £80 000 required for setting out the New Model Army in the spring of 1645.[27]

Inevitably, there was dissatisfaction at the unprecedentedly high levels of taxation. This was felt not only by those who deplored the outcome of the struggles of 1641–2 and questioned the legality of the impositions, but also among parliament's own supporters. The excise, in particular, provoked much resentment and complaints that it had led to price increases, while it became increasingly apparent that the repayment of the sums advanced as loans, and indeed interest on the capital, would take some time. It was not only the merchants and the wealthier citizens who had to wait for reimbursement, for the loans had been raised from a wider spectrum of the population; that floated in October 1643 raised £92 858 from 2047 subscribers, the majority of whom each contributed between £20 and £100.[28] Despite the problems and resentments, with competent organisation, perhaps aided by the difficulties of evasion, especially in the well-regulated City parishes, parliament's officers were able to exploit London's wealth to support the war effort. This was a resource which the king was simply unable to match, despite the affluence of some of his supporters.

The tax burden was one of the aspects considered by a writer who, in 1648, pondered the relative advantages of life in the town and the village in time of war. Taxation, he decided, was one of the drawbacks of the town, as were the compulsion to take up arms as a citizen-soldier and the risk of famine and disease during sieges. He concluded that the village was the safer place to live.[29] Nevertheless, London provided a refuge during the Civil War for those who felt threatened or vulnerable in the countryside. They included clergymen such as William Taylor, who held the living of Cirencester but moved to London after that town was sacked in 1643,[30] John Tombes, the vicar of Leominster, and Walter Cradock and members of his church at Llanvaches in Monmouthshire, who first sought shelter in Bristol and then, following its capture by the royalists in July 1643, in London.[31]

Others who arrived in London were drawn there not so much to escape the hazards they faced elsewhere but because of the opportunity which it presented for debate, change and reform. Religious exiles who had emigrated during the years of the Laudian ascendancy returned from the Netherlands and New England. Many of the clergy wished to contribute to and influence the deliberations on ecclesiastical reform of the Westminster Assembly, established in July 1643. The debate was not restricted to the clergy, for many Londoners had an informed interest in religious issues. The Bohemian intellectual Jan Comenius arrived in London in 1641 and was impressed to see how many members of a congregation not only gave attentive interest to the sermon, but also made shorthand notes.[32] There were even fears that the discussions were becoming too involved and prolonged and that there was a danger that opportunities for reform would be missed. In 1644 Edmund Calamy complained that Londoners had spent too much time considering church discipline and in doing so had 'almost disputed away their repentance'.[33]

Comenius was also struck by the number of bookshops. With the lifting of censorship as the authority of the church courts collapsed, there was a veritable explosion of printing after 1640. London's population had a high rate of literacy and the capital contained by far the largest share of the printing trade, producing all kinds of material during the 1640s. Material printed elsewhere was also circulated in the capital. The bookseller George Thomason collected a copy of every publication that he came across. This amounted to 24 items in 1640, 721 in 1641 and a staggering 2134

in 1642. Parliament's attempt at regulation, introduced in July
1643, reduced the number somewhat, but Thomason still collected
an average of 1413 items each year from 1643 to 1647, and the
number then rose again, to 2036 in 1648.[34] From faltering beginnings
in late 1641 and 1642 newsbooks became an established part of
the London scene, purveying news, information and propaganda
spiced with a degree of invective. By the beginning of 1644 a
dozen titles were available on London's streets each week and
throughout 1645 and the first quarter of 1646 an average of fourteen
appeared; Thomason collected 4044 newsbooks during the 1640s.
Not all of these supported parliament, for clandestinely printed
royalist newsbooks were also issued in the capital. They included
the long-running *Mercurius Aulicus*, which was printed in London
as well as in Oxford for much of the first Civil War.[35]

It was the availability of royalist items in London, the subversive
nature of some pamphlets and the objections of the Stationers'
Company to the fact that their copyright was disregarded in many
cases which caused parliament to attempt to regulate printing. Milton's
tracts on divorce were caught up in this, prompting his response in
favour of freedom of the press in *Areopagitica*, which contains a
splendidly evocative portrayal of the intellectual ferment in London:

> a city of refuge, the mansion-house of liberty, encompassed and
> surrounded with His protection; the shop of war hath not more
> anvils and hammers waking, to fashion out the plates and
> instruments of armed justice in defence of beleaguered truth,
> than there be pens and heads there, sitting by their studious
> lamps, musing, searching, revolving new notions and ideas
> wherewith to present, as with their homage and their fealty,
> the approaching Reformation; others as fast reading, trying all
> things, assenting to the force of reason and convincement.[36]

This was a far different atmosphere from that in the London of
the 1630s, when the ambitious men hanging around the court in
the hope of obtaining a profitable share in a project were akin to
'a band of hopeful adventurers swarming like bees around a
honeypot'.[37] Now the attraction for many was the opportunity to
shape the future rather than make immediate profit. Robert Baillie,
the Scottish divine, wrote that 'God is making here a new world'
and Samuel Hartlib urged Comenius to 'Come, come, come; it is
for the glory of God'.[38]

Hartlib and his circle had a wide agenda and through their extensive circle of correspondents they actively promoted the exchange and dissemination of knowledge and ideas. While some of their aims were unattainable, others, such as their efforts to promote agricultural improvement, did achieve practical success.[39] From their interest in educational reform emerged proposals for a university in London. The possibility had been mooted in the Westminster Assembly in 1643, primarily as an institution for training clergymen, and the idea was also put forward as a way of providing for refugees from Oxford University and students who were kept from their studies there by the war.[40] During the 1640s Hartlib's circle produced various plans for a federal university incorporating existing institutions, such as Gresham College; in their most mature form they described a university consisting of eleven colleges. Hartlib may have been the author of a pamphlet published in 1647 that was addressed to the lord mayor, aldermen and common council advocating 'the present Founding [of] an University in the Metropolis'. These schemes did not mature, however, and London's first university did not open until 1828.[41] On the other hand, the weekly meetings of scientists that began in London in the mid-1640s were later recognised as the precursors of the Royal Society.[42]

In such a climate of questioning and reform it was perhaps inevitable that the corporation itself should come under close scrutiny, and almost as inevitable that the Leveller John Lilburne should emerge as its chief critic. While incarcerated in the Tower in 1646 he was able to consult the copies of the City's charters that were kept there and develop points that he had raised earlier. In two pamphlets published in that year he attacked the existing system on the grounds that the commons' right of annual election of the lord mayor, sheriffs, aldermen and city officers had been denied them, and his calls for reform extended to demands for an investigation into the uses to which the City's finances were put. His complaints about the oligarchic nature of the City's government also included the organisation of the livery companies.[43] But agitation of this kind, even by so persuasive an advocate as Lilburne, was not going to bring about reform of the City's constitution, even though his demands were limited to the rights of the freemen of the City and he did not make any appeals for the extension of the freedom to those who were excluded from it. The changes made in 1642, as the radicals consolidated their position, had shifted the balance within the existing system rather than altered it. The radicals' political effectiveness had waned after 1643, but the moderates who held power at Guildhall during the mid-1640s did not attempt to reverse these arrangements.[44]

One reform that was attempted, with the support of the moderates, was the reorganisation of church government along Presbyterian lines. The Ordinance for the Election of Elders of August 1645 included a scheme for the capital in which the parishes were divided into twelve classes within the Province of London. Parliament ordered the implementation of the system in June 1646, despite objections from those who saw it as an enfeebled version of the full-blooded Scottish model which they had expected.[45] Some vestries moved briskly to adopt the system, elect elders and constitute themselves as presbyteries. The Fourth Classis, the only one for which records survive,[46] was formed in November 1646 and the First Synod of the Province of London met for the first time in May 1647.[47] Despite the undoubted numerical strength and organisation of the Presbyterians in London, the influence of the Presbyterian divines, the active encouragement of the Scottish commissioners, and the extent of political support, both on the common council and within parliament, the system was never fully adopted.[48] Only eight of the twelve proposed classes were formed and the example of the Fourth Classis shows that not all of the parishes within the eight classes adopted the system and were constituted as presbyteries.[49]

This reorganisation was carried out against a background of rising tension in the capital as the apparent puritan consensus disintegrated. The religious and intellectual freedom of the 1640s had allowed the separatists to emerge into the open, attracting increasing support and at the same time fragmenting as doctrinal issues were probed and debated.[50] To the dismay of those who desired and expected orderliness and conformity, some discussions were held by those who were not only not ordained but were from distinctly humble backgrounds. There were even weekly public lectures near Coleman Street in 1645 that were established by women, alarming both because of their success in attracting 'a world of people' and the 'confusion and disorder' that marked the discussions that followed the lectures.[51] To many in the City the existence of increasing numbers of Independents and sectaries outside the parish system threatened the breakdown of the order which that system represented. The sectaries, in particular, were regarded as the prime movers in the withholding of tithes, without which the parish clergy could not be maintained. Senior Presbyterian figures such as William Prynne and John Bastwick mounted a fierce attack during the mid-1640s that was ably supported by Thomas Edwards's caustic pen, most effectively in his brilliant polemic *Gangraena* (1646). This did much to discredit the separatists in the eyes of those fearful of a descent into religious, social and moral disorder. Indeed, social conservatism was an important ingredient in the support which the Presbyterians enjoyed.[52] The separatists, on the other hand, were all too aware that their freedom of worship was threatened by the Presbyterians' insistence on ecclesiastical uniformity, that they were in danger of exchanging Laudian for Presbyterian repression.

The reaction to the rise of the separatists produced a campaign of petitioning and lobbying, punctuated by such notable events as the expulsion of Henry Burton from his lectureship and the removal of the Presbyterian-turned-Independent John Goodwin from the living of St Stephen's Coleman Street. Burton was, with Prynne and Bastwick, one of the most celebrated victims of Laudian persecution, but despite his standing he was prevented from continuing his weekly lectures at St Mary Aldermanbury by a lock-out by the committee representing the subscribers who funded the lectures, while Goodwin had given offence by restricting the sacrament to those whom he regarded as the godly, thereby 'unchurching' many of the parishioners and effectively creating a separatist congregation within the parish system.[53] His ejection gives a false impression of the parishioners' loyalties, however, for the vestry represented only a section of the population and St Stephen's was still a centre of sectarian activity.[54] This limitation is also implicit in the evidence for the other parishes and, together with nomenclatural imprecision, makes it impossible to establish with any certainty the level of support for the separatists in the capital. It is glimpsed occasionally in the numbers presenting petitions; as many as 20 000 were said to have subscribed to that submitted to the House of Commons in May 1646. But even if this provides a reasonable indicator of the scale of their support, they were still a small minority.

Despite the rise of the separatists, which was anxiously chronicled by their opponents, the Presbyterians were still by far the most numerous group in the capital. Although the scheme for Presbyterian church government was never fully implemented and its proponents had run out of energy by the end of the decade, as their political counterparts had been eclipsed by the army and its allies among the Independents, what had been established apparently remained in place. Both the Fourth Classis and the Provincial Assembly continued to function throughout the period of the Commonwealth and Protectorate. Furthermore, on the tide of conservatism and reaction Anglican clergymen who had been sequestrated only a few years earlier returned to the City, initially on an occasional basis and later as lecturers and ministers.[55]

Although aware that overt political activity could provide their opponents with further opportunity to characterise them as dangerously subversive, the separatists also realised that ultimately they were dependent for their freedom to worship openly on political power rather than theological argument. They therefore petitioned parliament and lobbied and demonstrated at Guildhall in order to maintain attention on their campaign for religious toleration. They certainly provided a body of potential support for the Levellers, who emerged in the summer of 1646 as a political force with a much more radical and secular programme and acted as a focus not only for the separatists but also for those citizens whose grievances were as much economic as religious.[56] Skilful campaigning through pamphlets and petitions, cleverly orchestrated by Lilburne, gave the Levellers much publicity and they were able to attract many supporters to their cause during the late 1640s.

The political tensions between, on the one hand, the essentially conservative Presbyterians – whose position was strengthened by their successes at the common council elections in December 1646 – and, on the other, the radical Independents and Levellers, were set against a background of simmering discontent, which occasionally found practical expression. Taxation remained a major grievance and, even before the first Civil War had been brought to an end, in the summer of 1646 payment of the monthly assessments fell dramatically. Only a little over a quarter of the sums due from the City for the period June to September was received and, as payment was not enforced thereafter, the arrears continued to mount, reaching £64 337 by the summer of 1647 and £80 000 by October 1648. The excise, too, was immensely unpopular, not least with the butchers, and during riots in Smithfield in early 1647 the excise house was burnt down, together with its records.[57] The early months of 1647 also saw a new upsurge of agitation by the apprentices, focused largely on their dissatisfaction over the loss of holidays, coupled with a renewal of their objections to the number of foreigners trading in the capital. Early in 1647 they began a campaign of petitions and demonstrations for a monthly holiday to replace the days which had been lost. This was a concern which parliament needed to address in any case, in order to clarify the situation, and the campaign was eventually successful. On 10 June 1647 the second Tuesday of every month was designated as a holiday and the religious holidays were abolished.[58]

To this heady brew of religious and political tension, popular dissatisfaction, the political alignment of the City leadership with the Presbyterians in parliament and, in April 1647, the gaining of control of the City Militia Committee by the Presbyterians at Guildhall, was added the further spice of the discontented and dispossessed who drifted to London after the end of the war. They included ex-soldiers of both sides and royalists, some of whom were literally at a loose end and looking for opportunities, who were there to compound for their delinquency in order to avoid harsher punishment. Such men provided the material for a force to bolster the City's leaders in their opposition to the army. Following the tumults at Westminster in July 1647 – when parliament was invaded and the Members of both Houses intimidated – this force was placed under the command of three former parliamentarian generals. But the attempted counter-revolution within London collapsed in the face of the New Model's threat to occupy the City, a threat which it was able to carry out unopposed.[59]

There was considerable irony in the fact that London, which had not only escaped a royalist invasion during the war but had done so much to maintain the parliamentarian armies in the field, should find itself occupied by the most successful of those armies less than a year after the first Civil War had ended. Whatever the army's resentments regarding such matters as the citizens' withholding of the assessments, and therefore the soldiers' pay, the occupation was a peaceful one. Indeed, the troops, whose behaviour was exemplary, were even cheered when they paraded through the city on 7 August.[60] The capital therefore emerged unscathed from this experience, perhaps the one most feared by an early modern city at war, although apprehension regarding the soldiers' conduct remained. The Independents, at least, had cause to celebrate the failure of the Presbyterian coup, which was followed by the installation of a lord mayor, John Warner, acceptable to the army.

London avoided direct involvement in the second Civil War in 1648. Nevertheless, the aftermath of the war saw the return of the army to the City in December 1648 and the purge of the House of Commons by Colonel Pride. Once again, the annual common council elections played a crucial part in determining control of the corporation. Those who in 1647 had petitioned for a personal treaty with the king were disbarred from the elections on 21 December, producing a dramatic change, with over a half of the councillors supplanted and the radicals achieving a dominant position. In contrast to the summer of 1647, the behaviour of the troops was not above reproach in the eyes of many citizens, while, from the army's point of view, the tax strike that had begun in 1646 was finally brought to an end.[61]

III

In some ways London's experience of war during the 1640s was comparable in kind, if not in scale, with that of the provincial towns and cities. Their citizens, too, were presented with the opportunity to profit from supplying the military, and their role as the centres of the administrative frameworks created by both sides in order to finance and organise their efforts brought further employment. The commissariats' requirements were not only for clothing, footwear, arms and horses on a large scale, but also for food and drink, and a range of goods and services. At Gloucester the garrison employed carpenters, masons, blacksmiths, iron-founders, cutlers, gunsmiths, a book-binder, shoemakers, wood-cutters, charcoal-burners, a ropemaker, coopers, vintners, apothecaries, surgeons, carters and boatmen.[62] Unskilled labour was required for the construction and maintenance of the defences and at most towns a citadel as well.

As in London, the war provided the conditions in which it was possible to challenge the *status quo* in civil government and religion, resulting in political purges of the governing body and the displacement of clergy. Unlike London, those towns which were garrisoned faced the problem of satisfying the demands of a military government operating independently of the corporation. Clashes of interest and jurisdiction occurred even where the loyalties of the military and civil administrations coincided, and where they conflicted the most prominent citizens faced not only removal from office, but heavy fines and even imprisonment. Contentions between the military and civilians were most acute in the areas directly affected by the fighting. Only roughly one-sixth of the larger English towns, and only Norwich among the regional capitals, lay in East Anglia and the South East, outside the war zone. Few of those within the disputed areas escaped unscathed and Londoners' fears of siege, assault and the quartering of troops became a reality for the citizens of many towns, together with high taxation, an influx of refugees, epidemic disease, enlistment, the destruction of property, economic dislocation and acute shortages of food and fuel during sieges.

Several of the larger cities suffered severely. Newcastle's economy was disrupted by the parliamentarians' blockade of the Tyne, the city was captured after a destructive assault by the Scottish army in 1644 and it experienced a severe outbreak of plague in the following year. York, too, was badly affected. Although the war was not the fundamental cause of the city's problems, they were undoubtedly exacerbated by the conflict, particularly the long siege of the city in 1644. Recovery was a very slow process that lasted throughout the second half of the century.[63] Bristol was stormed by the royalists in 1643 and by the New Model in 1645. It suffered high levels of mortality, especially during an outbreak of typhus in 1643 and a severe plague epidemic in 1645.[64] When recaptured by the parliamentarians in that year the city was 'more like a prison than a City, and the people more like Prisoners than Citizens; being brought low with taxations, so poor in Habit, and so dejected in countenance'.[65] Exeter was also besieged and changed hands twice, although by treaty rather than assault, and it, too, experienced a typhus epidemic in 1643. By the end of the war virtually all of its suburbs had been destroyed. The effects of the war in the West Country, especially the disruption of the cloth industry, and parliamentarian blockades of the Exe when the city was in royalist hands combined to inflict considerable damage to its trade.[66]

Few of the towns of the second rank within the war zone were unaffected by the Civil Wars, and many endured at least one siege, in some cases culminating in a destructive assault. For these, the benefits brought by military expenditure had to be set against the injurious effects of war. Even Oxford, a potential gainer at London's expense by the removal there of the court, was in a squalid and impoverished state by the time it surrendered in 1646.

The royalist occupation had brought new business, but also over-crowding, with all of the attendant practical problems. During the war years there had been a typhus epidemic, a major fire and heavy impositions, with the university, which was operating on a much reduced scale, mulcted as heavily as the citizens.[67] Nor did all of those towns within the areas under parliamentarian control in the first Civil War escape. Colchester, for example, was a clothing town well away from the fighting, and potentially a beneficiary from the war, until its occupation by the royalists in 1648 led to a particularly hard-fought and damaging siege, topped by a hefty fine imposed on the town by the victorious parliamentarians for harbouring the royalist army.[68]

Seen in this context, London had not lost ground against the other major English cities, all of which, except Norwich, suffered much more directly and seriously from the conflict than did the metropolis. Their problems and the disruption of internal trade inevitably had a detrimental effect on London, but its role in the national economy was such that alternative sources of supply and routes to the capital were developed, rather than new markets elsewhere.

IV

By the outbreak of the Civil War London was a large and complex city, its size and growth fascinating contemporaries and alarming the governments of the early Stuarts. It experienced a remarkably rapid expansion of population in the first half of the seventeenth century, fuelled by immigration and unchecked by three severe outbreaks of bubonic plague. Such expansion inevitably affected all of the capital's component parts: the City itself, governed by the corporation, and the growing suburbs, especially those to the east and the west, and the south bank. In Chapter 1 Rosemary Weinstein examines the character of these areas and the contrasts between them in terms of their relative wealth, economic and social structure, and health, as well as the changes that were taking place in the years before the Civil War. The burgeoning population required the expansion of many of the older industries and services, and new ones, such as glass-making and ceramics, were developed. With the demand for housing, the built-up area grew ever outwards, and the face of the capital was also changing, with the introduction, under the patronage of the court, of the classical architectural styles which were favoured by Inigo Jones, but were not necessarily to the taste of the bulk of the populace. There was a similar contrast between the popular culture of the citizens and that of the gentry, who increasingly spent a part of the year in the capital, on the one hand, and the polite culture of the court and its followers on the other.

In Chapter 2 Robert Ashton examines the shifting loyalties of the City authorities during the 1640s, looking at the events of 1641–2, the counter-revolution in London in 1647, and the capital's role in the second Civil War in the following year. He shows how the disenchantment and exasperation of the City with the policies of Charles I's government during the 1630s were being steadily assuaged during late 1641, but that the process was halted by the elections to common council in December, which helped to secure London for the parliament's cause. There were marked parallels between parliament's actions in curtailing the prerogative of the crown and the shift in power within the City's government. There was also an affinity of outlook in 1647, with conservative, Presbyterian, groups dominant both in parliament and at Guildhall. The balance was upset, firstly by the army's seizure of the king in early June and, secondly, by the reconstitution, in late July, of the City Militia Committee by parliament, acting under pressure from the army, which was alarmed at the Committee's role in building a counter-revolutionary force in the capital. The subsequent crowd disturbances culminated in the invasion of parliament. This gave the army ample justification for its occupation of London in early August, which, as in 1642, was followed by a purge of the aldermanate. Professor Ashton argues that this experience was a major reason for London's non-involvement in the second Civil War, together with the dropping of charges of impeachment against the former lord mayor and aldermen who had been incarcerated in the Tower since the failed counter-revolution of the previous year, and the appointment of Philip Skippon to command of the militia.

Control of London's militia had been no less crucial to control of the capital itself during the crisis which preceded the outbreak of the first Civil War. In Chapter 3 Lawson Nagel details the process by which command of the militia was secured by Pym's allies in the City, and the subsequent changes in its organisation. During the crucial first few weeks of 1642 the new Committee of

Safety, shortly to become the Militia Committee, was established by common council and was subsequently given considerable powers by the House of Commons. In particular, the right to call out the militia, formerly vested in the lord mayor, was now transferred to the whole corporation. The Commons then further intervened to limit the lord mayor's authority and extend the Committee's influence. Shortly afterwards the king virtually conceded control of the Tower when he appointed the puritan Sir John Conyers to succeed Sir John Byron as its Lieutenant. While these moves were vital in making London safe for the parliamentary cause, they also had a wider significance, perceived by both sides, for the control of the militia elsewhere. The Militia Committee reorganised and expanded the trained bands during the spring of 1642 and London also contributed officers and men, although not the militia regiments, to the field army raised by the earl of Essex during the summer. By the time that the militia had halted the king's advance on London at Turnham Green in November it had, as Dr Nagel shows, undergone a number of significant changes in command structure and organisation since the beginning of the year.

The militia regiments were London's chief military asset, vital for the defence of the capital, as they demonstrated at Turnham Green, and on occasion an invaluable component of the parliamentarian armies. At full strength the militia and the auxiliary regiments, raised in 1643, mustered 20 000 foot and two regiments of horse, a force that was larger than the population of any provincial city except Norwich. The performance of the militia in the Second Bishops' War had done much to bring the military value of all militia forces into contempt, but, as Keith Roberts shows in Chapter 4, this was unjustified as far as the London trained bands were concerned. They had not served in the Second Bishops' War and their conduct in the Civil War far exceeded expectation. This was attributable partly to the commitment, deriving from a strong sense of community, of the militia soldiers themselves and partly to the success of the training provided by the Society of the Artillery Garden.

The Society should be seen in the context of the continental urban military guilds and due credit given to its members' awareness of current military practices. Their expertise was employed to train their men to use modern Dutch infantry practices, intended to be employed in set-piece battles. Such preparation gave the trained bands the capability of being far more than just a local defence force, and when their potential for service with the field armies was realised by their conduct with the earl of Essex's army on the Gloucester campaign, the strategic balance in southern England was considerably altered. Their training made them less suitable for the kind of campaigns waged by Sir William Waller, however, and their experience under his command was distinctly less happy than that undertaken under Essex. Indeed, the trained bands' service with Waller has tended to tarnish their reputation.

The freedom of the trained bands, and indeed of Essex's army, to operate away from London was only possible because the capital was protected by extensive fortifications. These were the longest continuous defensive circuit to have been built in Britain since Roman times and their construction, by the thousands who appeared each day during the spring of 1643 to carry out the work, reflected both the willingness of the citizens to support the parliamentary cause at a difficult time and their concern for the defence of their city and community. Their achievement is impressive, not least for the degree of organisation involved. As Victor Smith and Peter Kelsey show in Chapter 5, although these fortifications were of a relatively unsophisticated nature in terms of contemporary continental urban defences, they were effective both in freeing the parliamentary forces to operate without constantly having to cover the capital and as a security circuit enabling passage into and out of London to be controlled. Curiously, there is no known contemporary plan of the fortifications, but from descriptions of the 1640s and later cartographic and name evidence it is possible to trace the line of the works and identify their features. Although their demolition was ordered in 1647, some remains were still recognisable well into the nineteenth century and indeed the vestiges of a fort can still be identified in the south-east corner of Hyde Park.

The size and quality of the trained bands and the encircling fortifications gave London considerable military strength. Yet the possibility of a royalist victory has generally been considered in military terms, with speculations on the likely effects of the mobilisation of support for the king in Kent, followed by co-ordinated attacks down the Thames valley and from the south-east of the capital. The seeds of the idea of an apparently coherent royalist strategy for an attack on the capital were sown by Charles himself, through his agent Henry Heron, who was in London early in 1643. In fact, as Ian Roy discusses in Chapter 6, the king mounted a political and propaganda offensive, seeing London in terms of a loyal population misled by a malicious clique and believing that the majority of citizens were untainted by the religious and political radicalism of the new leadership in the City. Despite the difficulties between the crown and the City in the 1630s and resentment of the role played by the London crowd during the crisis of 1641–2, the king's entourage regarded the radicals and puritans as a manipulative and unrepresentative minority. This view was encouraged by the existence of royalist supporters among the City's élite and the agitations of a numerous peace party in 1643. But the king's attempts to persuade the citizens to return to their true allegiance were nullified, not least by the discovery of the plot organised by Tompkins and Challoner in the spring of 1643, which exposed his duplicity in pursuing negotiations while encouraging an armed coup. That support for the peace party and for the king's cause had fallen away in the summer of 1643 was recognised by the author of the brilliant royalist satire *A Letter from Mercurius Civicus to Mercurius Rusticus*. He used his extensive knowledge to outline and condemn the process by which the radicals had achieved control of the capital. Denouncing the city as one of the causes of the Civil War and the chief support of the parliamentarian cause, the author – probably John Berkenhead – took a gloomy view of the likelihood of Londoners returning to their rightful loyalty to the king and saw the solution to the rebellion in terms of forcibly bringing the capital to heel.

The measures aimed at disrupting the city's economy were unlikely to help the king to regain the citizens' loyalty, for the economic malaise had been one of the underlying causes of popular discontent with the government in the early 1640s and the war had exacerbated the problems. It had undoubtedly brought some benefits, but also added to the city's difficulties, inevitably so, given the extent of London's integration in the national economy, which was increasingly disrupted. These gains and losses, and the ability of the city's economy to respond to the changes in the short-term, are examined in Chapter 7. London benefited from the presence of parliament, its role as the headquarters of parliamentarian administration, and the supply of a range of goods and military equipment to the troops. But problems were caused by an acute shortage of fuel resulting from parliament's own blockade of the ports from which coal was shipped to London, the royalist occupation of many of the areas that served as both suppliers and markets for the capital, the absence of men with the forces, low levels of overseas trade, the unwillingness of those who normally brought business to the capital to travel there during the war, and the absence of the royal court and its satellites. Although alternative supplies were found – there do not seem to have been grain shortages in London during the war, for example – the necessary adjustments to very changed conditions took time to effect and some of the problems, such as the absence of the court, were insoluble so long as the war continued. Some citizens undoubtedly gained from the opportunities which the war provided, but many others complained that their businesses suffered. At a time of exceptionally high taxation the capital also had to cope with the increasing numbers of poor, provision for the wounded and for royalist prisoners, and an upsurge in the number of plague victims. It seems that the net effect of the war upon the metropolitan economy was a negative one, that London was a loser rather than a gainer during the years of the first Civil War.

Wartime disruption did not displace London from its position at the centre of political and cultural life, and it remained the stage for national political spectacles. In Chapter 8 Ian Gentles examines its role as the setting for large-scale political funerals during the 1640s, which contrasted with Charles I's neglect of public ceremonial and the burials of his unpopular ministers; the necessary restraint at Buckingham's funeral and the private interments of Strafford and Laud. His study looks at four such funerals, each of which provided the opportunity for political propaganda, contrasting the official ones of John Pym, one of the leaders in the Commons, and the earl of Essex, parliament's popular former Lord General, with the unofficial revolutionary celebrations at the interments of Colonel Thomas Rainborowe and a private soldier, Robert Lockyer.

The official funerals were orderly, closely regulated affairs, designed to focus attention on the greatness of the deceased, both of whom had died naturally, and therefore of the cause which they had served. Those of the two Levellers were of a different character, for both men had met a violent death, Rainborowe at the hands of royalists and Lockyer by a parliamentarian firing squad, and the message of those attending their funerals was one

of defiance, that their cause would not be impaired by these kill-
ings. While all four funerals attracted large numbers of participants and onlookers, that of Lockyer was particularly well attended,
a measure of support for the Levellers in London. In each case,
there was a significance attached to those who attended and those
who stayed away, for by stressing the continuity of the individual's cause, his mourners could not but draw attention to the
divisions within the parliamentarian movement.

Despite the political divisions within London and the optimis-
tic views of some senior royalists that they could be exploited,
the adherence of London to the parliamentary cause during the
first Civil War was never in doubt. Nevertheless, the citizens'
enthusiasm was neither unqualified nor unchanging. The militia
did not serve with the field armies after 1644, nor indeed did the
capital supply more than a small fraction of the recruits required
from it for the New Model Army in 1645. Because of the experi-
ences of its soldiers in the field during the first two-and-a-half
years of the war, perhaps, too, a growing dissatisfaction with their
performance among the parliamentarian commanders, and a more
general war-weariness in the capital, London virtually ceased to
provide troops for the armies at the end of 1644. To this extent
at least, its reputation as a virtually inexhaustible supplier of
manpower has to be qualified. The tax strikes from 1646 onwards
may be seen as a reflection of the same dissatisfaction, that London had borne more than its fair share of the burden of the war.
Its role as a supplier of the parliamentary forces may also re-
quire reassessment, at least in terms of its function as a producer,
rather than importer and distributor, of arms. The response of its
gunmakers and cutlers to the needs of the armies during the
Bishops' Wars had been sluggish and it may not have had the
means to quickly adapt and develop into a large-scale arms
manufacturer during the civil wars.

Yet whatever problems the war brought to London and its citizens, it demonstrated, perhaps even enhanced, the capital's central importance, both economically and politically. The folly of
losing the support of large groups within the City's élite and the
citizenry at a time when there was an organised and determined
opposition in parliament had brought the king's government to
its knees, and failure to retrieve the situation ultimately lost him
the ensuing civil war. The control of other areas and cities was
no substitute for being able to draw on London's wealth and

manpower; its militia was a potent weapon, its citizens were prepared to work and fight to defend their community, its financial resources were unrivalled, and it remained the focus of the political nation. This much must have been obvious before 1642, but potential power is one thing, that which has been demonstrated in practice is quite another. London's role in the Civil War provided a lesson for the future.

Notes

1. F. Tönies (ed.), Thomas Hobbes, *Behemoth or The Long Parliament* (London, 1889), p. 202. BL, Thomason Tracts, E377(27) John Lightfoot, *A Sermon Preached Before the Honourable House of Commons At their Publique Fast, Holden in Margarets Westminster Febr. 24 1646/47* (1647), p. 27. This is reproduced in R. Jeffs (ed.), *The English Revolution I: Fast Sermons to Parliament*, vol. 27 (London, 1971), pp. 157–95.
2. See below, Chapter 2. For London's role in the events of 1640–2 and their background see: V. Pearl, *London and the Outbreak of the Puritan Revolution* (Oxford, 1961), R. Ashton, *The City and the Court 1603–1643* (Cambridge, 1979), and R. Brenner, *Merchants and Revolution. Commercial Change, Political Conflict, and London's Overseas Traders, 1550–1653* (Cambridge, 1993). The wider picture is provided in: B. Manning, *The English People and the English Revolution* (2nd edn, London, 1991), Chapters 1–4, and A. Fletcher, *The Outbreak of the English Civil War* (London, 1981).
3. R. Clifton, 'Fear of Popery' in C. Russell (ed.), *The Origins of the English Civil War* (London, 1973), pp. 156–60. For the background to Catholicism at Court see, C. Hibberd, *Charles I and the Popish Plot* (Chapel Hill, 1983).
4. S. R. Smith, 'Almost Revolutionaries: the London Apprentices during the Civil Wars', *The Huntington Library Quarterly*, XLII (1978–9), 313–16.
5. Pearl, *London and the Outbreak*, p. 279.
6. Pearl, *London and the Outbreak*, p. 224. Manning, *English People*, p. 142.
7. Manning, *English People*, p. 63.
8. K. J. Lindley, 'London and popular freedom in the 1640s', in R. C. Richardson and G. M. Ridden (eds), *Freedom and the English Revolution. Essays in history and literature* (Manchester, 1986), pp. 121–2.
9. K. J. Lindley, 'Riot Prevention and Control in Early Stuart London', *Trans. of the Royal Historical Soc.*, fifth series, 33 (1983), 113. For attacks on brothels see, T. Harris, *London Crowds in the Reign of Charles II* (Cambridge, 1987), pp. 22–4.
10. Pearl, *London and the Outbreak*, pp. 119, 131–2.
11. J. Morrill, 'The Religious Context of the English Civil War', *Trans.*

of the Royal Historical Soc., fifth series, 34 (1984), 166.

12. P. S. Seaver, *The Puritan Lecturships. The Politics of Religious Dissent 1560–1662* (Stanford, 1970), pp. 9–10, 54, 68–70, 127–31, 171, 190, 203–4, 238–66, 274–5.

13. Pearl, *London and the Outbreak*, p. 183. D. A. Kirby, 'The Radicals of St Stephen Coleman Street, London, 1624–42', *The Guildhall Miscellany*, III (1970), 98–118.

14. Lindley, 'London and popular freedom', pp. 126–7.

15. Fletcher, *Outbreak*, pp. 107, 118.

16. M. Tolmie, *The Triumph of the Saints. The Separate Churches of London 1616–1649* (Cambridge, 1977), p. 37. Manning, *English People*, p. 94. P. Gregg, *Free-born John. A biography of John Lilburne* (London, 1961), pp. 91–2. Lindley, 'London and popular freedom', p. 132.

17. Brenner, *Merchants and Revolution*, esp. pp. 374–89. K. J. Lindley, 'London's citizenry in the English Revolution', in R. C. Richardson (ed.), *Town and Countryside in the English Revolution* (Manchester, 1992), pp. 19–45.

18. S. R. Smith, 'The Social and Geographical Origins of the London Apprentices, 1630–1660', *The Guildhall Miscellany*, IV (1973), 202–4.

19. Smith, 'Almost Revolutionaries', 317.

20. J. Knowles, 'The Spectacle of the Realm: civic consciousness, rhetoric and ritual in early modern London', in J. R. Mulryne and M. Shewring (eds), *Theatre and Government under the early Stuarts* (Cambridge, 1993), pp. 172–3.

21. *A & O*, I, pp. 26–7. R. Hutton, *The Rise and Fall of Merry England: The Ritual Year 1400–1700* (Oxford, 1994), pp. 202, 206–11. R. Ashton, *Counter-Revolution. The Second Civil War and its Origins, 1646–1648* (New Haven and London, 1994), pp. 190–1, 237–40.

22. P. S. Seaver, *Wallington's World: A Puritan Artisan in Seventeenth-Century London* (London, 1985), pp. 10, 38, 169–70.

23. V. Pearl, 'Change and Stability in Seventeenth-century London', *The London Journal*, 5 (1979), 3–34, reprinted in J. Barry (ed.), *The Tudor and Stuart Town* (London, 1990), pp. 139–65.

24. J. Boulton, *Neighbourhood and Society. A London Suburb in the Seventeenth Century* (Cambridge, 1987).

25. M. Ashley, *Financial and Commercial Policy under the Cromwellian Protectorate* (2nd edn, London, 1962), pp. 12, 51.

26. J. Morrill (ed.), *Reactions to the English Civil War* (London, 1982), p. 19.

27. This was agreed to upon the condition that no changes be made to Fairfax's list of officers for the New Model Army. I. Gentles, 'The Choosing of Officers for the New Model Army', *Historical Research*, LXVII (1994), 282, 285.

28. W. P. Harper, 'Public Borrowing 1640–1660. With special reference to Government Borrowing in the City of London between 1640 and 1650' (unpublished M.Sc.(Econ.) thesis, University of London, 1927), pp. 86–7.

29. Sheffield University Library, Hartlib papers, 70/2. I owe this reference to the kindness of Dr Joan Thirsk.

30. Seaver, *Puritan Lectureships*, p. 286.
31. Tolmie, *Saints*, pp. 53, 62, 94, 109.
32. Pearl, 'Change and Stability', 6.
33. C. Hill, *The English Bible and the Seventeenth-Century Revolution* (London, 1993), p. 200.
34. *Catalogue of the Pamphlets, Books, Newspapers, and Manuscripts . . . collected by George Thomason, 1640–1661*, I (London, 1908), p. xxi. *A & O*, I, pp. 184–6.
35. J. Frank, *The Beginnings of the English Newspaper 1620–1660* (Cambridge, Mass., 1961), pp. 21–8, 42, 50, 56–7, 75, 102, 113, 271.
36. *Areopagitica; A Speech of Mr. John Milton For the Liberty of Unlicensed Printing, To the Parliament of England* (London, 1644).
37. J. Thirsk, 'The Crown as projector on its own estates, from Elizabeth I to Charles I', in R. W. Hoyle (ed.), *The Estates of the English Crown, 1558–1640* (Cambridge, 1992), p. 324.
38. Manning, *English People*, p. 51. C. Webster, *The Great Instauration: Science, Medicine and Reform 1626–1660* (London, 1975), p. 77.
39. J. Thirsk (ed.), *The Agrarian History of England and Wales, volume V, 1640–1750: II Agrarian Change* (Cambridge, 1985), pp. 547–59.
40. *LJ*, VI, 1643–44, pp. 319–20.
41. Webster, *Great Instauration*, pp. 221–3. *Motives Grounded upon the Word of God* (London, 1647). N. Harte, *The University of London 1836–1986* (London, 1986), pp. 50, 61, 63.
42. Webster, *Great Instauration*, pp. 51–61, 488. C. V. Wedgwood, 'The Scientists and the English Civil War' in *History and Hope* (London, 1989), pp. 369–73.
43. Gregg, *Free-born John*, pp. 147–50. BL, Thomason Tracts, E356(12) *The Charters of London* (1646); E359(17) *London's Liberty in Chains* (1646).
44. Pearl, *London and the Outbreak*, esp. pp. 246–50; Idem, 'Change and Stability', 14. J. E. Farnell, 'The Social and Intellectual Basis of London's Role in the English Civil Wars', *Journal of Modern History*, 49 (1977), 641–60. Brenner, *Merchants and Revolutionaries*, pp. 460–1.
45. *A & O*, I, pp. 750–3.
46. C. E. Surman (ed.), *The Register-Booke of the Fourth Classis in the Province of London* (Harleian Soc., vols 82, 83, 1953).
47. Tai Liu, 'The Founding of the London Provincial Assembly, 1645–47', *Guildhall Studies in London History*, III (1978), 109–34.
48. For the role of the Scots commissioners see, V. Pearl, 'London Puritans and Scotch Fifth Columnists: a Mid-Seventeenth-century Phenomenon', in A. E. J. Hollaender and W. Kellaway (eds), *Studies in London History Presented to Philip Jones* (London, 1969), pp. 317–31.
49. Tai Liu, *Puritan London. A Study of Religion and Society in the City Parishes* (Newark, Del., and London, 1986), pp. 54–89.
50. Tolmie, *Saints*, p. 141. Lindley, 'London and popular freedom', 130–1.
51. Tolmie, *Saints*, p. 81.
52. M. Mahony, 'Presbyterianism in the City of London, 1645–1647', *Historical Journal*, 22 (1979), 93–114.
53. S. R. Gardiner, *History of the Great Civil War 1642–1649* (reprinted,

Moreton-in-Marsh, 1987), III, p. 9. Tolmie, *Saints*, pp. 110–16.

54. Liu, *Puritan London*, pp. 82–3.
55. Liu, *Puritan London*, pp. 132–43.
56. Tolmie, *Saints*, pp. 148–50.
57. I. Gentles, *The New Model Army in England, Ireland and Scotland, 1645–1653* (Oxford, 1992), pp. 196–7. Ashton, *Counter-Revolution*, pp. 77–8, 188–9, 194.
58. Hutton, *Merry England*, pp. 211–12. Smith, 'Almost Revolutionaries', 318.
59. V. Pearl, 'London's Counter-Revolution', in G. E. Aylmer (ed.), *The Interregnum: The Quest for Settlement 1646–1660* (London, 1972), pp. 29–56. Gentles, *New Model Army*, pp. 178–97. Ashton, *Counter-Revolution*, pp. 137–9, 178–85, 349–55.
60. Gentles, *New Model Army*, p. 194.
61. I. Gentles, 'The Struggle for London in the Second Civil War', *The Historical Journal*, 26 (1983), 277–305. For the shifts in power following the elections in December 1648 and the abortive attempts to democratise Common Hall and the livery companies see, J. E. Farnell, 'The Usurpation of Honest London Householders: Barebone's Parliament', *English Historical Review*, LXXXII (1967), 24–46, and Brenner, *Merchants and Revolution*, pp. 542–7.
62. D. Evans, 'Gloucester's Civil War Trades and Industries, 1642–46', *Trans. of the Bristol and Gloucestershire Archaeological Soc.*, 110 (1992), 137–47.
63. D. Scott, 'Politics and government in York, 1640–1662', in Richardson (ed.), *Town and Countryside*, p. 67. S. Porter, *Destruction in the English Civil Wars* (Stroud, 1994), pp. 85, 105–6.
64. P. Slack, *The Impact of Plague in Tudor and Stuart England* (London, 1985), pp. 120–3, 314–15.
65. Joshua Sprigge, *Anglia Rediviva* (London, 1647), p. 119.
66. Slack, *Plague*, pp. 117–18. W. B. Stephens, *Seventeenth-century Exeter: a study of industrial and commercial development, 1625–1688* (Exeter, 1958), pp. 59–63. M. J. Stoyle, '"Whole Streets Converted in Ashes": Property Destruction in Exeter during the English Civil War', *Southern History*, 16 (1994), 67–84.
67. I. Roy, 'The city of Oxford, 1640–60', in Richardson (ed.), *Town and Countryside*, pp. 141–54.
68. B. P. Lyndon, 'The Parliament's army in Essex, 1648', *Journal of the Society for Army Historical Research*, LIX (1981), 140–60. VCH, *Essex*, IX (London, 1994), pp. 73–5, 263, 313–14, 323.

1

London at the Outbreak of the Civil War

Rosemary Weinstein

By the outbreak of the Civil War in 1642, London stretched for over five miles from Stepney to Westminster along the north bank of the Thames and, south of the river, through Lambeth and Southwark to Rotherhithe. During the period 1600 to 1650, the population of the built-up area grew from some 200 000 to 375 000, an estimated 7 per cent of the national total. In fact, because some migrants to London later returned to the provinces, this underrepresents the proportion who came to the capital, and it is possible that as many as one out of every six English people now spent part of their lives in London.[1]

A huge influx of migrants, chiefly from the provinces, but also including many aliens, or 'strangers', from overseas, helped create this rapid growth, which continued despite major epidemics of bubonic plague in 1603, 1625 and 1636, each claiming about one-fifth of the population of the city, and generally high mortality rates at other times, due to various endemic diseases. Many newcomers were poor, subsistence migrants from the country, yet others came as apprentices in time-honoured fashion or to study at the Inns of Court (where admissions quadrupled between 1580 and 1640), to attend to legal or commercial business, parliament or the royal court. Increasing numbers of country gentry escaped the boredom of rural life and arrived in London for the 'season' (autumn to spring), a practice the crown tried to curtail in the 1620s and 1630s, but which developed more fully after the Restoration.

This influx of country gentry required suitable accommodation both to buy and rent, and the demand prompted the development of the 'west end'. Vigorous suburban growth all round the capital brought problems of overcrowding, epidemics, building control, crime and disorder, unregulated crafts and industries. From 1580 the crown had unsuccessfully tried to control this growth, issuing a series of proclamations to that end. In the 1630s new tactics were employed – the crown issued licences to build (under supervision and to certain specified standards) for a fee; those who could not afford a building licence might suffer imprisonment for illegal building and they also risked having their buildings demolished.[2] An abortive attempt to 'incorporate', and hence control, London's suburbs by the Privy Council in 1636 fuelled the mounting tension between crown and City. The 1630s were indeed a stressful decade: the granting of monopolies and problems regarding the Londonderry plantation added to the dissatisfaction and friction between the City and the crown, as Professor Ashton has described.[3]

The London of the 1630s to the 1660s is most vividly portrayed by the detailed drawings and engravings of Wenceslaus Hollar, a Bohemian artist staying at Arundel House under the patronage of the earl of Arundel. Hollar's 'long view' or panorama of London, published in Antwerp in 1647, shows the extent of the 'metropolis', as it was then called,[4] from the probable viewpoint of Southwark Cathedral. Some new landmarks had appeared during the 1630s: a watergate in classical style adorns the riverside entrance to York House, the new mansion of the duke of Buckingham, south of the Strand, and a great classical portico by Inigo Jones, Surveyor General of Works, incongruously attached to the west end of the gothic St Paul's, now dominates the approach to the walled City from Ludgate. Out of view north of the Strand, the first of London's 'squares', so called, has been built by the earl of Bedford at Covent Garden, also under Jones's influence. North and south banks of the Thames are linked by one bridge, London Bridge, lined with buildings, except where those at its northern end had been destroyed by fire in 1633. Substantial houses, including Winchester House (former palace of the Chancellor of England), crowd the Bankside. Here, too, we have a last glimpse of the Globe Theatre, closed at the outbreak of war in 1642, then demolished in 1644, with the Bear Pit adjacent, their names already confused and transposed.

North of the river, outside the City walls on the north-east side, the 'Agas' map (published in 1633) reveals ribbon development northwards up Bishopsgate Street. Here, too, 'many fair houses for receipt and lodging of worshipful persons' covered the site of the dissolved hospital of St Mary, Shoreditch. There were also large houses for aristocratic residents up Aldersgate Street on the north-western side of the City, whilst the poorer village of Clerkenwell had already become absorbed into the spreading metropolis a little further to the north. There was further development around the Inns of Court, west of the Fleet River, off Chancery Lane, as they grew in size and influence up to 1640, and houses spread along the Strand to the court suburb of Westminster. Each of these areas had its own residential and industrial characteristics. This chapter provides an overview of the growth of the City and its various suburbs by 1640, which had such a profound influence in shaping the capital's future residential and industrial development.

By 1640 the population of the walled City and its extra-mural parishes was some 135 000, already outstripped by the surrounding suburbs. Here was the country's chief port, handling both overseas and coastal trade, its main cloth market, at Blackwell Hall, Guildhall, seat of City government, the Royal Exchange, the nation's chief business place for merchants, and over 100 halls of its guilds or livery companies with their long-established privileges, traditions and great wealth, the bases of London's mercantile élite. Opportunities for office holding in parish, ward and civic life were numerous for those living within the network of parishes.[5]

By 1620 patterns of overseas trade were changing: goods from the Far East shipped by the East India Company (established in 1600) already produced 5 per cent of imports in the way of spices (especially pepper, cloves and nutmeg), raw silks, calico, indigo, and saltpetre for gunpowder. Trade with Virginia developed from the 1620s, and tobacco, the main commodity, was imported in growing quantities; smoking was common among all classes by the Civil War. London merchants then re-exported a proportion of these colonial goods to the continent, helping the balance of payments.[6]

Of exports overseas, textiles amounted to some 87 per cent of the total in 1640, about half of which consisted of the lighter and cheaper New Draperies, and of equal value to the exports of traditional broadcloths. The broadcloth industry was languishing, and these lighter cloths (bays, says and frisadoes) provided a vital new element. Dyeing of cloth in England was of variable success, but one notable Dutch inventor, Cornelius Drebbel, discovered a brilliant scarlet dye, and set up a dye works at Bow in collaboration with his son-in-law, a dyer from Leiden. This flourished in the 1630s.[7]

Although some of the greater fortunes were made in overseas trade, many merchants were equally successful as coastal traders. About a half of a sample of 140 merchant aldermen trading between 1600 and 1625 were involved in domestic trade – shipping general wholesale goods, especially grain, cheese and other foodstuffs, provincial cloths, and so on.[8] As London's population expanded, so food supply had to increase: by 1637 cereal imports into London stood at 95 714 quarters, a five-fold increase since 1580. North-east Kent was an especially important source, although areas further afield, such as Sussex, Norfolk and the south Midlands, were also stimulated to produce supplies.[9] London housewives benefited from markets at Newgate, Leadenhall, Billingsgate and Queenhythe, Cheapside and Gracechurch Street, selling a wide range of produce.

Manufacturing and selling are the two essential aspects of any craft or industry. Within the early seventeenth-century City, it has been estimated that manufacturing occupied 40 per cent of the workforce and retail trades 36 per cent (a rise from 28 per cent in 1600), but in the suburbs many more people made goods.[10] The move of manufacturing to the suburbs, where there was more space and lower rents, accelerated during the seventeenth century, especially for the dirtier and noisier industries. Between 1600 and 1640 clothing remained the dominant industry both in the intra- and extra-mural City, with the metal, leather and building trades also prominent. Metal workers increased their share of the market considerably. The number of pewterers, for example, rose from some 50 in 1600 to 350 by 1640, such was the demand for pewter utensils. Pewterers were especially numerous in Billingsgate and Bishopsgate wards.[11]

The medieval tradition of clustering of similar crafts continued in certain areas, although occupations were very mixed in most parishes, with few craftsmen living near their company halls. Some new crafts appeared at this time, such as those of calenderer (cloth presser), distiller, watchmaker and glass-maker, whilst others disappeared, being absorbed by more dominant crafts. The Watchmakers, Spectacle-makers and Gunmakers were three of the newly formed and incorporated companies in the 1630s.

Fine glass had been a novelty in London until Jacob Verzelini established his glasshouse at Crutched Friars in the City in 1572, and at Broad Street glasshouse (the former refectory of the Austin Friars) in 1580 – a precinct shared with Dutch watchmakers. Continued by Sir Robert Mansell from 1615 to 1656, this latter glasshouse specialised in wine and beer glasses, with some stems of 'extraordinary fashion' in the elaborate Venetian style. An investigation of the Returns of Aliens for 1635 produced evidence of immigrant glass-makers in the two parishes closest to the glasshouses: All Hallows London Wall and St Peter le Poor – presumably all were employed by Mansell as part of his skilled immigrant workforce.[12] Of the six glass-makers, four were Italians, one French and one a looking-glass maker from Hamburg. Glass-making was also established at the former Blackfriars and Whitefriars sites and in the developing industrial suburb of Southwark. Aliens totalled only an estimated 3622 in London in 1635, yet their contribution to innovative techniques was outstanding.

John Stow, in his *Survey of London* (1598), noted the dispersal of crafts from their traditional, medieval, locations to various other areas within the City, also how the wealthy tended to congregate together in 'fayre houses' in the best streets. This zoning of the better-off into certain parishes (usually the central ones) has been demonstrated by other means. Finlay used a listing of every householder in eighty-seven of the ninety-seven intra-mural and seven extra-mural parishes in 1638, which gives the moderate rent of each house and the tithe paid.[13] He demonstrated that already there was a clear social stratification, with substantial householders, whose property was valued at £20 rent or more, living in the central parishes, whilst the poorer lived around the City walls and riverside; all subject, of course, to a certain amount of intermingling of rich and poor within the various parishes.

What social conditions resulted from this stratification? That is, was it healthier in these better-off central parishes? Slack's research on the urban impact of bubonic plague indicates that in the epidemics of 1603, 1625, 1636 and 1665, those parishes were indeed less affected, whilst the poorer and more populous ones close to the walls and riverside suffered increasingly.[14] Certain slums, such as Bridewell and nearby Blackfriars, close to the mouth of the Fleet River, were amongst the worst hit. Plague was thus associated with the poor and over-populated dwellings, wherever they might be located. It was certainly noted by seventeenth-century commentators as spreading from the 'unregulated suburbs'.[15]

The most enlightened authorities were the elders of the Dutch Church in Austin Friars, who discussed whether the disease was a contagion or a 'miasma' (airborne) and who appointed surgeons to care for their congregation, segregating those affected. Slack points out that the inspiration for these new ideas had come from Charles I's Huguenot physician, Sir Theodore de Mayerne, who appears to have been the first to have believed that rodents (rats, mice and weasels) could be plague carriers, not cats and dogs, as was the common notion. Unfortunately, no new measures were taken by the crown as a result of these insights and Mayerne's report to Charles in 1631; the king thus missed a great opportunity for enlightened and humanitarian reform of public health.[16]

As noted above, manufacturing was in general moving away from the walled City to suburban areas for a variety of causes: direct prohibition of noxious trades, the lower rents and greater workshop space available, and guild interference, especially the obligatory seven-year apprenticeship. Some 90 000 people now lived east of the City and the area became especially noted for its shipbuilding industries. At first the impact was of relatively poor and small-scale housing and workshops. Stow deplored the Whitechapel area, thinking it 'no small blemish for so famous a city to have so unsavoury and unseemly an entry'.[17] Tenements were 'small and base', cottages 'filthy', and streets 'pestered' with tenements, which were filling up the former agricultural landscape, with its small market gardens. In the extra-mural parish of St Botolph Aldgate, the proportion of manufacturing workers (leather sellers, smiths, cutlers, tailors, weavers, porters, labourers, bakers, butchers and those belonging to the maritime trades) increased from 48 per cent to 72 per cent between 1600 and 1640, although formal apprenticeship of the City companies appears to have been in decline.[18]

Further east, in St Dunstan Stepney, there was greater occupational specialism, with maritime trades ranging from ships' carpenters and other artisans to ships' masters. Many immigrants were attracted to these developing trades. London's commercial expansion and overseas trade during the seventeenth century led to an enormous demand for ocean-going ships and maritime skills. Shipbuilding yards at Blackwall, an East India Company yard, Limehouse, Wapping and Ratcliffe flourished as a result. Between 1625 and 1635, for example, John Grave of Limehouse built one ship of 250–300 tons annually.[19]

In what conditions did people live in these areas, and how did their health and wealth (or poverty) compare with those in the suburb of Southwark or those in the developing 'west end'? In parts of Shadwell and Tower Liberty identified by Power in the 1650 parliamentary surveys, 89 per cent of houses were of one or two storeys and contained an average of four rooms each, compared with 6.7 rooms per house in the 'west end' at the same date.[20] Over 95 per cent of these 'east end' houses were built of timber and boards, rather than brick, and were in single occupation, and one-third (33.2 per cent) of the 918 houses had gardens, compared with 42.9 per cent of the 448 'west end' houses.

Apart from the smallness of the houses, a further notable characteristic of the 'east end' was its poverty: out of a total of 1543 households, 51.9 per cent were 'non-chargeable', that is, they were not liable for taxes, compared with only 18 per cent so categorised in the west. Not only was it poorer in the 'east end' but, as might be expected, less healthy too: Stepney's burials were 50 per cent more numerous than its baptisms, with an even worse ratio of 58.9 per cent burials above baptisms in Whitechapel. In 1636 over half of all deaths in Shadwell and over 60 per cent in Whitechapel were plague victims, as recorded in the Bills of Mortality for that year, compared with an average of 41.8 per cent of plague deaths in the 'west end'. Poverty and crime went together: in the suburban precinct of St Katherine's there were only two constables to 490 householders and there were five or six to 1575 householders in Stepney. This compared with the City's high ratio of constables to householders, with, for example, four constables to 260 householders in Cornhill.[21] The court records of the Middlesex sessions indicate a high level of robbery, burglary and violent assault in these suburban areas.

The conditions in the eastern suburbs were likely to apply to the similarly poor and industrial areas south of the river, which had a population of 45 000. Boulton's analysis of the Boroughside district of St Saviour's parish, Southwark, revealed the wide network of social relationships between householders and institutions within the area.[22] The average household, rather than house, size was a mean of 3.8 individuals, comparable with other urban areas such as Cambridge and Canterbury at this date, and north of the river (4.3 individuals) by 1695. Poorer households typically had fewer persons than the wealthy central ones.[23]

Boulton further refined notions of poverty and distribution of wealth, showing that in Boroughside these did not conform to the supposed 'pyramidal norm' with a small number of wealthy at the top of the pyramid and a large number of poor at the base, but rather that the middle ranks of householders (43 per cent) swelled out with those who did not have enough surplus income to contribute to local taxation, although they could earn enough to maintain their families without assistance in normal years. The truly poor (usually pensioners) comprised a much smaller proportion of householders (26 per cent). The middling and poor made up 51.9 per cent of 'non-chargeable' householders in Power's study of the 'east end', compared with 69 per cent in Boroughside (43 per cent middling and 26 per cent poor).[24] Clearly, there was a potentially greater problem in Southwark of a vulnerable majority who might need to seek poor relief in times of hardship, and more recent work has similarly identified this category of 'middling poor' in other City parishes. Was Boroughside also less healthy than other areas? On the contrary, mortality rates in 1625 indicate that Boroughside was as healthy as parishes within the City walls and better than the peripheral and extra-mural ones such as All Hallows' London Wall and St Botolph Bishopsgate, according to the crisis mortality ratio determining plague severity that year.[25]

Occupationally, Boroughside and other Southwark parishes showed a degree of occupational zoning, with food and drink retailing in Boroughside, watermen in the Clink Liberty and Paris Garden, and seamen in St Olave's. Leather dressing, tanning, candle- and soap-manufacture were long-established industries in the area. Not all units of production were the traditional small-scale ones. Indeed, Thomas Overman, soap boiler, ran one of the biggest such businesses in London, with an output of 550 tons of soap a year, amounting to one-quarter of the new Company of Soap-makers' total output in 1637–8.[26]

Dutch immigrants settled especially in east Southwark and made a great contribution to certain new and specialised industries, such as brewing, felt- and hat-making, dyeing and textile manufacture. From the 1540s, Dutch glass-makers had been operating in Southwark, an industry which developed here, as in the City, in the first half of the seventeenth century, under Sir Robert Mansell, the major monopolist, with an emphasis on drinking glasses, bottles and window glass. A coal-fired furnace, representing important new technology compared with the earlier wood firing, was in operation as early as 1611 at Winchester House glassworks.[27] At Pickleherring Quay and Montague Close, a luxury pottery of tin-glazed earthenware ('delft') was established and flourished widely until the nineteenth century.[28] It was these new ceramic technologies especially which made Southwark and the adjacent suburbs of Lambeth, Bermondsey and Rotherhithe an industrial area of note in later centuries.[29] Not all was industrial grime and poverty south of the river, however, and the delights and temptations of nearby Bankside, with its theatres, bear-pits and brothels, would have been a welcome retreat for many locals.

The suburbs to the west of the City – the burgeoning 'west end' – contained some 35 000 people by 1640.[30] Development here was in stark contrast to the poorer industrial suburbs to the south and east. An architectural revolution began here in the 1620s and 1630s that represents London's unique contribution to urban architectural development. How did this come about?

The prime mover was Francis, fourth earl of Bedford, who was keen to develop his estate of Covent Garden between the Strand and Long Acre (originally the Convent Garden of Westminster Abbey) that had been acquired by his family at the Dissolution. In 1631 the earl paid £2000 for a licence to develop his estate, one of the stipulations being that only one family should occupy each house. The plans were examined both by the Commissioners for Building and the king. Indeed, Charles I's desire to create a civilised and beautiful 'west end' was laudable enough, although his true motives appear to have been financial; to bring in money from licences.[31] A further speculative development during the 1630s was that of Lincoln's Inn Fields by a Bedfordshire developer, William Newton, of which the only architectural survivor is Lindsey House of *c*.1640.

The Italianate hand of Inigo Jones was to be seen not only in the 'west end', but also in the City. There was, most notably, his great portico for St Paul's of 1633 mentioned above, to which Charles I personally contributed £10 000. (Much bitterness was caused by Jones's high-handed action in partly demolishing the adjacent parish church of St Gregory because of its awkward proximity to St Paul's.) Of great medical and architectural interest was Jones's oval anatomy theatre built for the Barber Surgeons next to their hall in Monkwell Street, Cripplegate, in 1637. Others followed in his steps: Nicholas Stone, Jones's assistant, built the new hall of the Goldsmiths' Company in 1635,[32] and Peter Mills,

later appointed City Bricklayer, possibly designed the stone door-
way, dated 1633, and an internal doorcase of *c*.1635 at St Helen
Bishopsgate. Mills may also have been responsible for the church
of St Michael le Querne at the west end of Cheapside, where the
parishioners are recorded as standing their ground more firmly
than their neighbours at St Gregory's. Colvin has shown how the
negotiations between the king's Surveyor, Jones, and the parish
reveal the direct confrontation between the architectural ideas of
the court and those of the ordinary citizens of London.[33] The church
was eventually rebuilt between 1638 and 1640 in the manner favoured by the parishioners, who were 'not overawed' by their
confrontation with 'Mr Surveyor' Jones.

The intention of the earl of Bedford (now out of favour at court)
was to erect houses and buildings at Covent Garden 'fit for the
habitations of gentlemen and men of ability' and to exclude the
poorer classes.[34] Other aristocratic landlords had similar ideas:
by 1638 over 1361 houses had been built between Drury Lane,
Holborn, the Strand and St Martin's Lane. Peers, ambitious for
favours at court, and bored country gentry, quickly acquired these.
Yet the 'west end' was far from being homogeneous, despite the
earl's intentions. Power distinguished five areas of differing wealth:
Piccadilly, the Strand, High Holborn, Long Acre and Westminster.[35] High Holborn and Long Acre generally had some of the
lowest value property and Piccadilly was developed after 1630
with small properties of one and two storeys. The Strand was
the most desirable area, whilst demand for accommodation was
greatest in Westminster, where rents were high for small and
crowded properties, frequently no more than 'sheds', near the court.

The growth of shops in the Strand was notable. Some shopkeepers, like the goldsmiths, had moved here from Cheapside,
following the fashionable world westwards, especially after the
development of the earl of Salisbury's New Exchange near Dur-
ham House in 1609. 'The people of London began to expend ex-
travagantly', Stow complained. Of thirty-four houses on one plot
studied by Power there were two saddlers, two shoemakers, two
cutlers and two chandlers, a sempster, goldsmith, tailor, spectacle-
maker, confectioners, apothecary and a milliner, providing for
both everyday and specialist needs.[36] Hackney carriages, a recent
innovation in public transport for Londoners, could be obtained
from the rank by the Maypole in the Strand, and there were Sedan
chairs, too, for shorter journeys. From 1637 there were some 200

carrier services to provincial towns such as Oxford, Cambridge and further afield; people travelled more widely, and news, fashions, ideas and goods spread ever outwards from the capital.

Domestic comforts and living standards percolated down the class structure as wealth levels increased. A generation later a coachman of St Martin in the Fields possessed a silver tankard, a silver cup, two silver spoons and a silver wine taster, amongst other goods.[37] London was experiencing a consumer boom, not only due to rising levels of population but a *per capita* rise in the average consumption of goods and services.[38]

Londoners from all parts of the metropolis could enjoy popular, improvised pleasures such as drinking in the ubiquitous alehouses, smoking tobacco, playing cards and gambling. In summer there were walks in Moorfields north of the City walls, or a grander promenade or coach ride in Hyde Park, recently opened to the public. In St James's Park there was a menagerie with exotic beasts, some brought back from the new Virginia colony, to investigate,[39] and trips could be taken downriver to Deptford to visit the *Golden Hind*, left slowly rotting there after Drake's voyage round the world, and the greatest ships ever seen, being built in the royal dockyards nearby. There were new and rare plants and curiosities at the Tradescants' house in Lambeth, and the sculptures and classical collections of the earl of Arundel at Arundel House in the Strand, for those with more refined tastes. Surviving examples from both collections can still be seen in the Ashmolean Museum. The curious could investigate a glass furnace, the royal tombs at Westminster Abbey, an execution, or the zoo at the Tower of London, and all could gaze at a royal procession, like that of Marie de Medici, Queen Mother of France, traversing Cheapside in 1638.

Witch hunts remained something of a patriotic sport, with public interest stimulated by pamphlets, sermons, drama and the law. Witches' spells could be warded off with new methods of counter-witchcraft: stoneware bottles containing charms intended to cause sympathetic injury and pain to the 'witch' were corked and buried, or thrown into rivers. A notable 'building sacrifice' was discovered bricked into a first-floor chimney-breast at Lauderdale House, Highgate, during renovations in the 1960s. Live chickens and domestic artefacts had been inserted there during the early years of the seventeenth century.[40]

Traditional religious festivals had declined since the Reformation, although early Stuart Londoners could still enjoy processions on Shrove Tuesday, Ascension Day, with the beating of parish bounds, May Day, with dancing round the May-pole in the Strand, Midsummer's civic pageants when the City giants Gog and Magog were carried aloft, and Bartholomew Fair on 25 August at Smithfield, vividly evoked by Ben Jonson in his play of that name.[41]

Under James I the annual lord mayor's show became increasingly spectacular, with barges and floats elaborately decorated in allusion to the particular lord mayor's name and livery company. Anthony Munday was a notable producer of shows, and the playwrights Middleton, Webster and Heywood all competed to write and produce these pageants. These spectacles were open to all, unlike the masques at the royal court, the work of Inigo Jones and his rival Ben Jonson, at first seen in Jones's masterpiece, the Banqueting House, Whitehall, then later in his specially equipped Cockpit-in-Court theatre. These allegorical triumphs, lauding the Stuart monarchy, were a world away from the thunder and gore of tragedies by Webster, Marlowe and other playwrights at the 'popular' theatres. Londoners of all classes attended the Globe on Bankside, the Fortune, Blackfriars Theatre, and the Red Bull near the City, to revel in these.

By the 1620s a new Caroline repertoire, with plays of contemporary allusion and satire, was emerging in London's developing 'west end', aimed at the resident and the newly arrived gentry. Very aptly, the character of the speculative builder in Richard Brome's *The Weeding of the Covent Garden* (1632–34) draws attention to his need for 'worthy tenants' for his new houses, to maximise his profits. The first of the new theatres in the 'west end' was the Cockpit, Drury Lane (1616), followed by the Salisbury Court Theatre in 1629. Women now formed a larger part of the audience at these new playhouses, but entrance was dearer than at the 'popular' ones (6*d* compared with 1*d*), so keeping out the less affluent.

Butler argues persuasively for an 'independent sector' in the 'west end'.[42] There, regular theatre-goers, an informed and influential gentry grouping, who successfully evaded the king's attempts to force their return to the provinces, might be seen as a source of political opposition. Different groups and sections within society were beginning to act in new and unprecedented ways. For the first time, people at the top and bottom of society were linked within one movement – puritanism. Other sectors of the community were also developing independent voices: the spread of printing, especially newsletters, pamphlets, broadside ballads and sermons, stimulated increased literacy and a growing political and religious awareness. Artisans and mercantile élite were linked within the puritan movement. The Civil War could not have been won without popular support. That support was rapidly developing.

Notes

1. A. L. Beier and R. Finlay (eds), *London 1500–1700: The making of the metropolis* (London, 1986), p. 9.
2. N. G. Brett-James, *The Growth of Stuart London* (London, 1935), p. 110.
3. R. Ashton, *The City and the Court, 1603–1643* (Cambridge, 1979), pp. 157–76; and see Chapter 2, below.
4. The term was first used in 1636 in the Bills of Mortality of that year to denote the extended built-up area, that is, Greater London between Stepney and Westminster. Brett-James, *Growth of Stuart London*, p. 253.
5. V. Pearl, 'Change and Stability in Seventeenth-century London', *The London Journal*, 5 (1979), 3–34, reprinted in J. Barry (ed.), *The Tudor and Stuart Town* (London, 1990), pp. 139–65.
6. B. Dietz, 'Overseas trade and metropolitan growth', in Beier and Finlay (eds), *London 1500–1700*, p. 123.
7. David Ormrod, *The Dutch in London: The Influence of an Immigrant Community 1550–1800* (London, 1973), unpaged.
8. R. G. Lang, 'London's aldermen in business: 1600–1625', *Guildhall Miscellany*, 3 (1971), 242–64.
9. J. Chartres, 'Food consumption and internal trade', in Beier and Finlay (eds), *London 1500–1700*, p. 179.
10. A. L. Beier, 'Engine of manufacture: the trades of London', in Beier and Finlay (eds), *London 1500–1700*, pp. 150, 153.
11. J. Hatcher and T. C. Barker, *A History of British Pewter* (London, 1974), pp. 116, 119.
12. PRO, SP16/305/11(17) Returns of Aliens, 1635. Discussed by I. Scouloudi in *Returns of Strangers in the Metropolis 1593, 1627, 1635, 1639. A Study of an Active Minority*, Huguenot Soc. of London Quarto Series Publications, LVII (1985).
13. R. Finlay, *Population and Metropolis: The Demography of London 1580–1650* (Cambridge, 1981), pp. 70–82.
14. P. Slack, *The Impact of Plague in Tudor and Stuart England* (London, 1985), pp. 144–72.
15. Slack, *Plague*, p. 153.
16. Slack, *Plague*, pp. 218–19.

17. C. L. Kingsford (ed.), John Stow, *A Survey of London* (Oxford, 1908), pp. 11, 71–2.
18. Beier and Finlay (eds), *London 1500–1700*, pp. 10, 153.
19. Dietz, 'Overseas trade', p. 129 and n. 39.
20. M. J. Power, 'The East and West in Early-Modern London', in E. W. Ives, R. J. Knecht and J. J. Scarisbrick, *Wealth and Power in Tudor England* (London, 1978), pp. 167–85.
21. Pearl, 'Change and Stability'.
22. J. Boulton, *Neighbourhood and Society. A London Suburb in the Seventeenth Century* (Cambridge, 1987).
23. Boulton, *Neighbourhood and Society*, p. 123.
24. Boulton, *Neighbourhood and Society*, p. 115.
25. Boulton, *Neighbourhood and Society*, pp. 47–8.
26. Boulton, *Neighbourhood and Society*, p. 78.
27. R. J. Charleston, *English Glass and the Glass Used in England, circa 400–1940* (London, 1984), pp. 61, 74.
28. A. F. Britton, *London Delftware* (London, 1986).
29. VCH, *Surrey*, II (London, 1905), pp. 259, 281–93.
30. R. Finlay and B. Shearer, 'Population growth and suburban expansion', in Beier and Finlay (eds), *London 1500–1700*, p. 45.
31. F. H. W. Sheppard (ed.), *The Survey of London*, XXXVI (London, 1970), p. 26. Ashton, *The City and the Court*, pp. 157–76.
32. G. Worsley, 'Inigo Jones: Lonely Genius or Practical Examplar?', *Journal of the British Archaeological Association*, CXLVI (1993), 102–12.
33. H. Colvin, 'Inigo Jones and the Church of St Michael le Querne', *The London Journal*, 12 (1986), 39.
34. For Bedford's petition to Charles I see, *CSPD*, 1629–31, p. 220. See also, L. Stone, *The Crisis of the Aristocracy 1558–1641* (Oxford, 1979), pp. 357–63.
35. Power, 'East and West', p. 170.
36. Power, 'East and West', p. 176.
37. GLRO, DRO AM/P1/1675/42, Inventory of the goods of Thomas Frith, coachman, 1675.
38. Hatcher and Barker, *British Pewter*, p. 130.
39. R. Weinstein, 'Some Menagerie Accounts of James I', *Transactions of the London and Middlesex Archaeological Soc.*, 31 (1980), 133–41.
40. Museum of London collections.
41. P. Burke, 'Popular Culture in Seventeenth Century London', in B. Reay (ed.), *Popular Culture in Seventeenth Century England* (London, 1988), pp. 35–8. See also, R. Ashton, 'Popular Entertainment and Social Control in Later Elizabethan and Early Stuart London', *The London Journal*, 9 (1983), 3–19.
42. M. Butler, *Theatre and Crisis 1632–1642* (Cambridge, 1987), p. 109. See also, A. Gurr, *The Shakespearean Stage 1574–1642* (Cambridge, 1992).

2

Insurgency, Counter-Insurgency and Inaction: Three Phases in the Role of the City in the Great Rebellion*

Robert Ashton

I

Hardly less familiar than the verdict which attaches paramount importance to the City of London's roundhead rather than cavalier sympathies in parliament's victory over Charles I in the first Civil War is the fact that almost as soon as this victory had been won, the City authorities began to behave rather as if they had been overtaken by events; as if their primary need was now, if not to reverse, at least to apply a sharp brake to what many of them viewed as an alarming turn of events. In consequence, municipal sympathies during the second half of the 1640s were crucially different from what they had been between 1640 and 1645. The present essay offers some observations on the different and often conflicting interpretations of the City's role in the politics of the 1640s which have appeared in print over the past four decades.[1] It concentrates its attention on three main episodes in London's Civil War history. The first of these is why and how London became parliamentarian rather than royalist in 1642. The second relates to what has been called London's Counter-Revolution in the summer of 1647, when obviously the City was having second thoughts about the distinctly sour fruits of parliament's triumph in 1646. The third relates to London's role, if any, in the second Civil War which broke out in the spring of 1648.

II

Why did the City support parliament rather than the king in the first Civil War? Few if any historians today would have anything to say for the simple view on which many of us were brought up as undergraduates. This is the view that the City – in both its senses as the government of the square mile between Temple Bar and Aldgate and the business activities carried on within that area – was bound to be implacably hostile to the policies of a central government which, not believing that man's self-love is God's Providence, was strongly interventionist and imposed what citizens today would regard as intolerable restrictions on the freedom of economic enterprise.

What is wrong with this view is not that it misrepresents the attitude of the central government, which was indeed restrictionist and interventionist, but that it misrepresents the attitude of the business élite of the day. For this inescapably restrictive and interventionist scenario unquestionably offered distinct opportunities to certain sorts of private enterprise. These opportunities arose out of the twin circumstances in which, firstly, the government pursued restrictive economic policies, and, secondly, unlike modern interventionist governments, totally lacked the administrative means to pursue these policies unaided. And this is where private enterprise comes in. Many seventeenth-century businessmen – and notably the economic élite of the City – found some of the most attractive fields for their energies and investment not so much in that free enterprise which burks at economic restrictionism, but, on the contrary, in acting as agencies of that restrictionism. In a word, lacking a modern civil service and with only the most rudimentary administrative machinery at its disposal, the central government sought to fill the gap by using private enterprise.

If modern parallels must be sought, the relations between the city business élite and government are akin far less to those between the City and (say) a modern Labour government than perhaps to those between business and government in some third world countries today. In these circumstances it is hardly surprising that an analysis of the economic interests of the vast majority of the City aldermen in early Stuart England reveals that they were economic concessionaires *par excellence*; that is, concessionaires of the government.[2] Some of them held patents of monopoly; others held economic licences; others a variety of rights to implement government policies; and, most of all, directorships in the great chartered companies. These latter organisations were anything but organs of free enterprise. On the contrary, they were bodies exercising restrictive rights to engage in many branches of overseas trade from which lesser mortals were rigidly excluded. One concludes therefore that, as economic concessionaires, the interests of this business élite, far from being opposed to, would in normal circumstances be very much in harmony with, those of a restrictionist government. One of the questions posed in this essay is whether this apparent community of economic interest could survive when circumstances were not normal.

This is not for a moment to suggest that the considerations which made for this harmony were solely economic. No less important was the fact that, as 'men set apart' – a favourite seventeenth-century phrase – in positions of authority, it was natural – at least in normal circumstances – for the City Fathers to do their utmost to bolster royal authority. This they did in the certain knowledge that the order and authority which they valued so highly were indivisible, and that anything which made for a diminution of the king's prestige and authority could not but rub off on their own.

It will doubtless be objected that what has been said so far appears to highlight considerations which made for the maintenance rather than the disintegration of the community of interest between the crown and the City, and certainly does not suggest reasons for the latter to espouse the parliamentary side in the Civil War. However, by the end of Charles I's Personal Rule in 1640, that harmony and community of interest between government and City had taken some very hard knocks. In this the City's experience was not unlike that of the rest of the political nation, although there are historians who would disagree with this view and would argue that the harmony between crown and City had remained unaffected by the events of the reign of Charles I.[3] Which of these views comes nearest to the truth is a matter of likelihood rather than certainty. This essay will contend that the circumstances of the third and fourth decades of the seventeenth century were such as to constitute a crisis in the relations between the crown and the business and municipal élites of the City.

Every student of the period is familiar with the fact that when what was to become the Long Parliament met for the first time in November 1640, the great majority of the newly elected MPs came to Westminster thoroughly disenchanted with the Personal Rule of Charles I. They came ready to embark on a programme of reforming the excesses of the so-called Eleven Years Tyranny – Ship Money, forest fines, non-parliamentary taxation, innovative ceremony and ritualism in worship, and so on – and to set about ensuring by legislation that parliament could not be dissolved without its own consent and would in future meet regularly.

The City had shared in this disenchantment, partly for the same, but also for its own, autonomous, reasons. Under Charles I the City governors had had to face an all-out attack by the central government on, for example, their alleged mismanagement of the Londonderry plantation in Ulster; on their suspected sharp practice over the sale of the royal lands which had been conveyed to trustees of the City to sell and use the proceeds to pay off creditors of the crown who had subscribed to loans which had been raised through the Corporation of London, some of them as far back as 1617; and on a number of other matters. In addition, a variety of government initiatives vis-à-vis London had occasioned widespread City disapproval. Such were the support which Charles and his father had given to splinter craft organisations breaking from the parent gilds and companies; and the horrid shock which was afforded in 1636 by the royal creation of a Corporation of the Suburbs. This had rights of control not only in the out-parishes, but also in the so-called 'Liberties' or enclaves within the square mile over which the City had no jurisdiction. Almost equally offensive were the activities of the royal commission for regulating building since, like the Corporation of the Suburbs, this was concerned less with upholding standards than with making money by licensing their non-observance.[4]

As if this was not enough, the value of many of the interests of the City élite as economic concessionaires, and therefore the community of economic interest binding them to crown and court, had been attenuated by other royal policies. These threatened not so much domestic concessionary interests such as patentees and licensees and the vesting of public control in the hands of private individuals, as the exclusive privileges of some of the chartered companies in foreign trade; concessions which bulked much larger among the economic interests of the aldermen and other members of the civic élite than did domestic concessions such as customs farms and licences.

In a book published a decade and a half ago the present writer provided chapter and verse for this weakening of the economic ties linking the crown and the business élite and for the view that the latter and some of their hitherto most acerbic critics in parliament were in process of becoming reconciled, especially during the parliament of 1628–9 when co-operation over the non-payment of unparliamentary tonnage and poundage was particularly in evidence.[5] This thesis has recently been questioned by an eminent American historian, who, while admitting some degree of reconciliation between the companies and their former parliamentary critics in 1628–9, views both this and the attenuation of company links with the crown as at most very temporary phenomena.[6] However, these are not matters which admit of any definitive judgement and all that can be said is that the issue ultimately turns on the amount of weight which one is inclined to attach to what the present writer would regard as the flagrant and manifest disregard shown by the government of Charles I for the interests of its main sources of support in the City.

One example must suffice to illustrate this process. During the 1630s the great East India Company had to endure not only the depredations of the court-backed privateers Kynaston and Bonnell, but, far worse, the competition of Sir William Courteen's rival organisation that was strongly backed at court and licensed by the crown.[7] Aldermanic concessionaires in the early seventeenth century – unlike their aldermanic successors today – did not relish economic competition, and were disinclined to shrug such things off as matters of minor importance.

But even if the above version of events is accepted, it is not by itself a sufficient explanation of why the City of London took parliament's side in the Civil War. History is rarely so obligingly simple as this. One problem which every historian of the Civil War has to face up to is why was it that, in a parliament which had been overwhelmingly alienated in 1640 by the policies of Charles I's Personal Rule, there had developed by the beginning of 1642 a substantial minority of MPs – including many of the erstwhile supporters of reform – who now firmly set their faces against the plans of John Pym and his associates for further reform. For it was one thing to put to rights the royal excesses of the 1630s – Ship Money, forest fines, unparliamentary taxation, and so on. It was quite another to push the reform process so far as to challenge royal control of the militia and the unfettered right of the king to appoint his own ministers. It was one thing to seek to restore the true Protestant religion of the Elizabethan settlement and to put an end to the ceremonies and ritualism associated with the name of Archbishop William Laud. But had not the reaction gone too far when the Book of Common Prayer was set aside, and tinkers and button-makers were preaching from London pulpits, and – if some of the more lurid accounts are to be credited – men and women sectaries of the most extreme sort were to be found dancing naked in church? As the Kentish MP and former enthusiastic reformer Sir Edward Dering remarked, 'One absurdity leads in a thousand, and when you are down the hill of error, there is no bottom but in hell and that is bottomless too'.[8]

Dering's misgivings were shared by many of those City governors who had been supporters of limited reform in 1640 but were now protesting that enough was enough. In fact, in the City as in parliament, there was a reaction against what was increasingly regarded as the extremism of Pym and his associates. Moreover, this was aided by the apparent new-found moderation of the king himself. It is difficult to imagine a more striking contrast than that between the arbitrary and tactless behaviour of the crown towards the City during the 1630s and the new face of royal policies in the ten months or so before the outbreak of the Civil War. The lord mayor and his colleagues were given ample grounds for hoping that much of the damage done to the City by royal policies in the 1630s would now be put to rights: the City's confiscated estates in Ulster would be restored; the detested Corporation of the Suburbs would disappear into limbo; and there would be welcome alterations to the City's charter.

Conciliation and rapprochement reached their high point in the magnificent banquet given by the City for the king on 25 November 1641 on Charles's return from Scotland. Having displayed on more than one previous occasion a contemptuous disregard for the City's desire to fête him in the traditional manner, Charles now made amends. The lord mayor was informed by the queen of the king's intention to pass through the city on his return from Scotland, and the aldermen resolved that he should be received 'in as great shew and glory as at any time heretofore hath been performed to any Prince'. Charles was met by a deputation of citizens near Balmes, the country house of a former lord mayor, Alderman Sir George Whitmore, and then conducted to Guildhall, where he was feasted and conferred titles of honour on some City notabilities. Indeed 'the whole day seemed to be spent in a kind of emulation ... between their Majesties and the City; the citizens blessing and praying for their Majesties ... and their Majesties returning the same blessings upon ... the citizens'.[9] This and other exercises in mutual reconciliation gave firm grounds for hoping that the citizens' hearts would be captured by King Charles and lost to King Pym. The latter's fortunes had just reached a critical juncture as he launched his own statement of political faith and programme for further instalments of reform, the so-called Grand Remonstrance, in parliament.

How then was it that the City came to support the parliament and not the king when it came to civil war that summer? This paper has argued that the City, like the majority of MPs, had been disenchanted – to put it mildly – by the royal policies of the 1630s. But it has also argued that the crown made up much of its lost ground later in 1641. If the City government had indeed been won back for King Charles, there would surely have to be either a change in the personnel and/or the attitudes of the City rulers if it was to be made safe for King Pym. And this is in fact what happened.

The first crucial development here was one which ran completely counter to the process of reconciliation between the City government and the king and court. The elections to the common council in December 1641 produced a comfortable majority for those who supported Pym's policies of further reform. And just as Pym went ahead with that policy in parliament, so did those who now dominated common council go ahead with theirs, if anything with greater success. The striking parallel between events in the City and at Westminster is colourfully characterised for us by one pamphleteer with the aid of a musical metaphor. 'Thus', writes *Mercurius Civicus*, 'a faction in the City conspired with a faction in the parliament ...' and so 'as two strings set to the same tune ... on two severall violls ... if you touch one, the other by consent renders the same sound, so the house of Commons and the common-councell of this City were now grown to such a sympathy, that the notions and endeavours of one were the work of both'.[10]

There is here space only to outline the main parallels in the City to what was going on in parliament in 1642 which in any case have been made familiar largely through the pioneering researches of Dr Valerie Pearl.[11] First, the newly elected common council set up in January a new Committee of Safety and its allies in parliament decreed that the lord mayor had no choice but to summon common council whenever that committee required it. Thus, just as the Triennial Act and the Act that parliament could not be dissolved without its own consent had curtailed the king's prerogative power to call and dissolve parliaments when, and only when, he wished, so did this order reduce the lord mayor's analagous power to summon common council.[12] There was no getting away from this. When, for instance, in March the lord mayor pleaded illness as his excuse for not summoning common council as demanded by the Committee of Safety, he was brusquely told by parliament to appoint a locum tenens, and, on his refusal to do this, one was appointed for him. Scant regard was paid to a report to the House of Commons by an *ad hoc* committee of six aldermen to the effect that there was no precedent for the appointment of such a locum tenens save in times of the sickness of a lord mayor and then only on his nomination.[13] This is perhaps unsurprising since the aldermanry itself was already coming under the critical scrutiny of the reformers.

From January 1642 the aldermanic bench was gradually reconstituted as its more conservative members died, resigned, or some excuse was found for their dismissal.[14] Moreover, the aldermen's powers vis-à-vis the common council were reduced. Even if the reported outburst of a former lord mayor, Sir Henry Garway, at a Common Hall in January 1643 is apocryphal, his sentiments would have evoked sympathetic echoes among many other aldermen:

> ... there be some among us, we did not think two years ago to have met here, and yet we were wont to see an alderman coming a dozen years off ... I have been Lord Mayor myself, in a pleasanter time than this, and should have some share still in the government. Before God, I have no more authority in the city than a porter, not so much as an Aldermanbury porter. If to be governed by people whose authority we know not, and by rules which no body ever heard of ... be a sign of arbitrary power, we have as much of it as heart can wish.[15]

The climax had come in the summer of 1642, when the royalist lord mayor, Sir Richard Gurney, was deposed, sent to the Tower and replaced by Pym's City ally Isaac Pennington. The Recorder, Sir Thomas Gardiner, suffered a similar fate. The picture of parallel tendencies in parliament and City is now complete.[16] While there were still royalists in high places in the City, some of whom took part in a failed coup in 1643 which cost some of them their lives, the City was now firmly lined up alongside parliament in a civil war which most moderate citizens and MPs regarded as being not so much against the king as for king and parliament.

III

Five years later, in 1647, it was less easy to take such a comfortable view of the consequences of the City's stand in the first Civil War, and this situation forms the background to London's Counter-Revolution of July 1647.[17] The war had been brought to a successful conclusion a year or so earlier. In February 1647 the king, who had fled to the Scots the previous May, had been handed over by them to parliament. Parliament had held him in comfortable confinement at Holdenby House in Northamptonshire and was renewing its overtures for a peace settlement with him on terms which it and the Scots had agreed during the previous year at Newcastle. These prospects were shattered on 4 June by an event which lies at the epicentre of the political earthquake to which we now turn.

That event was the abduction of the king by a small but determined detachment of soldiers led by a junior officer. Had the king remained at Holdenby in the custody of parliament – a parliament dominated by the cautious and conservative Presbyterian faction – there is no reason to believe that London's Counter-Revolution would have taken place at all; or, at the very least, that it would have taken the form it did. But with the army holding the trump card in its hands in the person of the king, and now advancing its own terms – or at least those of its Independent parliamentary allies – for a settlement, this was quite a different matter. According to the army's own version of events, it had abducted the king as what today would be described as a pre-emptive strike to prevent the raising of a counter-revolutionary force at home accompanied by an invasion from Scotland; designs to bring the disobedient army to heel and to impose a settlement unacceptable to it and its parliamentary Independent allies.[18]

In the summer of 1647 then, the City and its Presbyterian allies in parliament attempted to raise an anti-army force. The main elements of this force were: firstly, the so-called reformadoes, that is, soldiers who had been disbanded from armies other than the New Model; secondly, deserters from the New Model itself, and the City and its parliamentary allies offered generous inducements to soldiers to desert the colours; and thirdly, out of the City's own militia, which, by an Ordinance of early May, was put under the control of a newly reorganised City Militia Committee dominated by the City allies of the parliamentary Presbyterian majority and therefore by persons hostile to the New Model Army.[19]

Not surprisingly, that army took alarm and, as well as bringing articles of impeachment against the eleven principal Presbyterian MPs, it more than once threatened to march on and occupy London. That certainly would have been as arbitrary and inexcusable an act as its abduction of the king had been, and it was only with difficulty that the Lord General, Sir Thomas Fairfax, restrained his more hot-headed colleagues from forcing a march on London.[20] When the army did finally occupy London on 6 August circumstances had crucially changed in such a way as to allow it to claim plausibly that it was now acting with complete constitutional propriety; for it was doing so in order to restore the integrity of parliament which had been grossly violated by the perpetrators of counter-revolutionary disturbances in London and Westminster in late July.[21] It is to these that we now turn our attention.

On 23 July parliament had, under pressure from the army, reconstituted the City Militia Committee which had been one of the media through which a counter-revolutionary force had been built in London.[22] The result of the new Militia Ordinance was to provoke violent disturbances which the City fathers seem to have done nothing to discourage. When the newly reconstituted Militia Committee had its first meeting at Guildhall, its members were violently assaulted by some young men, many of whom were probably apprentices, who threatened that 'if they came there again, they would hange their gutts about their eares. And never left them till they had Compelled them to rise, and, as they went, followed them with ill language'. But this was nothing compared with the astonishing events which were to follow on 26 July.

On that day a violent mob consisting mainly of reformadoes and apprentices but also including cavaliers, who, no doubt, played a crucial part in inciting the others, assaulted parliament itself. The occasion was the presenting of a petition asking for the revocation of the new Militia Ordinance of 23 July and – significantly – asking for the king to be brought to London to negotiate a final peace settlement. One admittedly hostile observer tells us that when the deputation of aldermen and common councilmen bringing the petition to parliament was told that the Militia Ordinance of 23 July could not be rescinded, they told the accompanying crowd that 'they had done what they could, and that it now rested in them to play their parts'. Their parts turned out to be the storming of parliament and the violent intimidation of both Houses. Some of the mob, we are told, even mingled with MPs in the House of Commons and took part in voting themselves; voting, that is, for the rescinding of the new Militia Ordinance and the bringing of the king 'in safety and honour' to London to negotiate.[23] The effect of this outrageous intimidation of parliament was to drive away large numbers of MPs and the Speakers of both Houses to take refuge with the army. But this deterred our counter-revolutionaries not at all. New Speakers were elected, and the Presbyterian rump of a parliament proceeded to align itself with the counter-revolution.

How far had the City government itself played a directing role in all this, or how far had events run beyond its control? It should first be clear that what had happened as a result of the disturbances of 26 July conformed closely enough with what had been the aims of City policy before the outburst: that is, the rescinding of the Militia Ordinance of 23 July; the invitation to the king to treat personally in London; and the recall to the House of Commons of the eleven Presbyterian MPs who had had to withdraw when the army had threatened to impeach them. There can be no doubt that the City governors had wanted these things, even if they disapproved of the violent and tumultuous way in which they had been brought about. But did their responsibility extend any further than this? In his letter of 29 July Lord General Fairfax informed the lord mayor and his colleagues that he had been 'assured from Eye and Ear Witnesses that divers of the Common Council gave great Encouragement to it'.[24] At the very least, it is arguable that the idea of using apprentices, reformadoes and even wild cavaliers as their surrogates to intimidate parliament might commend itself at least to some of the City governors. One observer describes how one of the aldermen, James Bunce, and some common councilmen had stood in Palace Yard at Westminster directing the tumultuous operations.[25] Another – the earl of Leicester, no less – tells how:

> At the same time came some of the Aldermen, the Sherriffes and a part of the Common Counsell to . . . Parliament . . . which shews that the said multitude came hither upon the excitation of the Common Counsell, for, as soone as they had theyr desires, they dismissed the multitude and sent them away to theyr homes.[26]

Naturally one would not expect this picture to be confirmed by the official City record of events. The common council Journal for 26 July tells us that when the common council was informed of the tumult at Westminster, it ordered some of its members to go down to Westminster 'and use their best endeavour by all gentle means . . . to appease the said multitude and to free the said house from danger'.[27] Not surprisingly, these words convey no suggestion of incitement to riot; at most only of acquiescence, though, of course, much depends on the precise meaning one attaches to the notion of appeasing the mob. But at the very least the City authorities could be charged with not doing anything positive to protect the parliament from the mob's attentions. As John Rushworth, the Secretary of the Army Council, admittedly a not unbiased observer, puts it: 'the militia stirred not and the Lord Mayor would not. The Sheriffs came in person with some 40 halberdiers which was all the militia of the City that appeared for the Parliament'.[28]

The Presbyterian rump of a parliament and its City allies desperately prepared to withstand the now apparently inevitable on-slaught of the New Model Army. They appointed the seasoned anti-New Model generals, Edward Massey, Sir William Waller and Sydenham Poynz, to the command of a defence force which, as these generals later protested, ought to have been strong enough to repel Fairfax's army – it was later reckoned that there were about 10 000 men under arms in London at that time. But – and on this Massey, Waller and Poynz were agreed – they were let down by what they scornfully described as the pusillanimity of the City fathers.[29] Accordingly the army, now brimming over with virtue in its role of restorer of the integrity of parliament and of the Speakers and the fugitive MPs to their seats, occupied London on 6 August.

Before the July tumults it had been the army, the abductor of the king and defier of the parliament's order to disband, which had appeared as the constitutional aggressor. In contrast, its role was now that of restorer of the constitution; of the integrity of a parliament which had been outrageously disrupted by tumults which, if not incited, had at least been connived at, by the City government. The lord mayor and his colleagues could obviously expect no mercy. Just as the royalist lord mayor Sir Richard Gurney had been replaced by Isaac Pennington in 1642, so, in 1647, was the current lord mayor Sir John Gayre, who, for all his earlier opposition to royal policies, was now a royalist in all but name, replaced by the radical Independent John Warner. History, of course, never repeats itself, but to many contemporaries it must have seemed to be coming close to doing just that. Like Gurney in 1642, Gayre and his closest aldermanic colleagues soon found themselves in the Tower, of which Fairfax was now appointed Constable. The new Constable in turn replaced the Lieutenant of the Tower, Colonel West, a prominent counter-revolutionary of the July days, with his own nominee, Colonel Tichborne, a Londoner but one of a radical political persuasion.[30]

Before the army's occupation of London, there had been every effort by the City authorities and their associates to build up an atmosphere of terror and apprehension at the plunder and rapine which would be the citizens' lot if the army was ever allowed to occupy London;[31] not least because the main reason why the soldiers' pay was months in arrears was that the City was heavily in arrears in paying its share of the monthly assessment towards the maintenance of the army. Yet the behaviour of the occupying soldiers belied this gloomy prediction. Their disciplined and orderly demeanour stood in marked contrast to the outrageous conduct of the so-called reformadoes, or disbanded soldiers, who had formed the core of London's defence force over the previous weeks.

The aldermen made the best of a very bad job and went down in their gowns to Westminster on 6 August for a very different purpose from that which had taken some of them there on 26 July; this time to observe the army formally escorting the Speakers and fugitive MPs back to parliament from which they had been driven by the tumult of 26 July. Of the soldiers, one Londoner, Thomas Juxon, an enthusiastic supporter of the army, observed in his diary that there was 'not . . . soe much as an apple tooke by any of them'. Coming from this source, the observation is not surprising, but the unexceptionable behaviour of the soldiers is also testified by other observers who certainly cannot be described as friends of the army.[32] This contrast between the disorderliness of the reformadoes in London's now disintegrated defence force and the discipline of the New Model soldiers is of crucial significance in understanding the City's role in the third and last of our case studies; the City's role in the second Civil War in the summer of 1648.

IV

In the summer of 1647, there had been a major (but failed) counter-revolution in London, but no response elsewhere in the country – there had been a very minor rising in Glamorgan in June, but nothing else. Above all, the expected invasion from Scotland or behalf of the king and against the army had not materialised. In 1648, by contrast, there was a Scottish invasion; a series of internal revolts in north and south Wales, the Welsh Marches, Kent, Essex, Surrey, parts of East Anglia, the east and west Midlands, and the northern counties. But this time there was no rising in London. Why was this? A distinguished Canadian historian sees as the crucial factor the putting of the London militia under the command of Major-General Philip Skippon, a trusted New Model Army infantry commander who was also – and this helped – pious Presbyterian in religion even if not in politics.[33]

Skippon had been chosen in preference to Major-General Richard Browne. Described by one of his partisans as 'a Citizen bred and one that loveth the City heartily . . . and . . . loveth government and order',[34] Browne was suspected by many others as someone who would have been happy to co-operate both with English insurgents and Scottish invaders. Certainly the tight control exercised by Skippon over London's security is an important factor. Nevertheless, it is arguable that the most important reason why the City kept its hands clean in the summer of 1648, as emphatically had not done a year earlier, is that it had learnt from its unhappy experience on that earlier occasion, and no rightly calculated that it was likely to do better through co-operation and quiescence.

Although there had again been strained relations between the City and the army in the closing months of 1647 over the City's laxity in paying its tax arrears, with further consequent delays in the payment of the soldiers, there were some indications of an unwonted cordiality in the following February, when lord mayor Warner, who, unlike his predecessor Gayre who was still languishing in the Tower, was *persona grata* to the army, entertained Lord General Fairfax, his principal subordinates and some of the army's parliamentary allies at a banquet. There 'the Fife and Drum played all dinner while, and, to make up the Harmony, the Citie Trumpeters afforded great melody'. Harmony was indeed the keynote of the occasion and was further marked by post-prandial speeches which were mutual assurances of good affection.[35] As Colonel Overton, the governor of Hull, observed in a letter a week later, the army no longer had anything to fear from the City which had 'nothing left to hedge in the cuckoo, or to head their headless multitudes. The militia, Tower and army is all our own and nothing theirs, except their wealth and voices, and that not unquestionable'.[36]

This was perhaps more than a trifle over-optimistic. In view of their memories of the events of July 1647 and of the current expectations of the Scottish Engagers that their traditional allies in the City would rise in their favour when they invaded England to restore the king to power, it is hardly surprising to find a continued uneasiness in the army about the City's intentions. On 23 April one John Everard deposed in an affidavit that, while lying in bed at an inn in Windsor, he had overheard a conversation in the adjoining room between high-ranking army officers to the effect that the army was planning to disarm the City so as to prevent it from joining forces with the expected Scottish invaders. Everard's revelations fostered a state of alarm bordering on panic in the City, where chains were raised in the streets and other defensive measures were adopted. Parliament pooh-poohed the alleged army design against the City, but the incident had temporarily revived something of the tense atmosphere of the previous summer.[37] The situation was restored, partly by Skippon's appointment to the command of the London militia which made such army occupation unnecessary; but more, as a result of the dropping of the charges of impeachment in May and June against

ex-lord mayor Gayre and his aldermanic colleagues who had been
in the Tower since the previous August on account of their part
in the July counter-revolution. That slate was now wiped con-
veniently clean.[38]

Thus, in 1648, although the Scots did invade, and the Home
Counties rebelled, the City refused to rise in support of the Scots
or to allow the Kent insurgents passage through London. Chas-
tened by its experience in 1647, the City kept its head clear and
its hands clean in 1648, while the tight grip kept by Skippon on
its defence forces was in marked contrast to their mobilisation
for counter-revolutionary purposes in 1647. The City's quiescence
now reaped the rich reward which all its counter-revolutionary
militancy in 1647 had failed to achieve; arrangements for an un-
conditional peace treaty with the king in the Isle of Wight. Patience
had indeed been rewarded.

The sequel is, of course, familiar. The army was enraged at the
renewal of negotiations with Charles I, who, not without reason,
it regarded as responsible for the renewed bloodshed of the second Civil War. Having defeated the king's forces a second time,
was it now to watch idly while the parliament, as it seemed, was
about to concede the war aims of the losers in the war? It will be
recalled that when the army had occupied London in August 1647,
it had claimed to be acting to restore parliament's integrity which
had been shattered by outrageous violence which had been connived at by the City authorities. When, horrified by what seemed
the likelihood of the negotiations with the king being attended
with success and what the army believed was a betrayal of all it
had fought for in two wars, it once again occupied London in
December 1648, it was itself to do what it had condemned the
Londoners for doing in 1647: to shatter parliament's integrity,
this time by the event known to History as Pride's Purge. Compared with the momentous consequences of this event – the trial
and execution of the king and establishment of a republic – the
army's other object in occupying London, to force the City to
cough up its tax arrears so the soldiers could be paid, is rather
small beer. So are the citizens' protests at having to provide
premises and 3800 beds and bedding for the occupying soldiers,[39]
who this time were to show themselves to be less disciplined
and restrained than they had been sixteen months earlier; at least
if the subsequent complaints about rape and plunder are anything to go by.[40]

Notes

* This paper is a revised version of the Sir Lionel Denny Lecture given for the Worshipful Company of Barber Surgeons in the Museum of London in April 1993.

1. The main publications in question are: V. Pearl, *London and the Outbreak of the Puritan Revolution* (London, 1961); Idem, 'London Puritans and Scotch Fifth Columnists: a Mid-Seventeenth-century Phenomenon', in A. E. J. Hollaender and W. Kellaway (eds), *Studies in London History Presented to Philip Jones* (London, 1969), pp. 317–31; Idem, 'London's Counter-Revolution', in G. E. Aylmer (ed.), *The Interregnum: The Quest for Settlement 1646–1660* (London, 1972), pp. 29–56; R. Ashton, *The City and the Court, 1603–1643* (Cambridge, 1979); Idem, 'Charles I and the City', in F. J. Fisher (ed.), *Essays in the Economic and Social History of Tudor and Stuart England* (Cambridge, 1961), pp. 138–63; Idem, 'Conflicts of Concessionary Interest in Early Stuart England', in D. C. Coleman and A. H. John (eds), *Trade, Government and Economy in Pre-Industrial England* (London, 1976), pp. 113–31; R. Brenner, *Merchants and Revolution. Commercial Change, Political Conflict, and London's Overseas Traders 1550–1653* (Cambridge, 1993); Idem, 'The Civil War Politics of London's Merchant Community', *Past & Present*, 58 (1973), 53–107.
2. This at least is common ground between the authorities cited in note 1, who, however, differ on much else.
3. The view which is put forward here is developed in more detail in Ashton, *The City and the Court*; Idem, 'Charles I and the City'; Idem, 'Conflicts of Concessionary Interest'. For differing views, see Pearl, *London and the Outbreak*; Brenner, *Merchants and Revolution*; Idem, 'Civil War Politics'.
4. For a more detailed treatment of these and other causes of contention see Ashton, *The City and the Court*, pp. 43–82, 177–200. On the Londonderry plantation see also, T. W. Moody, *The Londonderry Plantation 1609–1641* (Belfast, 1939). On the City and the Royal Contract Estates see also R. Ashton, *The Crown and the Money Market 1603–1640* (Oxford, 1960), pp. 132–53.
5. See Ashton, *The City and the Court*, esp. pp. 149–59.
6. See Brenner, *Merchants and Revolution*, esp. pp. 199–239, 281–91.
7. On the Crown's relations with the East India Company and other chartered companies, see Ashton, *The City and the Court*, pp. 121–41; Idem, 'Charles I and the City', pp. 149–59. For a very different emphasis see Brenner, *Merchants and Revolution*, esp. pp. 281–91.
8. Sir Edward Dering, *A Collection of Speeches* (1642), p. 101.
9. 'Ovatio Carolina: The Triumph of King Charles, or the Triumphant Manner and Order of Receiving His Majesty into the City of London the Twenty-Fifth of November, Anno Dom. 1641, upon His Safe and Happy Return from Scotland', *Harleian Miscellany*, v (1810), pp. 86–103.
10. *A Letter from Mercurius Civicus to Mercurius Rusticus* (Oxford, 1643),

reprinted in W. Scott (ed.), *Lord Somers Tracts*, IV (London, 1810), p. 592. For a full account of the Common Council elections see Pearl, *London and the Outbreak*, pp. 132–41, which supersedes M. C. Wren, 'The Disputed Elections in London in 1641', *English Historical Review*, LXIV (1949), 34–52.

11. The fullest account of these events is in Pearl, *London and the Outbreak*, pp. 125–59. In my view, however, Dr Pearl underestimates the extent to which royal policies aroused opposition in the City before December 1641. On this see Ashton, *The City and the Court*, esp. pp. 201–21.

12. *LJ*, IV, p. 510. *CJ*, II, pp. 376, 662–3. *A Letter*, pp. 591–2.

13. *LJ*, V, pp. 210, 229. *CJ*, II, p. 688. HMC, *Fifth Report*, pt.i, pp. 37, 39.

14. For full details see Pearl, *London and the Outbreak*, esp. pp. 145–55.

15. 'A Speech made by Alderman Garroway at a Common Hall on Tuesday the Seventeenth of January 1642 [i.e. 1643]', *Harleian Miscellany*, V (1810), p. 226.

16. Details relating to Gurney's and Gardiner's dismissal and the diminution of aldermanic power are drawn from, CLRO, Repertory [of Court of Aldermen], LV, f. 456v. *LJ*, V, pp. 72, 192, 280, 284. *CJ*, II, pp. 484, 492, 657, 662–3. HMC, *House of Lords MSS XI, Addenda 1514–1714*, p. 320; *Fifth Report*, pt.i, pp. 24, 36, 37, 42; *Twelfth Report*, pt.ii, p. 321. *A Letter*, p. 594.

17. As it is described in the important essay by V. Pearl, 'London's Counter-Revolution', in Aylmer (ed.), *The Interregnum*, pp. 29–56.

18. For statements treating the abduction as one form or another of pre-emptive strike, see, for example, BL, Thomason Tracts, E391(10) *A Copy of the Paper delivered by Cornet Joyce* (June 1647), pp. 4–5; E393(1) *A true impartiall Narration concerning the Armies Preservation of the King*, (June 1647), esp. pp. 2–9; E399(5) *New Propositions from the Armie propounded by Cornet Joyce*, (July, 1647), unpaged. *The Parliamentary or Constitutional History of England . . . collected by several hands*, XV, p. 47.

19. A detailed account of the arrangements for the counter-revolutionary force and the army's measures against it is given in R. Ashton, *Counter-Revolution. The Second Civil War and its Origins, 1646–1648* (New Haven and London, 1994), pp. 379–90.

20. BL, Thomason Tracts, E400(37) *The Intentions of the Armie plainely discovered* (31 July 1647), p. 3, represents Colonel Edward Whalley as one such person.

21. That these events would justify the army marching on London was a point made as early as 27 July, the day following the disturbances, in a letter from John Rushworth, the Secretary of the Army Council, to the Lord General's father, Ferdinando Lord Fairfax, BL, Add. MS 29,747, ff. 15–16. For the declaration by the Lord General and his Council of War of their intention to restore the MPs who had fled to the army following the disturbances of 26 July see BL, Thomason Tracts, E401(4) *A Declaration from his Excellencie . . . and his Councell of Warre* (August 1647), pp. 3–5. *Parliamentary History*, XVI, pp. 210–12, 225–37. For a longer declaration to the same effect

see, BL, Thomason Tracts, E401(2) *passim*. The most famous and effective of all accounts justifying the army's action is its lengthy Remonstrance of 18 August: *Parliamentary History*, XVI, pp. 251–73.

22. *CJ*, V, pp. 254, 255, 256–7. *A & O*, I, pp. 990–1.
23. Much of the detail of these events of 23 and 26 July is derived from the Journal of the admittedly Independent Londoner, Thomas Juxon: Dr Williams's Library, MS 24.50, ff. 112v–13v. For a similar emphasis in an account of the riot of 26 July, see the pro-army newsletter of that date, C. H. Firth (ed.), *The Clarke Papers*, I (Camden Soc., new series, XLIX, 1891), pp. 217–18.
24. CLRO, Journals of Common Council, XL, 1641–49, f. 243v. *LJ*, IX, p. 360. J. Rushworth (ed.), *Historical Collections [of Private Passages of State]* . . ., VI (1721), p. 647. BL, Thomason Tracts, E400(23) *Two Letters from His Excellency* (July 1647), pp. 1–2.
25. Dr Williams's Library, MS 24.50, f. 113v (Juxon's Journal).
26. R. W. Blencoe (ed.), *Sydney Papers. Consisting of a Journal of the Earl of Leicester and Original letters of Algernon Sydney* (London, 1825), pp. 25–6.
27. CLRO, Journals of Common Council, XL, f. 240v.
28. R. Bell (ed.), *Memorials [of the Civil War comprising the Correspondence of the Fairfax Family]* (London, 1849), I, pp. 380–3.
29. See [W. Waller], *Vindication of the Character and Conduct of Sir William Waller Knight* (London, 1793 edn), pp. 188–9. BL, Thomason Tracts, E401(12) *The Declaration of General Massey and Colonell Generall Poyntz* (8 Aug. 1647), esp. pp. 1–2, 4. For a more hostile and dismissive account of the City defence force by Thomas Juxon see Dr Williams's Library, MS 24.50, f. 116.
30. *CSPD*, 1645–47, pp. 598–9 (Perfect Occurrences, no. 32). *LJ*, IX, p. 375. *CJ*, V, p. 269. BL, Thomason Tracts, E401(15) *Two Speeches Made by the Speakers of both Houses* (Aug. 1647), pp. 3–4. For Juxon's account see, Dr Williams's Library, MS 24.50, f. 119.
31. See, for example, HMC, *10th Report Appendix IV, Captain Stewart's MSS*, p. 97; BL, Thomason Tracts, E393(28) *A Letter written from a Person of Worth* (22 June 1647); E396(17) *Certain seasonable Queries* (3 July 1647), pp. 2–3; E400(35) *Eighteen Queries* (2 Aug. 1647), p. 4; Worcester College, Oxford, pamphlet collection, *Queries Propounded to all well-affected Citizens* . . . (1647), pp. 1–2. For the opposite view, seeing the likely occupation of the city as a boon to be welcomed, see BL, Thomason Tracts, E396(1) *Reasons why the House of Commons ought . . . to suspend the Members charged by the Army* (July 1647), p. 9 (corrected pagination).
32. See, for example, BL, Thomason Tracts, E404(34) *A Religious Retreat Sounded to a Religious Army* (27 Aug. 1647), pp. 2–3. For Juxon's account, Dr Williams's Library, MS 24.50, ff. 118v–19v. For a scathing comment on the gloomy predictions of London Presbyterian parsons see BL, Thomason Tracts, E438(10) *The Pulpit Incendiary* (4 May 1647), p. 42. For less favourable verdicts on the soldiers' behaviour see BL, Thomason Tracts, E419(6) *The Army Anatomized* (4 Dec. 1647), pp. 29–30; E422(9) *The Petition of Right of the Free-*

holders and Freemen . . . (8 Jan. 1648), p. 13; Clement Walker, *The History of Independency* (1648), pp. 18–19.

33. On this see I. Gentles, 'The Struggle for London in the Second Civil War', *Historical Journal*, XXVI (1983), 277–305.

34. BL, Thomason Tracts, E449(35) *The Honest Citizen* . . . (3 May 1648), p. 5.

35. BL, Thomason Tracts, E426(13) *The Kingdomes Weekly Post*, no. 6, 2–9 Feb. 1648, p. 44. All Souls College, Oxford, Codrington Library, pamphlets, *The manner of* . . . *Sir Thomas Fairfax* . . . *entertainment* (Feb. 1648), pp. 4–6.

36. Bell, *Memorials*, II, p. 11.

37. BL, 669.f12(10). CLRO, Journals of Common Council, XL, ff. 267v, 269, 270–1. Rushworth, *Historical Collections*, VII, pp. 1070, 1072–4. HMC, *MSS of the Earl of Ancaster*, p. 414; *Seventh Report, House of Lords MSS*, p. 23. BL, Thomason Tracts, E437(2) *A Declaration of the Lord Major* [sic] *Aldermen and Common-Councel* . . . (25 April 1648), pp. 1–3; E437(2) *The true Answer of the Parliament to the Petition of the Lord Major* [sic] (25 April 1648), defective pagination. All Souls College, Oxford, Codrington Library, pamphlets, *The Humble Petition of the Lord Major* [sic] *Aldermen and Commons* (25 April 1648), pp. 3–12. S. R. Gardiner (ed.), *The Hamilton Papers* . . . (Camden Soc., new series, XXVI, 1880), pp. 190–1.

38. CLRO, Journals of Common Council, XL, ff. 277, 279, 281. *LJ*, X, pp. 278, 296, 303, 307, 308. Rushworth, *Historical Collections*, VII, pp. 1124–6, 1134. BL, Thomason Tracts, E445(24) *Two Petitions to the Lords and Commons* (June 1648), p. 5. *Parliamentary History*, XVII, pp. 171–3, 197. For the articles which had been brought against the aldermen in April see, *LJ*, X, pp. 213–15, 217–19; *Parliamentary History*, XVII, pp. 96–103.

39. CLRO, Journals of Common Council, XL, ff. 307, 307v. BL, Thomason Tracts, E475(39) *The Impeachment Demands and Proposals of the Army* (December 1648), unpaged; E479(40) *A Declaration concerning the supply of bedding* (Dec. 1648), pp. 6–7.

40. Examples are in, CLRO, Repertory LIX, ff. 333r–v; B. Whitelocke, *Memorials of the English Affairs 1625–1660* (London, 1682), defective pagination (entry dated 6 Jan. 1648/9).

3

'A Great Bouncing at Every Man's Door': The Struggle for London's Militia in 1642

Lawson Nagel

The political crisis in London which preceded the Civil War was paralleled by a no less important contest for control of its trained bands. In the climate of mistrust and fear produced by the breakdown between the king and his parliament during the dramatic days of December and January 1641–2, security became a pressing issue. It was not only a matter of the continuing need to maintain public order in the face of crowd disturbances, but also of having the military means to defeat a royalist coup. The London trained bands – at that stage a force of 6000 men in four regiments – could provide both the security so urgently required and the germ of an army. Both the parliamentary leaders and their supporters among the new rulers of London, who were in the process of taking power on the corporation, were aware of the futility of acquiring political control over the capital if the trained bands were to come under the command of a potentially hostile leadership. Not only was it inconceivable that either party could establish effective command over London without their support, but the outcome of the contest for control there could provide a precedent for acquiring command over the militia forces elsewhere. Securing the allegiance of the trained bands was, therefore, an urgent priority for the parliamentarian leaders and their allies as 1641 drew to a close.

At the end of December it was reported from London that 'the citizens for the most part shut up their shops, and all gentlemen provide themselves with arms as in a time of open hostility'.[1] Tension had been rising since the king's return to the capital on 25 November. The Westminster trained bands had been guarding the Houses of Parliament for some weeks under the command of the earl of Essex, Captain-General south of the Trent during the king's absence, in accordance with an order from parliament. Essex's authority expired when Charles returned, and the king naturally gave the command of the guard to the courtier earl of Dorset, Lord Lieutenant of Middlesex. On Monday 29 November 'some hundreds of the citizens came down with swords and staves, and accosted some of the Members to desire their votes for the putting down of Bishops ... the Lord Dorset came forth and caused the guard to thrust them out'. The MP Sir Simonds D'Ewes was worried: 'For [Dorset] to bid the musketeers discharge upon so many citizens and the pikemen run them through, we may well consider how dangerous effects it might have produced'.[2] The following day the Commons dismissed the guard, explaining to the king that they would 'rather run any hazard than admit of a precedent so dangerous' as to have a guard under the command of anyone not chosen by themselves.[3]

The Commons' dismissal of the guards on 30 November was not the end of the matter, and the trained bands of Westminster and Middlesex continued to be pawns in the manoeuvring of king and parliament throughout December. On 10 December a new guard appeared around the Houses, and it was discovered that they were from St Clement Danes and the Savoy, sent down to Westminster by the Justices of the Peace in accordance with a writ from the king in anticipation of a rumoured riot. (This guard, consisting of halberdiers rather than musketeers and pikemen, was in fact a 'strong guard' and technically not a company of the trained bands.) The guard was immediately dismissed by parliament, and one of the Justices was sent to the Tower for this breach of privilege.[4] On 16 December, however, the Commons themselves ordered that the Westminster trained bands should attend on the following Wednesday, when a solemn fast would be observed and a sermon preached.[5] Then on 27 December the Privy Council, in turn, ordered them to attend the Palace of Whitehall 'for a defence against tumultuous risings', and they continued to man the courts of guard at Whitehall until the king's withdrawal from the capital on 10 January.[6]

Throughout the troubled days of December, the London trained bands were kept busy in trying to maintain order within the City itself. On 13 December there was a riot in Newgate, and the prisoners gained temporary control until the trained bands arrived and forced them to surrender.[7] On the fast day, 22 December, a special watch was kept during the City's observance while the Westminster men guarded the Houses of Parliament.[8] On 28 December it was reported that the king had ordered the lord mayor to call out his trained bands to put down disorders in the City.[9] Two days later, with the Westminster and Middlesex men guarding Whitehall on the king's orders, the parliamentary leader John Pym suggested to the Commons that the London trained bands should be sent to guard parliament.

This motion was at first defeated, to the relief of Sir Simonds D'Ewes: 'The Cittizens are not all the sonnes of one mother nor of one minde', he said, 'and wee knowe not how in such a case they may be divided amongst themselves, and if wee should send to them and not succeede it were much better for us not to sende'. D'Ewes noted that he was 'very much troubled' by Pym's motion, 'because I feared that the remedie which hee had proposed would bee almost of as dangerous consequences as the designs pretended' – a reference to the rumoured plot to invade the Houses and attack the Members.[10] Later in the day, however, Pym tried again, claiming new reasons.

The bishops, who had been prevented by the mob outside from taking their places in the House of Lords, had protested that in such circumstances the parliament could hardly be called a 'free' and legally valid one. Pym and his followers responded not only by packing the twelve protesting bishops off to the Tower in record time, but also by carrying through a motion to petition the king for a guard from the City, to be commanded by the earl of Essex. This motion was a watered-down version of Pym's earlier proposal that the Commons should communicate directly with the City, but the House of Lords nevertheless refused to support the petition. On the evening of 31 December, shortly before rising for the weekend, the Commons sent Denzil Holles and seven other MPs to petition the king in the name of the Commons alone, and 'the King told them that if it were delivered to him in writing hee would consider of it'.[11]

Towards the end of December 1641, while these momentous events were taking place in and around Westminster, there were also important changes in the government of the City of London.

The annual ward meetings of the freemen to elect common councilmen for the ensuing year took place on 21 December, but this time many of the wards disregarded the tradition of confirming long-serving and 'able' men in office. Instead, the king's opponents among the aldermen and other prominent citizens made use of the 'fears and jealousies' of these troubled days, according to a later royalist pamphleteer, to

> instill into their fellow-citizens how much it concerned them to make choyce of godly men (so they miscall themselves) and such as would oppose the popish party, under which notion they comprehend all such as stand well affected to the government established, whether ecclesiasticall or civill. They accuse the old common-councell-men as men not zelous for religion, ready to comply with the court for loanes of monies; and, which was worse, many had not only set their hands to, but were active in promoting the intended petition for episcopacy and the booke of common prayer. These objections . . . so prevailed with these silly men, (who thought all to be in danger, unlesse the government were put into new hands,) that, in most wards, the old common-councel-men were turned out, and new chosen in, wholly devoted to the puritan faction.[12]

The exact number of 'new men' elected in December has not been established, but there is no doubt that several of the king's most prominent supporters in the City were voted out and replaced by men who would prove to be staunch supporters of the parliamentary cause in the coming months.[13]

The 'new men' would traditionally have taken their places in common council on the Monday after Epiphany (6 January), but events were moving too swiftly for such legal niceties to be observed when the City's official stance in support of king or parliament was at stake. On 31 December the king ordered the lord mayor to call a common council meeting and sent a representative to inform the members of the late tumults at Westminster, asking them to take steps to prevent their recurrence. The 'new men' attended this meeting, led by the prominent puritan John Fowke, and mixed in with the current members. A few of the royalist common councilmen noticed this and wanted to raise the matter as a point of order, but the matter was hushed up out of respect for the king's representative and because the only business to be decided was common council's answer to the king's message. This premature acceptance of the 'new men' by common council was to have far-reaching consequences, however, for the next meeting would, under their leadership, effectively vote for a *coup d'état* in the City.[14]

The king, having 'considered of' the Commons' request for a guard from the London trained bands under the earl of Essex, sent his reply on Monday 3 January when the House reassembled at Westminster; he 'denyed their requests, as conceiving there was no need thereof'.[15] That same afternoon he began his long-awaited counter-attack when the Attorney General accused the five leaders of the opposition in the Commons, together with Lord Mandeville, of high treason. The Commons voted that night to send an order on their own authority to the lord mayor, aldermen and common council to put the trained bands in readiness, and the king responded around midnight by sending a warrant to the lord mayor forbidding the use of the trained bands except by royal directive, and then gave authority for them to be used to disperse any further tumults, by shooting if necessary. The royalist lord mayor was therefore able in good conscience to call out the trained bands on Tuesday 4 January in accordance with the king's warrant, while simultaneously appearing to comply with the order of the Commons. That day 'in divers parts of the City and Burrough of Southwarke they kept their shops shut and stood on their Guard, fearing some insurrection'.[16] But two important questions remained unanswered: under whose authority were the trained bands ultimately operating, and who were the potential 'rebels' they were guarding the City against?

Answers to these questions were being prepared at Guildhall on Tuesday morning. Although the trained bands had always been called out only on the lord mayor's direct order, the Commons had now gone over his head by sending their message to the aldermen and common councilmen as well; the leaders of the Commons were well aware of the lord mayor's royalist opinions. And when common council assembled to deal with the Commons' message on 4 January, we can be sure that the 'new men' – the recently elected but not-yet-installed members – were present, in view of their known attendance on 31 December and 5 January and the nature of the decision which common council now made. A committee of twelve common councilmen and six aldermen was chosen to undertake measures for the safety of the City.[17] Of the common councilmen elected to this Committee of Safety, at least two were 'new men',[18] and all the others already had proved themselves to be outspoken opponents of royal policy. Three of the six aldermen were also allied to the parliamentary cause; of the three 'lukewarm' aldermen, one would resign a fortnight later and the other two would be expelled in September.[19] Presumably the royalist members of common council wanted nothing to do with such a committee as this; in any case, whether through their apathy or through their being outvoted at the 'packed' meeting on 4 January, common council had now committed itself to armed resistance to the 'malignant party', and had chosen its most vociferous supporters of parliament to supervise that resistance.

The vote of common council which established the Committee of Safety did not specify how its powers were to relate to the lord mayor's authority over the trained bands, but it was obvious that a conflict must arise sooner rather than later. That afternoon the king went in person to the House of Commons in his attempt to arrest the Five Members. Finding that they had fled to the City, he ordered the lord mayor to summon a common council meeting on the following day and went himself to demand the accused men. The newly elected and irregularly admitted John Fowke, now a member of the Committee of Safety as well, made a 'saucy, insolent speech' in reply,[20] and when the king left Guildhall it was the Committee of Safety which prepared a draft response to the king's address. This consisted of a petition listing the grievances of the parliamentary and puritan party and supporting the accused men, and it was accepted by common council – a clear sign that the radicals represented on the Committee were now in control.[21]

On Thursday 6 January, when the Commons assembled (as a committee of the whole House) at Merchant Taylors' Hall in the City, they were met and welcomed by a committee of common council 'consisting of the most eminent persons . . . for their disaffection to the Government of Church and State' who had appointed a guard of 'Substantial Citizens in arms' to protect the Commons.[22] There can be little doubt that the City deputation consisted of the new Committee of Safety, but the guard on Merchant Taylors' Hall is not specifically stated to have been provided by the trained bands. It seems likely that the guard was made up of volunteers who were 'well affected' to parliament; the lord mayor's authority over the trained bands had not yet been challenged.

That challenge was not long in coming, however. Between 9 and 10 o'clock that night, as the tense and fearful citizens lay worrying what the king's next move would be, someone informed the watchmen at Ludgate that royalist supporters were plotting to seize the City that very night. (This rumour appears to have been the result of the accidental discharge of a carbine by a trooper enlisted for the Irish campaign, together with the noise produced by a party of roistering and duelling courtiers at a tavern in Covent Garden – although a later royalist writer claimed that the rumour was spread by the parliamentarian leaders themselves 'to see what party they had in the city'.)[23] Acting on this news, 'divers persons' demanded that the lord mayor call out the trained bands to meet the royalist threat, but he refused to do so, having received no proof of any such danger. His orders went unheeded; there was 'great bouncing at every man's door to be up in their arms presently and to stand on their guard . . . So the gates were shut and the cullisses let down, and the chains put across the corners of our streets, and every man ready on his arms'. The fear in the City was so great that several pregnant women reportedly miscarried and the wife of Alderman Thomas Adams died of fright, but the royalist forces did not materialise, and after a few hours everyone returned home.[24]

As far as the king and Privy Council were concerned, the calling out of the trained bands against the lord mayor's orders was a serious development – a local precedent for parliament's attempt to wrest control of the national militia from the king. The Council wrote to the lord mayor on Saturday 8 January, ordering him to find out who was responsible for the unauthorised raising of the trained bands and to reveal the names of those who originally importuned him to call them out. At this point the Commons immediately interjected, and within a matter of hours they had passed a series of motions of great consequence. It was resolved that the citizens' action had been in accordance with their duty; that commissions of lieutenancy granted by the king to administer the militia forces were illegal; that the lord mayor's authority over the London trained bands derived from such a commission; that the lord mayor, aldermen and common council, or a majority of them, could give orders to the trained bands; that the trained bands of the City could operate throughout Middlesex; that the sheriffs of the City could and should provide a guard from the *posse comitatus* (in effect, from the trained bands) for the protection of parliament, as was usual with lower courts of law; that Philip Skippon, the Captain Leader of the Society of the Artillery Garden and a professional soldier, should be military commander of the London trained bands, subject not to the lord mayor but to a majority of the lord mayor, aldermen and common council; and that a committee of the Commons should meet with the City's Committee of Safety on Monday morning.[25]

By vesting the authority over the trained bands in the whole corporation rather than the lord mayor alone, the Commons gave the radical-dominated common council a voice in their use. The result of this decision was not clear-cut, however, since the lord mayor and most of the aldermen were opposed to the Commons' proceedings. There was also the question of what 'a majority' of the corporation meant: did the lord mayor and aldermen vote as houses, or did each of them vote only as individuals on the same basis as a common councilman? In any case, common council could not even meet without the lord mayor's co-operation, since it was he who had authority to summon them. The Commons' control over London's militia was, as yet, incomplete.[26]

The alternative provision, whereby the sheriffs could be ordered to provide a guard for parliament from the trained bands, was meanwhile being put into effect. On Saturday 8 January two of the City regiments (along with a number of other parliamentary supporters among the citizens) escorted Lord Mandeville and the Five Members to Grocers' Hall, where the Commons were sitting as a committee. On Monday, the joint committee of the Commons and the City's Committee of Safety ordered the trained bands of London, Westminster and the adjacent areas to be called to their colours under the command of Skippon, who was given the title of Sergeant-Major-General. Eight companies were to be drawn out for service on the following day, when they escorted the Commons in triumph back to Westminster – the king having fled to Hampton Court the night before – finally discharging the Westminster and Middlesex men from their guard duties in Whitehall.[27]

It is not known whether the latter actually took part in the parliamentary triumphal parade on 11 January, as they were now free to do, but the eight London companies under Skippon duly escorted Mandeville through the City to the Houses of Parliament while the Five Members went by water, with the Southwark trained bands guarding the South Bank. Each of the London soldiers had a printed copy of the previous summer's Protestation Oath for reformed religion and the privileges of parliament (now reprinted and generally distributed) fastened to the top of his pike or stuck into his hat or doublet – a gesture which was obviously stage-managed rather than spontaneous, and which does not necessarily signify the trained bands' unanimous support for parliament, since only those who had agreed to take the Protestation Oath were allowed to participate in the parade.[28] But there is no doubt that the parliamentary party now had a firm grip on the military forces of the capital, and two London regiments were ordered to guard the Houses of Parliament each day from now on. The king's belated offer to appoint a guard for the Houses from the London trained bands under the command of the royalist earl of Lindsey was not acted upon;[29] as far as the capital was concerned, the control of the militia had already passed from king to parliament.

The House of Commons, having confirmed the decisions made during the past few days while they were sitting as a committee at Grocers' Hall, now began to tighten their control over the London trained bands through the twin channels of the sheriffs and the corporation. On Thursday 13 January they drastically reduced the lord mayor's control over common council by ordering him to call a meeting 'as often and at such times as shall be desired by the ... Committee [of Safety]'. Two days later, they also ordered that the sheriffs 'shall issue warrants for raising such trained bands and other forces as Philip Skippon, Sergeant Major General, shall from time to time give order for', and they gave Skippon personal authority to call out the Southwark militia to relieve the City forces as required, although this was modified on 28 January to take account of the sheriff of Surrey's rights.[30] In each case, the sheriffs were now at the beck and call of Skippon as far as the calling-out of the trained bands was concerned, while the initiative in calling common council meetings (and therefore, in effect, determining the agenda) had passed to the most radical parliamentary supporters on the council itself.

It was presumably in accordance with the Committee of Safety's instructions that a meeting of common council was held on Wednesday 19 January while the Lords and Commons were meeting together as a joint committee of both Houses at Grocers' Hall. (Clarendon states that this latter adjournment to the City was merely a propaganda move by the parliamentary leaders, who, 'finding the general mettle somewhat to abate, and that they might keep up the apprehension of danger and the estimation of their darling the city', once again sought the protection of Londoners.)[31] The decisions of common council on this day reflected the concerns of the Committee of Safety: it was agreed that Skippon should have a pension of £300 per annum for life, or as long as he continued to serve as the City's Sergeant-Major-General; that each captain in the trained bands should have 50s for every day or night on duty for the payment of his officers; that watch-houses with chimneys should be constructed at the end of Broad Street, at Moorgate, at Bishopsgate, and on the wall between the last two; and that the lord mayor should issue precepts to the aldermen to draw up new lists of the inhabitants of their wards who were able to bear arms or to pay for them – this last being a preliminary to an increase in the number of men in the City's trained bands.[32] That night, the company which was then on duty guarding the grand committee of parliament at Grocers' Hall were 'feasted in a most bountifull manner' as a gesture of thanksgiving and support for the change in control over the City's militia.[33]

That change, however, was still felt to be incomplete. Despite the Committee of Safety's new power to force the lord mayor to call common council meetings, and despite the fact that the meeting on 19 January had passed a number of measures proposed by that Committee, the control over the trained bands was still vested in the lord mayor, aldermen and common council together in accordance with the Commons' vote of 8 January. The following is a royalist account of how the parliamentary seizure of military power in the City was perfected through the delegation of this control to the radical Committee of Safety on Saturday 22 January

There was a common-councell held, in which many things were debated: the court was continued long, untill one of the clock At last, tired out with long sitting, and willing to rise, Ven,[3] taking advantage of the present indisposition of the court to sit longer, ready to admit proposalls without any strict scanning ... produceth an order from the house of commons, by which they were desired to returne such men's names with whom the city thought fit to intrust the militia of London. The court, surprised with so unexpected a message, for the present not piercing into the reason for it, nor ... imagining that th men whose names they returned should have absolute powe to execute any thing of themselves, but only as a committee, to consult, and prepare, and report to the common-councell, as the limited power of all committees is . . . ordered that the names of the committee for the posture of defence should be sent to the house in returne to their order.[35]

When it later became clear that the Commons did not intend the Committee of Safety (known henceforth as the Militia Committee) to 'consult, prepare and report' but to take direct control, there were second thoughts and protests among the conservative elements in both common council and the City as a whole, including a petition to parliament signed by the lord mayor, a majority of the aldermen, and more than 300 other prominent citizens. This petition merely provided ammunition for parliament to prosecute the men who had organised it, since the parliamentary party had no intention of retreating from the great advantage they had gained by the creation of the Militia Committee. That Committee also retained its control over common council business and was given new authority to settle disputed elections to the council itself.[36] According to the same royalist account, the Committee 'being, by these dishonest practices, made lords of the militia, and being armed with as much power as will serve the most desperate treasonable designes which either Say or Pym should suggest, they now goe on without checke or controule, and beate downe all before them that stand in their way'.[37]

While the London militia was thus being brought under parliamentary control, other measures were being taken to secure the capital's great arsenal and fortress. On 12 January the Commons had ordered the sheriffs to post a guard around the Tower, drawn from the trained bands under Skippon's command. The royalist Lieutenant of the Tower, Sir John Byron, thus found himself blockaded by both land and water; he was also summoned by the House of Lords to give an account of the artillery and other military stores which had been brought into the Tower in late December and early January, but he refused to leave the Tower and go to Westminster until he had received permission from the king.[38] That permission came on about 20 January, and Byron duly made his report to the Lords, returning just in time to frustrate 'a great conspiracy':

Captain Skippon towards the evening marched very privately
when it was dark to the backside of the Tower, and stayed at
the iron gate with his men, which were about 500, where having continued a while with great silence, he sent one into the
Tower to the Serjeant who commanded the Hamleteers[39] that
night, that he should march out of the Tower with his men
and come to him. But the Serjeant desired to be excused, because, coming thither by my command, he durst not depart
without it. Upon this answer Skippon sent him a second message, that those terms were in vain, for he was sure I should
never come into the Tower again as Lieutenant; but since he
scrupled to come out of the Tower, he desired him to draw his
men up to the iron gate, and upon the shooting of a musket to
be ready to assist him. Whilst these things were in agitation I
returned from the Parliament, it being almost 10 o'clock at night
before I had my dismission, and so the plot was spoiled, but certainly the design was, in case I had been detained, to have surprised the Tower, and to have put in a Lieutenant of their own.[40]

Byron went on to claim that 'were it a time when the laws might
be impartially executed, Captain Skippon might be questioned
for his life for this attempt', but parliament passed an Ordinance
on 12 February approving Skippon's actions and stating that anyone
attempting to arrest him for them was an enemy of the commonwealth. By this time, too, the king had given in to parliament's
repeated demands for Byron's removal, backed up by Byron's
own pleas for freedom from 'the agony and vexation of that place',
and had consented to parliament's nomination of the puritan Sir
John Conyers to replace him – a decision which Clarendon thought
was 'such an instance of his yielding upon importunity that from
that time they thought themselves even possessed of the whole
militia of the kingdom'.[41]

The struggle for control of the militia did indeed switch from
being a London to being a national issue during the next few
months; the naming of the Committee of Safety as commissioners
of the London militia, the seizure of the Tower, and the dispersal of a small royalist cavalry force at Kingston upon Thames
during the second week of January had eliminated all practical
military opposition to parliament in the capital. Skippon continued to send two companies of the London trained bands to Westminster each day to guard the Houses of Parliament (or, as on

Shrove Tuesday, 22 February, to guard the Members as they attended sermons at St Margaret's), but by early March the danger had lessened so much that only one company was henceforth required.[42] Skippon himself had been added to the Militia Committee on 12 February at the Commons' request (having been made a freeman only the month before).[43]

The Venetian ambassador reported on 7 March that 'the City of London, whose mayor has always enjoyed the privilege of commanding the trained bands and of executing despotic powers for securing peace and safety, displays great resentment at an innovation practiced by Parliament in despoiling the mayor and aldermen of this advantage, appointing another individuals in their confidence to this office',[44] but the protests of the lord mayor and a number of the aldermen did not affect the powers granted to Skippon and the Militia Committee. Indeed, those powers were spelled out and confirmed in a new Ordinance for the London militia on 4 April; the Committee was to raise and train forces, appoint and remove officers, and lead men 'as well within the City as within any other part of this Realme of England or Dominion of Wales, according . . . as you shall receive directions from the said Lords and Commons'.[45]

The main concern of the Militia Committee during March and April was the programme to increase the number of men in the trained bands. As we have seen, a new listing of the inhabitants was ordered by common council on 19 January, and on 12 February it was specified that the trained bands should be increased from the current 6000 men to 8000 in forty companies. This required the reorganisation of the four existing regiments into six and the redrawing of the boundaries from which each unit drew its men, as well as the appointment of a number of new officers, and these tasks were accomplished by the Militia Committee early in April. A precept was then issued on 15 April requiring the aldermen and common councilmen in each ward to assist the captains in proceeding with the enrolment of the required number of men for the reorganised trained bands, on the basis of the lists of 'able' men which had been drawn up in January. The listing was to begin on Monday 18 April and continue from day to day until the correct numbers had been listed.[46]

Having obtained parliamentary authorisation on 3 May to 'draw the Trained Bands . . . into such usual and convenient places within three miles of the said City, as to them . . . shall seem fit for the training and exercising of the soldiers',[47] the Militia Committee fixed Tuesday 10 May as the date for the first general muster of the reformed trained bands, 'and accordingly, on that day, their own new Officer, Sergeant-Major-General Skippon, appeared in Finsbury fields, with all the train-bands of London, consisting of above eight thousand soldiers, disposed into six regiments, and under such captains and colonels as they had cause to confide in'.[48]

This first general muster of the reformed trained bands in Finsbury Fields was planned to be an event of great national significance. For the radical Militia Committee, it was designed to demonstrate the City's wholehearted support for the parliamentary cause and its willingness to take up arms in the defence of that cause; for the parliamentary leaders, it would also prove that the newly passed Militia Ordinance was being put into effect and would give a lead for the counties to follow. As Clarendon explained it, although the leadership 'had before sufficient evidence of the inclinations of the mean and common people to them, and reasonable assurance that those in authority would hardly be able to contain them, yet till this day they had no instance of the concurrence of the City in an act expressly unlawful'. Accordingly, the muster was to take the form of a public celebration attended by thousands of citizens and by many members of both Houses – the latter being accommodated in a specially erected tent and entertained by the City at enormous cost (£1000 according to Clarendon; £368 according to the City accounts).[49]

The muster duly took place without mishap, at least in the sense that none of the 8000 men of the trained bands sustained injuries during the skirmishing. The occasion was nevertheless marred by an unfortunate incident when Alderman Thomas Atkins, the Colonel of the Red Trained Band, proudly sitting his horse at the head of his newly enlarged regiment, was surprised by a sudden discharge of musketry. His embarrassing accident was recorded in satirical verses that were circulating within a few days and was to provide valuable material for royalist satirists during the Civil War.[50] A year and a half later, *Mercurius Aulicus* would refer to the time when Atkins 'was troubled with a yearning in his bowels'.[51] The aldermanic colonels of the London trained bands were, of course, appointed for political rather than military reasons, and perhaps it is not surprising that neither Atkins nor any of the other aldermen ever actually led their regiments on campaign during the war.

In general, however, the 'triumphant muster' of 10 May was a great success, and a week later a delegation from both Houses went to common council to return thanks to the City for this demonstration.[52] It also had the desired effect of encouraging the 'well-affected' in the counties to put the Militia Ordinance into practice, and during the following weeks the preparations for war continued on both sides. The king's formation of a bodyguard at York led to parliament's agreement on 10 June to propositions for bringing in money and plate to maintain a cavalry force. The London trained bands, meanwhile, remained responsible for guarding the Houses of Parliament, and an attempt was made on 13 June to identify defaulters; the Lords ordered a list to be drawn up of those citizens who 'find their own arms, or are appointed to wear other men's arms, and either refuse or do not attend the Parliament Houses or the several trainings'.[53] On 24 June, parliament ordered the Militia Committee to take charge of the arms and ammunition recently brought to the City from Hull and to store them in Leadenhall, Blackwell Hall, Guildhall, Apothecaries' Hall, Leathersellers' Hall, or other places they thought fit.[54] Early in July the Commons debated various proposals for raising volunteers for the service of parliament, and on 12 July both Houses finally voted to create an army to be commanded by the earl of Essex and resolved 'to live and die with him'.

The citizens of London responded with enthusiasm to the appeal for volunteers, and common council was ordered to appoint commissioners to assist Essex in the enlistments at the New Artillery Garden near Finsbury Fields on Tuesday 26 July. According to one newsbook, 5000 citizens were listed on that day and 3000 apprentices two days later, after the Lords had declared that they would automatically receive their freedoms on discharge from the army at the end of the conflict.[55] On the following Wednesday the Houses adjourned to watch the exercising of some of the new troops of horse in Tothill Fields, while one of the trained bands mustered for training in Finsbury Fields. The military enthusiasm of the citizens extended even to the children, for on 4 August 'a company of boys came with a drum to the Abbey in Westminster, and in the middle of divine service, the organs then playing, very irreverently came into the church and ... fell a-dancing with their hats on'.[56]

Meanwhile, other measures were being undertaken by the trained bands to secure the City from attack. London and its suburbs were to be searched for suspicious persons, resulting in the following report to the House of Commons on 17 August:

> At the house of the Queen's picturer in London hath been seen several parties of about forty persons at a time, and the house by the Trained Bands being begirt and entered, they privately conveyed themselves away, and narrow search being made about the house, they found a private way down into a vault under the ground, in which they might go a quarter of a mile, leading them to the Thames-side where they might privately take boat and escape.[57]

A week later,

> report was made to the House of Commons that in the house of one Mr Molleins in Baldwin's Gardens near Gray's Inn Lane, being searched by some of the Trained Bands, was found ammunition for 20 men, 2 great pieces of ordnance, one culverin, one great murdering-piece, and four small brass murdering-pieces.[58]

Within each parish of the City, posts and chains were to be set up or repaired to barricade the streets in case of enemy attack.[59] The newly raised regiments of the parliamentary army needed officers to command them, and an obvious source of supply was the Honourable Artillery Company – the most active members of which were already serving in the trained bands. Colonel Denzil Holles recruited two trained band lieutenants[60] to serve as captains over the apprentice butchers and dyers who were to make up his regiment, and one of them soon rose to become lieutenant-colonel after the cashiering of the 'goddam blade' who originally held that post.[61] Colonel John Hampden similarly obtained the services of a trained band lieutenant[62] as one of his captains, and also acquired Captain-Lieutenant William Barriffe, already the author of a celebrated drill book, as his major.[63] It might appear surprising that only these four trained band subalterns joined the regular army in the late summer; the explanation probably lies in the widely held belief that Essex's army would make short work of the cavaliers and the war would be over by Christmas.

Attitudes among the London officers soon changed as news of the royalist army's size and its movement towards the capital became known. By the middle of September, Captain Richard Browne of the Orange Regiment was raising a force of dragoons for the parliamentary army, and he soon appointed his lieutenant, Nathaniel Whetham, as a captain in this new regiment, of which he himself became colonel.[64] In the following month, parliament resolved to raise a second army specifically to guard the capital; the earl of Warwick was named commander-in-chief and new regiments were quickly recruited in London and Essex.

This time, the officers of the London trained bands eagerly accepted commissions as captains in the new units. Lieutenant-Colonel John Venn of the Yellow Regiment was named a colonel in Warwick's army, and he took with him Captain Thomas Buxton of the Orange Regiment, Captain-Lieutenant Jonathan Gauthorn of the Red, and Lieutenant William Stackhouse of the Green.[65] Philip Skippon, now the earl of Essex's Sergeant-Major-General, was also asked to raise a regiment in the City, and he called upon Lieutenant Roger Clay and Ensign Ralph Tusker of the Green Regiment, as well as Lieutenant Samuel Turner of the Yellow, to serve among his captains.[66] Lieutenant-Colonel George Langham of the White Trained Band, on being named to the colonelcy of a regiment in the new army, recruited Captain Samuel Carleton of the Blue Trained Band as his second-in-command, and his captains included the former Lieutenant Timothy Crusoe and Ensign Robert Thomson of the White Regiment, Lieutenant Thomas Jackson of the Green, and Lieutenant Thomas Clarke of the Red.[67] Finally, Lieutenant John Fenton of the Yellow Trained Band and Ensign Thomas Pride of the Orange were given captaincies in the new regiment of Colonel Henry Barclay.[68]

The positions left vacant by the departing trained band officers could be filled relatively easily through the promotion of subalterns and the granting of commissions to recent graduates of the Artillery Garden, but there were also vacancies in the 'other ranks'. The Commons heard on 15 September that 'divers Citizens &c. who were well able to maintain Arms are not of body to beare them, and that other some are able in body, but not able to buy them . . . and that there are divers Gentlemen and others who have been charged to maintain arms, as 1, 2, 3 a man, have refused and are gone to their country houses, leaving behind them neither Arms nor men in their absence to supply their places'. It was therefore ordered that new lists should be prepared of 'the names of the ablest and sufficientest men of all parishes, as well inmates as house-keepers, to carry Arms as shall be appointed them, and to enrole them in the number of the trained bands'.[69] Service in the City forces was thus no longer to be restricted to householders, and since there was apparently no procedure laid down for determining whether or not a man was able-bodied, the practice of paying substitutes probably became widespread. In the following month, common council specified that '12d a day and 12d a night be paid by owners of arms to those poore men who borrow them for service, on presentation of a ticket certifying good service signed by the captain'.[70]

Inability to bear arms and absence from the City were not the only reasons for non-attendance at musters, however; some of the citizens simply were unwilling to appear. On 23 September the lord mayor and aldermen noted that 'when they are commanded forth upon the service of this City . . . a very small number of men inrolled do make their appearance, and some of them appearing do depart from their colours before they be lodged, in contempt and great neglect of the said service'.[71] The constables in each ward accordingly were ordered to enforce attendance by the reluctant. In the following month, when parliament proposed that fifty men from each company should be drawn forth to join with forces from the Home Counties to guard the approaches to the capital, the suggestion was 'for the major part consented unto by every company, onely some few that did make some excuses, and desired to be exempted from going any further than to attend upon their Captains'.[72] There was no such hesitation on the part of the forty captains themselves, and in a ceremony at Guildhall on 16 October they 'unanimously entred into a solemne resolution to live and die with the Parliament, and to oblige themselves the more strictly thereunto, they all tooke the Protestation again'.[73]

The earl of Essex meanwhile had left the City to take charge of the main parliamentary army on 9 September, and his departure had been treated as a civic occasion: 'The Lord Generall tooke horse at Temple Barr . . . guarded with most of the Trained Bands of the City of London, in this manner riding from Temple Barre to Ludgate, from thence through Pauls church-yard into Cheapside, and so along to the Royall Exchange, turning downe from thence to Moore-gate and through that towards Islington'.[74] Essex first went to his headquarters at St Albans and then met his forces at Northampton and led them to Worcester, where they waited for the royalists to move from their own headquarters at Shrewsbury.

That move finally came on 12 October, but it was not in the direction of Worcester; instead, the royalist army began marching straight towards the capital. It was the news of this threat which prompted the proposal to draw out fifty men from each company of the trained bands for service in the Home Counties.

Common council, having considered the proposal and the reaction to it among the men of the trained bands, resolved instead that twelve complete companies should be chosen by lot to go out, commanded by their own captains to ensure cohesion and discipline. On 23 October, the day of the battle of Edgehill, the two chosen companies from each of the six trained bands marched out to secure Windsor Castle against the advancing royalists. Their stay at Windsor was short, partly because the local militia forces soon arrived to guard the town and castle, and partly because news had reached London that Essex's army was on its way back in front of the enemy. On 25 October, therefore, the twelve companies returned to London, bringing with them £3000 worth of plate and money 'which they found in the Towne and Castle; the most of it is said to belong to the King and the Cathedral [*sic*] there'.[75] Four days later a further change occurred when the new army regiment of Colonel John Venn, recruited in London and captained partly by former trained band officers, was sent to Windsor as a permanent garrison.

Other frantic preparations for the defence of the City were being made during the week following the battle of Edgehill. It was ordered that courts of guard were to be set up in each parish, and it was laid down that 'a competent number of the Trained Bands and Voluntiers belonging to every Parish shall day and night attend with their Armes in or neere to their Court of Guard, and shall seize and arrest all suspitious persons, Ammunition or Armes passing through their Parishes'.[76] The sheds lining the outside of the old City walls were to be pulled down, and all horses in the City were to be listed.[77] The trained bands were to take 'vigilant care of any conspiracy against the City whether by fire or otherwise, and there should be Pieces of Ordnance taken from Tower-hill and be planted in severall places of the City'.

Meanwhile, the citizens were busily constructing trenches and ramparts 'neere all the Roads and highwaies that come to the City, as about St James, St Gyles in the fields, beyond Islington, and about Pancras Church in the fields . . . and the Saylors are raysing of a Mount and Trenches at Mile-end-Green neere Stepney, where women of good fashion and others, as also children, labour hard at the worke'. On 25 October 'all the shops in and about London were shut by order from the Parliament, and every man was commanded to forbeare his Trade and imployment, that so with the more freedome and diligence they might secure and defend the City and Suburbs ... In obedience to this Order, divers of the Trained Bands watched and walked their rounds in and about London, and many hundreds of people laboured hard at the new fortifications'.[78] On that Saturday night the City's leading royalists were rounded up: 'That evening the Trained Bands of London ... apprehended divers Malignants in severall wards in London, some of them being Aldermen and other cittizens of good worth and divers of the Malignant Clergy'; these were imprisoned in Crosby House in Bishopsgate Street.[79]

The king's army moved more slowly than expected on its march towards London and the immediate crisis passed, but twenty companies of the trained bands continued to watch the City each night for the next fortnight while Essex hurried back to defend the capital. Colonel Venn's forces in Windsor Castle held off a royalist attack on 7 November, but five days later the two London-raised infantry regiments of Essex's army – those of Lord Brooke and Denzil Holles – were destroyed by Prince Rupert's forces at Brentford: 'the Trained Bands of the City of London that night stood all upon their guard and secured the Citie and Outworkes, and a great manie of them that night and the next morning went out towards Brainford'.[80] Bulstrode Whitelock takes up the story with his well-known description of the trained bands at Turnham Green on 13 November:

The City Bands marched forth very cheerfully under the Command of Major Generall Skippon, who made short, and encouraging Speeches to his Souldiers, which were to this purpose: 'Come my Boys, my brave Boys, let us pray heartily and fight heartily; I will run the same fortunes and hazards with you, remember the Cause is for God, and for the defence of your selves, your wives and children; Come my honest brave Boys, pray heartily and fight heartily, and God will bless us'. Thus he went all along with the Souldiers, talking to them, sometimes to one Company, and sometimes to another ... the Foot of the Army were in good plight, and well Armed, and were placed in the Body one Regiment of them, and another of the

City Band, one by another, and some were left for reserves . . . when [Essex] had spoken to them, the Souldiers would throw up their Capps and shout, crying 'Hey for old Robin' . . . The City Good-wives, and others, mindfull of their Husbands and Friends, sent many Cart loads of Provisions, and Wines, and good things to Turnham-green, with which the Souldiers were refreshed and made merry.[81]

In the end, the royalist army withdrew and left the troops to enjoy their picnic.[82]

Whitelocke's account implies that the London trained bands were eager and enthusiastic supporters of the parliamentary cause, but this is not the whole story. He also notes that 'the City were in much trouble, and different Opinions' when the request for support from the trained bands came down from parliament; it was lord mayor Pennington and the Militia Committee who succeeded in obtaining a favourable response from common council. The earl of Clarendon later recalled that he had 'heard many knowing men, and some who were then in the city regiments, say, that if the King had advanced and charged that massy body, it had presently given ground, and that the King had so great a party in every regiment that it would have made no resistance'.[83] Parliament also took the precaution of ordering the lord mayor 'to disarme all such of the trained Bands or others that should refuse to go out'.[84] But there are no records to show whether any were in fact disarmed, and the extent of royalist sympathies among the men of the trained bands cannot be determined.

On the Friday after the confrontation at Turnham Green there was a plan to send three regiments of the trained bands to Blackheath, where they would join with the Kentish militia to help protect that county from plundering by the king's army. In the event, however, the royalists retreated into Berkshire and the London forces remained at home.[85] They were not called upon to take the field again until the following year's campaigning was well under way, although their guard duties in the City continued throughout the winter and they were occasionally involved in searching the homes of 'malignants' or escorting royalist prisoners of war into the City. But the events of 1642 had brought important changes in the London trained bands: they were now under the control of a Militia Committee comprising some of the City's most radical supporters of parliament; they were commanded by officers whom the Militia Committee trusted; service was no longer restricted to 'substantial' householders; substitution was accepted; and the trained bands could be ordered to march out of the City and fight anywhere in the kingdom. None of them had yet been killed or wounded in battle – but it was now obvious that the war would not be over by Christmas after all.

Notes

1. *CSPD*, 1641–43, p. 214.
2. W. H. Coates, *The Journal of Sir Simonds D'Ewes* (London, 1942), p. 211.
3. *CJ*, II, p. 328.
4. *CJ*, II, p. 338. *LJ*, IV, p. 469.
5. BL, Thomason Tracts, E201(3) *Diurnall Occurences*, 13–20 Dec. 1641.
6. BL, Thomason Tracts, E201(8) *Diurnall Occurences*, 10–17 Jan. 1642. *CSPD*, 1641–43, pp. 216, 241.
7. *CSPD*, 1641–43, p. 201.
8. BL, Thomason Tracts, E201(3) *Diurnall Occurences*, 13–20 Dec. 1641.
9. *CSPD*, 1641–43, p. 214.
10. Coates, *Journal of Sir Simonds D'Ewes*, pp. 334n, 366.
11. S. R. Gardiner, *History of England* ... 1603–1642, x (London, 1884), p. 122. Coates, *Journal of Sir Simonds D'Ewes*, pp. 368, 372–3. *CJ*, II, p. 366.
12. *A Letter from Mercurius Civicus to Mercurius Rusticus*, reprinted in W. Scott (ed.), *Lord Somers Tracts*, IV (London, 1810), pp. 588–9.
13. V. Pearl, *London and the Outbreak of the Puritan Revolution* (Oxford, 1961), pp. 132–7.
14. *A Letter*, p. 589.
15. BL, Thomason Tracts, E201(7) *Diurnall Occurences*, 3–10 Jan. 1642.
16. Ibid. Coates, *Journal of Sir Simonds D'Ewes*, p. 376. Gardiner, *History of England*, x, p. 134.
17. Pearl, *London and the Outbreak*, pp. 139–40. CLRO, Journals of Common Council, XL, 1641–49, f. 11.
18. These were John Fowke and Alexander Normington. *A Letter*, p. 589.
19. These were Sir Nicholas Rainton, Sir John Gayre, Sir Jacob Garrard. CLRO, Journals of Common Council, XL.
20. *A Letter*, p. 589.
21. R. R. Sharpe, *London and the Kingdom* (London, 1894–5), II, p. 158. Pearl, *London and the Outbreak*, pp. 143–4.
22. W. D. Macray (ed.), Edward, Earl of Clarendon, *The History of the Rebellion and Civil Wars in England* (London, 1888), I, p. 488.
23. Coates, *Journal of Sir Simonds D'Ewes*, p. 392. BL, Thomason Tracts, E201(7) *Diurnall Occurences*, 3–10 Jan. 1642. *The Rebellion in Coven Garden* (London, 1642). *A Letter*, p. 587.

24. *CSPD*, 1641–43, p. 249. N. Wallington, *Historical Notices* (London, 1869), cited in Pearl, *London and the Outbreak*, p. 142. *Percival Boyd's Units: Citizens of London* (Society of Genealogists).
25. *CSPD*, 1641–43, p. 249.
26. Pearl, *London and the Outbreak*, pp. 144–7.
27. BL, Thomason Tracts, E201(7)(8) *Diurnall Occurences*, 3–10, 10–17 Jan. 1642.
28. Gardiner, *History of England*, x, p. 150. Coates, *Journal of Sir Simonds D'Ewes*, p. 401. Clarendon, *History*, I, pp. 508–10. Pearl, *London and the Outbreak*, p. 145.
29. BL, Thomason Tracts, E201(8) *Diurnall Occurences*, 10–17 Jan. 1642. *CSPD*, 1641–43, p. 251.
30. *CJ*, II, pp. 376, 382, 401.
31. Clarendon, *History*, I, p. 521.
32. CLRO, Journals of Common Council, XL, ff. 16, 16b.
33. BL, Thomason Tracts, E201(10) *Diurnall Occurences*, 17–24 Jan. 1642.
34. The radical City MP, John Venn.
35. *A Letter*, pp. 592–3. The author places this meeting 'before February was tenne dayes old', but the true date is given in, CLRO, Journals of Common Council, XL, f. 17.
36. Pearl, *London and the Outbreak*, pp. 138, 146–50.
37. *A Letter*, p. 594.
38. Gardiner, *History of England*, x, pp. 154–5.
39. The men of the Tower Hamlets provided the nightly guards for the Tower.
40. *CSPD*, 1641–43, p. 269.
41. *CJ*, II, p. 427. Clarendon, *History*, I, p. 558.
42. BL, Thomason Tracts, E201(19) *A Continuation of the true Diurnall*, 21–28 Feb. 1642. *CJ*, II, p. 468.
43. CLRO, Journals of Common Council, XL, f. 30.
44. *CSPVen*, 1640–42, pp. 2–3.
45. CLRO, Journals of Common Council, XL, f. 30.
46. CLRO, Letter Book QQ, ff. 19, 21, 38b.
47. *CJ*, II, p. 559.
48. Clarendon, *History*, II, p. 75.
49. Ibid. CLRO, MS 86.5.
50. *CSPD*, 1641–43, p. 323.
51. *Mercurius Aulicus*, 28 Sept. 1643, and cf. Pearl, *London and the Outbreak*, p. 312 n. 28.
52. Clarendon, *History*, II, p. 75. Sharpe, *London and the Kingdom*, II, p. 166.
53. *LJ*, v, p. 130.
54. *CJ*, II, p. 641.
55. BL, Thomason Tracts, E202(28) *A Perfect Diurnal of the Passages in Parliament*, 25 July–1 Aug. 1642.
56. BL, Thomason Tracts, E202(32) *A Perfect Diurnal of the Passages in Parliament*, 1–8 Aug. 1642.
57. BL, Thomason Tracts, E202(38) *An Exact and True Diurnall*, 15–22 Aug. 1642.

58. BL, Thomason Tracts, E202(39) *An Exact and True Diurnall*, 22–29 Aug. 1642.

59. BL, Thomason Tracts, E240(3) *A Perfect Diurnal*, 12–19 Sept. 1642.

60. George Hurlock of the Blue Regiment and William Burles of the Yellow. PRO, SP28/4, f. 110.

61. PRO, SP28/5, f. 24. Sir H. Ellis, 'Letters from a Subaltern Officer of the Earl of Essex's Army . . .', *Archaeologia*, XXXV (1864), p. 313.

62. Robert Farrington of the Blue Regiment. PRO, SP 28/2A pt 2, f. 259.

63. PRO, SP28/2B pt 1, f. 330. W. Barriffe, *Military Discipline, or the Young Artillery Man* (London, 1635).

64. BL, Thomason Tracts, E240(2) *England's Memorable Accidents*, 12–19 Sept. 1642.

65. PRO, SP28/262 pt 2, f. 219.

66. PRO, SP28/3B pt 1, f. 400.

67. PRO, SP28/6 pt 2, ff. 215, 294; SP28/140 pt 16.

68. PRO, SP28/262 pt 3, f. 448.

69. BL, Thomason Tracts, E240(3) *A Perfect Diurnall of the Passages in Parliament*, 12–19 Sept. 1642.

70. CLRO, Journals of Common Council, XL, f. 40b.

71. BL, Thomason Tracts, E118(29) *A Warrant . . . to all the Trained Bands of London*.

72. BL, Thomason Tracts, E123(24) *Certain Propositions . . . for the drawing out of fiftie in a Company*, 17 Oct. 1642.

73. BL, Thomason Tracts, E240(45) *England's Memorable Accidents*, 17–24 Oct. 1642.

74. BL, Thomason Tracts, E240(49) *Remarkable Passages*, 5–12 Sept. 1642.

75. BL, Thomason Tracts, E240(49) *England's Memorable Accidents*, 24–31 Oct. 1642. The six companies were Mainwaring's and Hooker's from the Red, Player's and Harvey's from the White, Geere's and Tichborne's from the Yellow, Foster's and Blackwell's from the Blue, Forster's and Owen Roe's from the Green, and Wilson's and Buxton's from the Orange; CLRO, Journals of Common Council, XL, f. 40b.

76. BL, Thomason Tracts, E242(2) *A Collection of Speciall Passages*, 17 Oct.– 1 Nov. 1642.

77. *CJ*, II, p. 826. *LJ*, V, p. 416.

78. BL, Thomason Tracts, E240(49) *England's Memorable Accidents*, 24–31 Oct. 1642.

79. BL, Thomason Tracts, E242(2) *A Collection of Speciall Passages*, 17 Oct.– 1 Nov. 1642. For a list of the prisoners see, *CSPD*, 1641–43, p. 403.

80. BL, Thomason Tracts, E242(14) *A Continuation of Certaine Speciall and Remarkable Passages*, 12–17 Nov. 1642.

81. B. Whitelocke, *Memorials of the English Affairs 1625–1660* (London, 1682), p. 62.

82. See page 115, note 53.

83. Clarendon, *History*, II, p. 396.

84. BL, Thomason Tracts, E242(14) *A Continuation of Certaine Speciall and Remarkable Passages*, 12–17 Nov. 1642.

85. BL, Thomason Tracts, E242(18) *A Perfect Diurnall of the Passages in Parliament*, 14–21 Nov. 1642.

4

Citizen Soldiers: The Military Power of the City of London

Keith Roberts

...he [King Charles] loosing for a long time none but toterdemalion Welch and Irish, whilest we lost Citizens of a City not inferiour to Rome.[1]

The central role of the City of London as a source for the supply of men, finance and military equipment for the parliamentary cause was evident to both royalists and parliamentarians from the outbreak of the Civil War. But if London was the key to the kingdom, the source, as one royalist pamphleteer wrote, of 'continual, not small distillations, but floods of men, money, ammunition, and armes descending from the head city, and metropolis of the kingdome',[2] then the key to London lay in control of its citizen militia, the London trained bands.

The sheer number of soldiers under the control of the City authorities during the Civil War was impressive. The London trained bands comprised 6000 men in four regiments before the Civil War and were increased to 8000 men in six regiments in April 1642. There was a further increase in 1643 when six regiments of auxiliaries were recruited from amongst London apprentices and citizens' sons and the suburban militias were brought under the control of the common council's Committee for London Militia. This added a further six regiments, one regiment of trained bands and one of auxiliaries from each of the suburbs: Westminster, the Tower Hamlets and Southwark. By September 1643 the Committee controlled eighteen regiments of foot, totalling some 20 000 men, and two regiments of volunteer cavalry.[3]

While the importance of the trained bands as a garrison for the City was immediately apparent to both sides, with thousands of armed citizens permanently *in situ*, the military assessment of the king and his advisers continued to view London as a source of financial and military supplies, and not as a military power in itself. This fatal error was a continuation of the court's attitude which, as Clarendon had commented, saw the City as a financial asset to be milked – 'a common stock not easy to be exhausted'[4] – and not as Londoners saw themselves; proud of their City, assertive of their privileges and conscious of the Classical parallels which could be drawn between London and republican Rome. The royalists' failure to appreciate the citizens' willingness to fight was compounded by an easy contempt of the actual military value of the London trained bands, and no thought was given to the potential danger if they were to be involved in campaigns outside the capital.

I

The European experience of King Charles's military advisers would have led them to discount the fighting potential of the London trained bands. The Dutch Revolt and the Thirty Years' War in Germany provided numerous examples of citizen militias active in defence of their own homes, but attempts in Germany to extend this to a citizen army, familiar in the military literature of the day as *Landrettung*, had failed.[5] Furthermore, although the London trained bands had not served in the Bishops' Wars, the conduct of other trained band soldiers who had would not have encouraged a contemporary analyst to believe that any trained band soldiers could be effective. Yet experience was to show that while the London trained bands had their shortcomings, including a consistent dislike among their members of the hardships of campaigning, the large numbers of infantry which they were able to provide and their ability to fight in set-piece battles made them a major military factor in the campaigns in southern England.

The process by which the London trained bands came to support the parliament is discussed by Lawson Nagel in Chapter 3 but the military factors which made their support worth having must be appreciated in terms of the peculiar circumstances of the military theory and practice of the early seventeenth century together with the attitudes and experience of London citizens.

During Queen Elizabeth's reign there had been a great controversy in England between the comparative advantages of traditional
English weapons, longbows and brown bills, and modern European
weapons, pike, caliver and musket, which were familiar to those
Englishmen who had served abroad as mercenaries or volunteers.
Many Englishmen retained a strong nostalgia for their traditional
weapons and pointed to famous victories in the past and the more
recent example of Flodden (9 September 1513) as an instance of
the victory of bows and bills over pikemen.[6] Others saw the success
of the Spanish army, first in Italy and then in the Low Countries,
as a model for modern armies and one which could only be matched
by copying its weapons and tactics.

Proponents of the modern Spanish style were successful in this
debate and the new militia created during Queen Elizabeth's reign
was gradually re-equipped on modern lines. This required a difference in emphasis in the organisation of the militia as modern
weapons were more expensive and the tactical styles necessary
to use them were more complex. This placed a limit upon the
burden which could be imposed upon the community to fund
the purchase of military equipment and find the time required
for training. In consequence, the mass levy was replaced by smaller
units of 'trained bands' that were trained to use new weapons
and tactics, supported by untrained men similarly equipped but
not regularly trained. The expense of providing modern equipment was divided amongst the community, but change was
gradual. The surviving returns of twenty-nine English counties
mustered in April 1588, in anticipation of an invasion mounted
by the Spanish Armada, show that longbows and bills still formed
a substantial element of militia equipment among both 'trained'
and 'untrained' men.[7]

The wealth of the City of London and its proximity to the Court
ensured that its militia's equipment met the highest standards
from an early stage and its first muster saw the selection of 3000
men, equipped as calivermen and pikemen, with arrangements
proposed for regular training in the Artillery Garden and St
George's Fields.[8] The selection of these men was originally organised by the City Guilds, but as the diplomatic situation worsened with the despatch of an English expeditionary force in 1585
to assist the Dutch in their rebellion against Spain, the trained
bands were reorganised in the following year, with each Alderman

being responsible for selecting the men from his ward.[9]

The events of the Armada crisis provided evidence of the strengths and, in the eyes of contemporary professional officers, weaknesses, of the London trained bands. Another generation of professional soldiers would hold very similar views in 1642. The strengths of the London trained bands in 1588 were that they provided a strong contingent of 6000 well-armed men and their officers were 'gallant, active and forward citizens having had experience, both abroad and at home' who were 'very sufficient and skilfull, to traine and teach common souldiers the managing of their peeces, pikes and halbards, to march, countermarch and ring'.[10]

This was supported by the objective assessment of a Spanish spy, Antonio de Vega, that 'The 6000 men raised in London meet for drill twice a week . . . are certainly very good troops considering they are recruits, and are well armed'. He also commented that they were 'commanded by merchants', and in the eyes of the earl of Leicester, commander of the London and other trained bands mustered at Tilbury, and a professional soldier, this was their weakness. Leicester's concern was shown in his comment, 'For your Londoners I se as the mattre stands, there servyce wyll be lytle except they have their owne captains' and 'having them I look for none at all by them when we shall mete the enymy. I know what burgers be well enough'.[11] He felt that however well trained and well armed they might be, since neither officers nor men had any actual experience in facing an enemy, the trained bands' formations would crumble away in the face of the Prince of Parma's veteran Spanish army.[12] Londoners were spared the acid test of their military ability as the defeat of the Spanish Armada ensured that Parma's army never landed. Londoners and the professional officers who had seen them retained their respective opinions of the military value of London's citizen soldiers.

The pacific policies of Elizabeth's successor, James I, led to stagnation within the trained bands at precisely the time when radical changes in military practice were being developed by the Dutch. The cutting edge of developing military theory and practice was now to be found not in the Spanish army which had formed the model in the later sixteenth century but in its opponent, the Dutch army which had been radically reformed and trained by Prince Maurice of Nassau. The Dutch had swiftly discovered that simply copying Spanish methods did not provide a successful counter to a veteran army, and in the 1590s Prince Maurice turned instead to devising a different system. The structured nature of his new theories, derived from Classical models, made a great impact on contemporary soldiers, as the admiring comments of the English professional, Henry Hexham, indicate: 'how careful and industrious Prince Maurice was of famous memory (the Father of Souldiers) to establish an uniforme Order and Discipline amongst us'.[13]

A uniform or standard response to orders was required for the new Dutch tactics, because although the soldiers would still fight in close-packed ranks, as the Spanish did, they also had to be capable of a swift and flexible response to different orders. Dutch soldiers were trained to fight in smaller units than the Spanish and their tactical deployment was intended to allow them to manoeuvre on the battlefield in support of one another. If they were to do so successfully, each soldier and each unit had to respond to the same orders in the same way and, to achieve this, common systems of orders and training were necessary.

Three factors were required if this system was to operate successfully; a thorough understanding of the principles involved, the continuous service of a standing army which created a core of experienced officers, non-commissioned officers and men, and regular wages or 'constant pay'. The last was essential because contemporaries considered it impossible to impose the discipline required for serious training unless the soldiers were regularly paid and, as the Dutch system was more complex to operate than the Spanish, more training was necessary. In the Dutch army, the wealth of the state made regular pay achievable, but among the Protestant German armies which copied Dutch tactics it was less certain.[14]

The English government's efforts to revitalise the militia were heightened following Prince Maurice's campaign in 1610 to secure the succession to the strategically placed Duchy of Cleves-Julich by a Protestant candidate. The campaign itself was nearly the cause of a broader European conflict some eight years before the Thirty Years' War erupted, and the highly publicised demonstrations of the battlefield deployment of the Dutch army (which included an English brigade) pointed clearly to the advantages of adopting the Dutch system.[15]

In adopting Dutch training methods, however, the English militia officers, and those with responsibility for ensuring that they were competent, inevitably faced the same three requirements as the

Dutch; the need to understand the theory, to obtain the experience through continuous service, and to provide regular pay. The actual military equipment required – pikes, calivers and muskets – was the same whether Spanish or Dutch systems were used, which often leads modern observers to make superficial judgements on the similarity of the two systems. The key difference in contemporary eyes was the flexibility offered by smaller units and the standard response to standard orders which the Dutch system demanded, and this required a more consistent approach to training than had been enforced previously.

Manuals, based on Dutch originals, were printed to improve understanding of the system itself,[16] but the leadership provided by the trained band officers was limited. The officers had to be men of local standing if they were to have any influence over their soldiers, but few had any military experience. Efforts were made to train both officers and soldiers, by continuing the previous Elizabethan system of Muster Masters and, in 1626, by the attachment of sergeants from the Dutch army as training officers.[17] However, the success of local and county musters, which should have addressed the need to build up some element of continuous practice, varied widely according to the energy and enthusiasm of the Lord Lieutenant and his deputies. The motivating force for the soldiers to train could not be pay, as militia service – with the requirement to purchase and maintain arms – was effectively a form of local taxation.

Nevertheless, government efforts succeeded in providing the framework for a modern militia. The trained bands were armed with modern weapons and a standard set of training instructions was produced in 1623.[18] Only the community itself could build upon this framework to create an effective force by 'discipline' and 'training', the first meaning the military theory itself and the second putting it into practice. Here the motivation was lacking and when finally called upon for service in the Bishops' Wars of 1639 and 1640 the trained bands showed neither a willingness to fight nor any marked ability to do so.[19]

The London regiments did not serve in the Bishops' Wars, but with those two débâcles as a national example of the militia in action, it may be asked why the London trained bands' service in the Civil War proved to be so markedly different to contemporaries' expectations. The answer lies partly in the sense of commitment felt by the soldiers themselves and partly in the urban parallel to the formal training efforts instigated by the Privy Council. This movement, the voluntary military companies, was inspired by the example of London and copied elsewhere in the country. The companies were based upon the revitalisation of an existing London model, the urban military guild, for which the new emphasis on the value of trained infantry in modern warfare offered new opportunities. The London Guild and those copied from it were popularly known as 'Artillery' or 'Military' companies.

The origins of the London Guild, the oldest of the English 'Military Companies', can be traced back at least to the reign of Henry VIII, who granted it a charter on 25 August 1537, probably formally acknowledging an existing group. The charter refers to the Guild of St George, but by 1588 the group was known by the location of its training ground in the City of London, the target range of England's Master Gunner, known as the Artillery Garden. By 1613 it was known as the 'Society practising Armes in the Artillery Garden' and later as the 'Society of the Artillery Garden'. The Society survives today as the Honourable Artillery Company.

The urban military guild was not an entirely English phenomenon and close comparisons can be drawn between the Society of the Artillery Garden in London and the *Schuttersgilden* or militia guilds which had originated in thirteenth-century Flanders.[20] These began as voluntary associations meeting for target practice and competitions, but their value as centres of excellence for bowmen, particularly crossbowmen, led to their formal acceptance as city guilds. There were similar guilds in the Netherlands in the fourteenth century and their popularity was demonstrated by a shooting competition at Doornik in 1394 which attracted competitors from *Schuttersgilden* at Utrecht, Den Briel, Gorkum, Schoonhoven, Schieden, Gouda, Amsterdam, Haarlem, Delft, Heusden, Geetruidenberg, Middelberg, 's Hertogenbosch and Dordrecht.[21]

Neither the *Schuttersgilden* in the Low Countries nor the Society of the Artillery Garden in London replaced the city authorities in overall control of the city militias, but where military threats existed their role as centres of excellence was expanded and selected members provided military leadership as officers of the militia. The Spanish campaigns in the Low Countries escalated this process as several Dutch cities faced the immediate threat of siege. In England, a general fear of Spanish invasion affected military preparations in London. In 1588 'Captains from the Artillery Garden' provided officers for the capital's trained bands mustered at Tilbury. Their efforts were sufficiently valued by the government that, when enthusiasm flagged, instructions were addressed to the lord mayor in 1591 stating that 'the Artillery Yarde belonginge to the Cittie beinge erected for the trayninge of yonge gent[lemen] in London ... hathe bin of late discontynued' and ordering that 'the same maie forthwith upon receipte hereof be renewed, beinge a matter verie requisete and necessarie for the benefitte of the common weale'.[22] There was a further impetus to revitalise the Guild after a period of stagnation during the opening years of the reign of James I. Military enthusiasts[23] took active measures to revive the Company in 1610 and petitioned the Privy Council two years later for permission to assemble 'to the end this their endeavour might not draw upon them any inconvenience or incurr the danger of the lawes, ordained for restrainte of Assemblies in Armes'. They supported their case by referring to:

> the examples of other flurishinge Citties and States in forraigne parts, together with a pressident of certaine worthie Cittizens of London, heretofor exercisinge Armes had moved the peticoners wth like zeale and affection to enable themselves to doe his Mats Service, and there Contry, and to applie themselves to some laudable exercise for their better knowledge and experience in the use of Armes.[24]

Apart from the evident attraction of military exercise after the pattern in Jacob de Gheyn's attractively illustrated *Exercise of Armes*, there was a genuine sense of the obligation for national defence amongst the leading citizens as a part of their civic responsibilities. This concept was expressed in a note which Marmaduke Rawder., a leading London merchant who joined the Society in 1612, made in his commonplace book in about 1635:

> For as much as the life of man holdeth on a travellers course continually as itt were under saile either in the calme of pease, or the tempestuous sea of warre. Itt behoveth every well governed Common wealth to bee prepared for the one and the other.[25]

By 1614 the Society's role as a training body was generally accepted within the City and all trained band Captains not already members were enrolled. The lapse in the Guild's activity had one significant effect, for it renewed its training entirely on the new Dutch model and so avoided the confusion of styles of training and military theory seen among militia soldiers at the close of the sixteenth century.[26]

With the professional soldier, Captain Edward Panton, as their Captain-Leader, or training officer, the Society of the Artillery Garden commenced weekly training in the handling of arms 'after the modern and best fashion and instruction then in use'. Membership of the Society soon became sought after as 'divers of the better sort of citizens of the best means and quality were desirous to be admitted into the Company, for their better instructing in military discipline'. A dispute between Panton and the Society, which wished to replace him with Captain John Bingham, led to a formal assessment of the quality of their training by a board including two of the leading professional soldiers in England, Sir Horatio Vere and Sir Edward Conway. Bingham was appointed, but the enquiry did show that the Society was being well-trained, as it found 'that haveing seene his [Panton's] trayning and the ordering of his men, they finde his disciplyne and teaching to be as good as they have seene in any bandes wheresoever'.[27]

The source of this new desire for military training lay not so much in the activity for its own sake as for the social prominence membership of the Society offered, with its military displays, social gatherings and feasts. The wealth of its members was sufficient for them to erect a 'strong and well-furnished armory' and to furnish it with 'Armes of severall sortes and of such extraordinary beauty, fashion and goodnesse for service, as are hard to be matched elsewhere'[28] – a deliberate parallel with the *Schuttergild* armouries in Dutch cities. The display of wealth, and by inference power and influence, was important to the mercantile élite which formed the Society, and its activities provided a legitimate and prominent way to do so. The new Dutch military discipline, with its emphasis on a set pattern of training, particularly infantry training, and its prestigious illustrated manual on arms handling,[29] provided a model against which performance could be measured. Military displays provided an opportunity to show both competence in an elaborate art and conspicuous wealth, through the skilled use of beautifully decorated expensive weapons. In this sense, a reasonable comparison can be drawn between the military exercises and displays of the Society and the Tourneys of the greater nobility.[30] Both provided the excuse of military training for an opportunity for the display of wealth and power.

Social reasons provided an impetus for training which replaced the regular soldier's need for pay as a motivating force, and created an enthusiasm for military exercises which was lacking in the national militia. It was not restricted solely to the Society of the Artillery Garden, but also influenced the ordinary soldiers of the trained band companies as they took the opportunity to follow a fashion set by the leading members of their communities. The most notable example was provided by the companies of Captains Edward Ditchfield and Henry Saunders, both members of the Society, who formed a separate association, called the Gentlemen of the Private and Loving Society of Cripplegate, in the early 1630s. This group mustered at six o'clock every morning in summer for an hour's training. According to William Barriffe, who commented admiringly on their enthusiasm, this provided 'no hindrance to mens more necessary callings. Yea it rather calls them the earlier unto it'. These enthusiasts 'neither beat drumme, display Ensigne, nor discharge Musket; but onely exercise their Postures, Motions and formes of Battell, with false fire in their pannes' at their early morning musters, a gesture their neighbours must have appreciated at that hour.[31]

This sense of emulation was not confined to London, as 'many countrey gentlemen of all shires resorted, and diligently observed their exercise of armes which they saw was excellent and being returned; they practised and used the same unto their trained bands in their countries'.[32] Other cities and towns sought permission from the Privy Council to follow 'the most worthy example of London, in the Artillerie Yard there, and of divers other citties and townes incorporate, when the exercise of armes and military discipline hath bin practiced and used'.[33] An indication of the national character of this movement can be seen in John Cruso's dedication of his translation in 1639 of the Sieur de Praissac's *Discours Militaires* 'To the Gentlemen of the Artillery and Militarie companies of this kingdome, and particularly of that in Norwich'.[34] This was also reflected in Edward Cecil's comment, made about 1635, that 'the exercising of Armes for foot

Companys is delighted in not onely in the Citty of London, but in all the principall Townes and Cittyes of the kingdome' and represented 'the humour of the times'.[35] Examples of applications to the Privy Council to form these voluntary companies are Coventry (1616), Colchester (1621), Bury St Edmunds (1622), Norwich (1625), Bristol (1625), Chester (1626), Gloucester (1626), Great Yarmouth (1626), Derby (1627), Ipswich (1629) and Nottingham (1629).[36] The military company at Norwich was sufficiently well regarded in 1633 for the Deputy-Lieutenants of Norfolk to send potential trained band officers there for training.[37] The value of the voluntary companies as a part of the English militia system was recognised in the American colonies and the formation of the Military Company of Boston was authorised by the Governor and Council of Boston on 17 March 1638. This company was being described as the Society of the Artillery Company by 1653.[38]

By the 1620s the Society had become a centre for military experiment and tuition, in default of a permanent military establishment. Its Captain-Leaders were usually professional soldiers[39] and one of them, Captain John Bingham, had such a good reputation that he was summoned by the Privy Council in January 1621 for specialist advice on the discussions for the formation of an army to support the Elector Palatine.[40] Its members provided some of the most influential books on military theory and practice[41] in English and were involved in military experiments in several areas, examples being the combination of the offensive qualities of firepower with the defensive qualities of the pike[42] and the optimum charge of gunpowder to be used in musketry.[43]

Nevertheless, the training of infantry in the Dutch style for battle in the grand manner – 'aux grands armées royales' – remained its major concern and the Society did not offer tuition in the broader practice of the new art of war found, for example, in the professional syllabus of Johann of Nassau's academy at Siegen.[44] The enthusiasm of the Society and the trained band soldiers it trained lay in military exercises the practical military value of which could be expanded into elaborate displays.[45] This served to train officers and men for set-piece battles, which required the ability to manoeuvre in large formations and maintain a series of volleys of musketry, but not for siege warfare or the small actions of war such as 'hedge-fighting' or surprisals.[46]

On the eve of the Civil War the strength of the trained bands lay in the training and leadership provided by officers from the Society, recently improved by the appointment in 1639 of the able professional soldier Philip Skippon as their Captain-Leader, and the sense of unity found where officers and soldiers were drawn from the same community. The political motivation of members of the Society reflected that of the City itself, as although, in theory, membership was restricted to 'men of good means and well affected', the real criterion for this voluntary organisation was social position rather than partisan political leanings. This broad spectrum certainly included some with radical religious and political views, and although the suggestion by a royalist newsletter in 1643 that 'Puritan' sympathisers had deliberately infiltrated the Society was extreme,[47] the text of sermons preached by invitation at the Society's general meetings before the Civil War tend to the godly. A sermon given by Obadiah Sedgewick on 18 October 1638 suggests that his audience would accept the connection between the duties of a 'Christian Souldier' and the concept that 'Armes well exercised prove the great security of the Commonwealth'. Dr Calybute Downing's sermon preached two years later was more obviously radical. Downing mixed direct flattery – comparing the Society's efforts with the militia of ancient Rome in his careful description of its members as 'the Chief Legionaries of this royall City' – with the radical suggestion that they were 'the guard of good Laws' and the comment that it was possible to have the 'worst of government under the best of Princes'.[48]

Any existing disaffection of rank-and-file members of the Society had been exacerbated by the king's interference in the election of their officials during a lengthy dispute between them, the Court of Aldermen and the Privy Council, which lasted from February 1632 to July 1634. This had reduced attendance at the Society's military exercises to the extent that by 1634 the Society's turnout 'hath been so small that it hath seemed only to have the name of a Company'. The compromise solution to this dispute had not satisfied any of the parties concerned, but the Society had gradually recovered, particularly after a new initiative for militia training in April 1635. Those members of the Society who valued military protocol, and by definition any citizens in a voluntary military company did, would have been seriously offended by the king's personal recommendation to the lord mayor and aldermen on 13 September 1635 to appoint one Captain John Fisher as Muster Master to the City of London. This post could be a lucrative one and recent attempts to create it in London had been resisted.[49] Petitions against the creation of this post were submitted by the lord mayor and aldermen, who considered it to be an unnecessary expense, and the Captain of the Society, who stated that his 'continual attendence and labour in exercising the principal citizens in martial discipline, whereby the forces of the City were always furnished with able commanders out of the Company, and the private soldiers made ready for the general musters' fitted him for the role if it was necessary to appoint such an officer. They were over-ruled, however, and Fisher's appointment was made under the Great Seal. The City's reaction may be gauged from the fact that Fisher was still seeking his arrears of pay in November 1639.[50]

II

At the outbreak of the Civil War loyalties in the Society were divided, as each member was influenced by his own business interests and religious or political views. Individual members fought on both sides during the war, although the majority of those who can be traced in service outside the trained bands favoured parliament. Others who may well have sympathised with the royalist cause remained inactive, as they were tied to London by their businesses and risked ruin by formally joining the king. The main impact of the Society on the conduct of the Civil War lay not in the efforts of individual officers, but in its provision of a pool from which men with appropriate political views could be drawn to provide officers for the trained bands. This would be shown during the Civil War itself and, following the revolt of the New Model Army, in the replacement of officers sympathetic to the Army with others more acceptable to the Presbyterian party in parliament.

The feelings of the citizens themselves in this critical period are hard to assess. There was certainly a highly charged atmosphere and considerable mistrust of the king's intentions, engendered by the public knowledge of his attempts during the Second Bishops' War to recruit soldiers from Ireland or hire mercenaries from Denmark, and of the Army Plots. This can only have been exacerbated by his armed attempt to arrest the Five Members on 4 January 1642 and the general atmosphere that this created explains the panic which gripped the City on the evening of 6 January in fear of a coup by, as it turned out, non-existent royalist mercenaries.

The significance of the loss of control over the trained bands by the royalist lord mayor was immediately apparent to the Privy Council, but they were unable to reverse it. The appointment of Philip Skippon, Captain-Leader of the Society, as commander of the London trained bands on 10 January and his attempt to seize the Tower of London by a ruse clearly showed that the king had lost control of London.[51]

After the indecisive battle at Edgehill on 23 October 1642, the London trained bands were persuaded to join with the earl of Essex's parliamentary army to oppose the king's march on London at Turnham Green. The political sympathies of the soldiers were not necessarily anti-royalist, but skillful propaganda depicted the king's army as a collection of rapacious mercenaries and the experience of other European cities was well known, with the sack of Antwerp in 1576 during the Dutch revolt and that of Magdeburg in 1631, during the Thirty Years' War, providing particularly horrific examples.[52] The sack of Brentford by Prince Rupert's forces on 12 November, and casualties amongst London volunteers in the regiments of Denzil Holles and Lord Brooke, can only have served to fuel the soldiers' fears.

Choices of loyalty in civil wars are always immensely difficult and the question of exactly where the sympathies of the trained band soldiers, and even some of their carefully chosen officers, lay, remained open. In the end their decision to come to the muster in strength, as they did, probably rested more on self interest than political allegiance; they marched to protect their homes and families. Parliament was fortunate that in Philip Skippon the trained bands had a leader who completely understood their concerns and whose encouragement of his men as he went from company to company provided the only certainty these men can have felt in an uncertain world; the defence of their homes and families under a trusted leader familiar to the trained bands as the Captain-Leader of the Society since 1639.[53] The outcome of Turnham Green meant that London was impregnable to a royalist army for as long as the trained bands supported parliament. The addition of their 8000 infantry, regardless of their actual capacity, to any army raised for parliament weighted the odds in its favour. It also meant that the militia had passed from vocal opposition to the king to direct military confrontation.

During February 1643 royalist propaganda included threats that London's trade would be interrupted and the citizens starved into submission unless they used their influence to persuade parliament to negotiate a peace. The successful campaigns of Sir Ralph Hopton in the West Country and the earl of Newcastle in the North increased Londoners' concerns that the royalist armies might converge on their city. The military elements of this strategy were unlikely to succeed and even after the successes of his regional armies Charles may never have intended anything more than a propaganda threat. However, it seemed all too plausible from the Londoners' perspective and, as the discovery of Edmund Waller's plans for a royalist coup in May showed, there was significant support for the king in the capital which could easily act as a focus for discontent if parliament's military situation continued to worsen. It was evident to any observer that the fall of Gloucester, coming so soon after the defeats of the armies of Lord Fairfax at Adwalton Moor on 30 June and Sir William Waller at Roundway Down on 13 July, followed by the loss of Bristol on 26 July, would have a serious effect on morale in London. The royalist decision to besiege Gloucester, rather than attempt a costly storm, was soundly based on the military information available, for the prevailing view in the royalist camp was:

> That the Enemy had no Army; nor, by all intelligence, was like to form any soon enough to be able to relieve it; and if they had an Army, that it were much better for his Majesty to force them to that distance from London, and to fight there, where he could be supplied with whatsoever he wanted, could choose his own ground, where his brave Body of Horse would be able to Defeat any Army they could raise, than to seek them in their own Quarters.[54]

Essex's army, depleted by sickness and desertion, was too weak to march by itself and the military realities of this situation were as evident to Essex and parliament as they were to the king's advisers. This led to appeals from Essex and a delegation from parliament[55] to the common council for assistance from the militia, trained band regiments and auxiliaries. Prompted by Essex's warning that it would be better 'to Fight with the Enemy at that distance, rather than to expect him at their own Walls, where they must be assured to see him as soon as Glocester should be reduced'[56] the common council agreed on the grounds that 'the City of London and parts adjacent cannot be long in safety, if that City [Gloucester] be lost, they have there upon resolved forthwith to send out a force both of Horse and Foot for the relief of the said City of Gloucester'.[57]

As at Turnham Green, self-defence was the key factor in the City's decisions and in the form in which they were expressed. From the trained bands' point of view their involvement was limited; they were taking part in a relief expedition with the intention of keeping the war away from London, not formally joining Essex's army for the duration of the war. This limited involvement was indicated by the temporary closure of the City's shops so that the businesses of those who marched with Essex would not suffer by the competition of those who stayed. The citizens' enthusiasm for this service was far from universal, but as they left the City their concerns were focused more on the physical dangers of the war than incipient royalism and, as Sergeant Henry Foster recorded, after reaching Brentford 'many of our citizens, who seemed very forward and willing at the first to march with us, yet upon some pretences and fair excuses returned home again, hiring others to go in their room; others returned home again the same night, before they came to Brainford'.[58]

If the citizens marching out were worried, so also were the families and friends they left at home. Sergeant Foster of the Red regiment of the trained bands recorded sadly the accidental shooting of a young soldier in his regiment on 5 September during a night alarm in the camp, commenting that his 'death will be much lamented by his parents and friends, from whom he received a letter but a few days before to return home'. The royalist newsletter *Mercurius Aulicus* reflected this concern in a similar letter, published in its issue for 3–9 September, which it claimed had been written on 5 September by one Susan Owen to her husband John, a soldier in the Blue regiment of trained bands, and intercepted by royalist patrols. The letter probably is genuine, perhaps with some additions from other intercepted letters and a little careful editing, as the concerns expressed are not political and a London readership would be well aware of the name of any citizen whose status made him liable for enrolment in a trained band company.

Most tender and deare heart, my kind affection remembred unto you. I am like never to see thee more I feare, and if you aske the reason why, the reason is this, either I am afraid the Cavaleers will kill thee or death will deprive thee of me, being full of greif for you, which I fear will cost me my life. I doe much greive that you be so hard-hearted to me, why could you not come home with Master Murfey on Saturday? could you not venture as well as he? but you did it on purpose to show your hatred to me. There is none of our Neighbours with you that hath a wife but Master Fletcher and Master Norwood and yourselfe, everybody can come but you. I have sent one to Oxford to get a passe for you to come home, but when you come you must use your wits; I am afraid if you do not come home I shall much dishonour God more than you can honour him, therefore if I do miscary, you shall answer for it, pitty me for Gods sake and come home. Will nothing prevaile with you? My cosen Jane is now with me and prayes for your speedy returne, for Gods sake come home, so with my prayer for you I rest your loving wife.[59]

Despite desertions, the City Brigade mustered 5000 men when it made its rendezvous with the earl of Essex. Foster estimated that this made the total parliament force around 15 000 men, a useful indication of the importance of the London contingent. Having successfully relieved Gloucester, Essex was forced to fight at Newbury on his return march and here the potential contribution of the London trained bands became apparent to both sides. The set-piece battle there was the style of fighting for which officers from the Society of the Artillery Garden had specifically trained their soldiers, but it was a combination of the confidence gained through training and the sense of unity found in regiments formed of neighbours, men from the same wards in the City, which kept them in the field. Sergeant Foster's account has a laconic style which only partly disguises the horror felt at his first action, when the royalist cannon 'did some execution amongst us at the first, and were somewhat dreadful when men's bowels and brains flew in our faces; But blessed bee to God that gave us courage, so that we kept our ground, and after a while feared them not'.

The trained band soldiers had fought well where many had expected them to run, standing instead 'like so many stakes before the shot of the cannon' and '[ac]quitting themselves like men of undaunted spirits, even our enemies themselves being judges'. This was a view echoed by Clarendon as 'the London train-bands and auxiliary regiments (of whose inexperience of danger, or any kind of service beyond the easy practice of the postures in the Artillery Garden, Men had till then too cheap an estimation) behaved themselves to wonder; and were in truth the preservation of that Army that day'.[60]

The bravery of the trained bands had more serious implications for the royalist cause than the mere survival of the parliament's army in an indecisive battle. At a stroke they had changed the strategic balance in southern England, as Clarendon noted:

> The City was so much united with the Parliament that it supplied their Army with such a body of their train-bands (without which it could never have marched) with what success could his Majesty [have] approached London, after the taking of Bristol, with his miserable Army? and would not then the whole body of the train-bands have defended that.[61]

There could be no question now of a march on London. The bloodless confrontation at Turnham Green had brought the trained bands into armed opposition in the presence of the king. Newbury committed them to actual warfare. As the opening quotation to this chapter shows, Londoners felt the loss of their casualties in this battle equally with their pride in their soldiers' performance. Had Essex been beaten at Newbury, the experience may well have taken the heart out of the City trained bands, but pride in their hard-won success made them responsive to future requests for military support.

After the battle of Newbury, London supplied further brigades of infantry in support of the main field army under Essex, the new Western Army of Sir William Waller and Major-General Richard Browne's garrison at Abingdon. Support remained the key to the trained bands' perspective of their participation in the war and they saw themselves as allied contingents serving under their own officers either for a specific period or for a specific objective. Essex remained popular with the contingents serving with him and, although desertion was always a problem, he had the added advantage of Philip Skippon as his Sergeant-Major-General to keep them in order. Sir William Waller, whose taste for winter campaigning did not stir much enthusiasm with soldiers thinking of their warm homes in the City, had an entirely different experience.

Waller was waging a different sort of war from the style taught by officers in the Society of the Artillery Garden. It featured sudden marches in foul weather, assaults on fortified points and hedge-fighting in wooded or broken ground, and the trained bands did not excel at this. His campaigns showed the weaknesses in the training offered by the Society, as both officers and men lacked practical experience in the small actions of war, and were not accustomed to fending for themselves in the countryside when supplies failed to appear. Discipline was also a problem, for the close relationship between officers and soldiers which stood the regiments in such good stead under fire also meant that officers took a sympathetic attitude to their soldiers' reactions to campaigning.

The crux of Waller's problem was a difference in perspective. He saw the trained bands as a contingent under his direct command and they did not. The shortage of infantry in his army led Waller to attempt to retain the services of the City regiments after their original period of service expired, and this led to friction. Waller's first campaign with the City regiments set the pattern which the rest would follow. After only two days in service at the siege of Basing House, the trained band soldiers were suffering from the harsh November weather and, as Waller reported:

the coldness of the night with fowle weather was a great discouragement to the London regiments, who were not used to this hardness in so much as the officers came to me and made itt their request they might be drawn off, with an intimation that many of the souldiours were hirelings, and their monye being spent, they began to thinke of their returne. The first remonstrance in this kinde was made by the field officers, the second by the captaines and inferiour officers. This was a great surprise to me, but the weakness of my condition without them, inforced me to yeeld upon condition they would give me in their desires under their hands which they did.[62]

After recuperating for a few days in nearby Basingstoke, Waller returned to assault Basing House. During the attack, which failed, there was some confusion in the firing procedures of the Westminster trained bands. This resulted in the second and third ranks firing their muskets before the first was out of their way. The regiment lost some eighty men, shot in the back at close range by their comrades, and must have been thoroughly demoralised. Faced with the approach of a royalist army under Sir Ralph Hopton, Waller drew his force together to prepare to fight. But as he rode amongst them to give his orders he was 'saluted with a mutinous cry among the citty regiments of "Home, Home"'.[63]

Waller suppressed the immediate trouble by threatening to pistol the next man to speak and held a council of war to persuade the City regiments' officers to fight, only to have them return and advise him that their men would not march. Waller abandoned his attempt to take Basing House and returned to his base at Farnham. Although individual trained band soldiers were beginning to desert, he was able to shame most of those who remained into participating in a night march on Alton in view of the 'bad successe' of their service to date. However, when he proposed to follow this up with an attack on Arundel the soldiers responded that 'it was time enough for us to be upon our march homewards before Christmas' and refused.[64] The brigade was welcomed home in London on 20 December, in time for Christmas.

The brigade which replaced it served during the campaign which culminated in Waller's victory at Cheriton. Despite all his efforts to retain it, including his refusal to supply cavalry escorts for its march home, the brigade returned to London escorted by Colonel George Thompson's regiment of City horse, the latter also acting 'without and against order'.[65] The third and last brigade to serve with Waller did notably good service at his defeat at Cropredy Bridge, but proved mutinous thereafter. Waller's despair is evident in his comment that 'yesterday 400 out of one regiment quitted their colours' and his estimate that in all '2000 Londoners have run away'.[66] Worse was to follow, as with the death of their colonel and one of their captains from sickness, the remainder of one entire regiment marched home, officers and men together. Waller was not referring solely to Londoners when he wrote in his dispatch of 2 July to the Committee of Both Kingdoms, 'My Lords, I write these particularities to let you know that an army compounded of these men will never go through with their service, and till you have an army merely your own that you may command, it is in a manner impossible to do anything of importance', but he must have had them in mind.[67]

By the close of 1644 the City regiments had lost all enthusiasm for campaigning. Each of the three brigades which had served with Waller had left on bad terms with him and the three auxiliary regiments serving with Richard Browne at Abingdon were so decimated by desertion that they had to be combined into one regiment in January 1645. Even the earl of Essex began to lack credibility after he abandoned his infantry, including two City auxiliary regiments, at Lostwithiel in Cornwall. In London itself garrison duties on the fortified Lines of Communication were becoming a burden to the soldiers who remained in the City by wasting time which could be more profitably spent in the pursuit of business. In October 1644 there was talk in the City in favour of raising a regiment specifically to garrison the fortifications, an instance of the citizens' growing disenchantment with any form of military service which may explain their support for the creation of, and advance of £80 000 towards, a New Model Army.

With the creation of the New Model, the trained band soldiers considered that their campaigns were at an end. In May 1645 a brigade was requested for service at the siege of Oxford and in June there was a further request for 500 musketeers to assist in the relief of Taunton,[68] but no City soldiers were forthcoming. Regular soldiers were still recruited in London, including cavalry and dragoons directly under the control of the City, but the citizen soldiers of the trained bands and auxiliaries had had enough. The citizens would still supply money for the war effort, but they were no longer prepared to die for it.

III

This war-weariness should have been evident to any observers in London, but there was one last attempt to use the City regiments as pawns in parliament's political struggles. As relations between parliament and the New Model deteriorated during 1647, the Presbyterian party within parliament sought to create a force of their own as a counter to the New Model. This was to be based on the trained band and auxiliary regiments of London and the suburbs, with the addition of new regiments recruited from among disbanded officers and men who had flocked to London to seek their arrears of pay.[69] Army sympathisers were removed from the Committee of London Militia, and from commands in the City regiments, and replaced by others who were more politically acceptable. Once again the pool of trained officers available from the Society of the Artillery Garden made new appointments among the officers possible, but the effectiveness of the regiments depended, as always, on their soldiers' willingness to fight.

New Model Army pamphleteers had a much clearer appreciation of the motivations and concerns of London citizens. They began by reminding the citizens of their joint efforts in the campaigns before the New Model was formed, but then went on to underline the point that where others had failed to win the war, the New Model had succeeded in a single campaign. Having driven home the point that the New Modellers were dangerous enemies, the pamphleteers drew attention to their lack of pay and the opportunity a wealthy City would offer to poor soldiers if they were ever beyond the control of their officers.

The New Model propaganda was well targeted and newsletters that it received from London showed that the trained band soldiers had no will to fight against the New Model Army, and neither parliament nor the common council could force them to do so. One newsletter, dated 14 June, reported that when orders were given to muster 'on paine of death' the 'trayned Bands would not budge, not 10 men of some companies appeared, and many companies none at all but the Officers; nay the very boyes in the streets jeered the drumms as they went about with their charge upon pain of death'.[70] Only the Westminster trained bands had appeared in significant numbers on this occasion. A further letter, dated 26 June, showed that their enthusiasm did not last long, and at a later muster when 'called out upon paine of death ... not one in 20 appeared'.[71] Five years after Turnham Green and with some experience of the realities of war, the citizen soldiers saw the New Model as a more dangerous opponent than the king's army and better disciplined if appeased. The Presbyterian party's plans to create a fresh army collapsed in the face of this attitude and the New Model's march on London became a triumphant parade.

IV

The citizen soldiers had made a significant contribution to the outcome of the Civil War, surprising all observers with their willingness to fight and their ability to do so in set-piece battles. Despite desertions and mutinies, the number of trained infantry which the City could provide, and the trained officers provided by the Society of the Artillery Garden, gave it the potential to be a major military power in its own right. This potential rested on consent rather than pay or politics, for these citizen soldiers could be persuaded that fighting would serve their best interests, but they could not be forced. They were always citizens first and soldiers second, their main concerns were their families and businesses, and the City, their community.

Notes

1. BL, Thomason Tracts, E69(12) *The Parliament Scout*, 22–29 Sept. 1643.
2. *A Letter from Mercurius Civicus to Mercurius Rusticus* (Oxford, 1643), reprinted in W. Scott (ed.), *Lord Somers Tracts*, IV (London, 1810), p. 598.
3. K. Roberts, *London and Liberty, Ensigns of the London Trained Bands* (Leigh on Sea, 1987), pp. 72–3, for details of the infantry. Six troops of volunteer cavalry were raised for the City in the autumn of 1642. These were formed into a regiment under Edmund Harvey in the following year and, in August 1643, a second regiment of eight troops was raised with Richard Turner as colonel. At full strength of 60 men and 11 officers per troop these fourteen troops together with the headquarters staff of both regiments would have mustered a total of around a thousand officers and men. Harvey and Turner were both members of the Society of the Artillery Garden.
4. W. D. Macray (ed.), Edward, Earl of Clarendon, *The History of the Rebellion and Civil Wars in England* (Oxford, 1888), I, p. 499.
5. Johann Jacobi Von Walhausen, *Defensio Patriae oder Landrettung* (Frankfurt am Main, 1623). E. Von Frauenholz, *Die Landesdefension in der Zeit des dreissigjahrigen Krieges* (Munich, 1939).
6. Sir John Smythe, *Certain Discourses* (London, 1590).
7. J. Tincey, *Elizabeth's Army & the Armada* (Leigh on Sea, 1988), pp. 49–51. BL, Harleian MS 168, ff. 166–71, An Abstract of the certificates returned from the Lieutenants of the able trayned & furnished men.
8. John Stowe, *Annales, or a Generall Chronicle of England continued and augmented by Edmund Howes* (London, 1631), p. 671.
9. G. G. Walker, 'The Trained Bands of London', *Journal of the Honourable Artillery Company*, XV (1937), 237.

10. Stowe, *Annales*, p. 744. The word 'peece' is used in this sense for an infantry firearm, caliver or musket.

11. PRO, SP 12/213/55, cited in L. Boynton, *The Elizabethan Militia 1558–1638* (London, 1967), p. 105.

12. The core of Parma's invasion force consisted of veteran tercios.

13. Henry Hexham, *Principles of the Art Militarie; Practised in the Warres of the United Netherlands* (London, 1637), dedication to Henry Rich, earl of Holland.

14. M. Lee (ed.), *Dudley Carleton to John Chamberlain 1603–1624: Jacobean Letters* (Princeton, New Jersey, 1972), p. 290. When referring to the mercenary soldiers raised by Count Ernst von Mansfeld and Duke Christian of Brunswick for service against the Emperor, Carleton remarked (9 March 1622) 'how they can be well paid or disciplined without pay, I must confesse I see not', a typical comment for the period. Carleton was the English ambassador at the Hague (1616–24) and his comment reflects Dutch military opinion and that of English officers in the Dutch service.

15. BL, Royal MSS 17B xxxii, George Waymouth, 'A Journall Relation of the service at the takeing in of the towne & castle of Gulicke this present yeare 1610; with a platt of the towne and castle as it is againe to be fortified'.

16. K. Roberts, 'Musters and May Games: The effect of changing military theory on the English militia', *Cromwelliana* (1991), pp. 5–9.

17. The sergeants were seconded from the eight English infantry regiments in Dutch service at this time. Each regiment consisted of a number of companies, varying between thirty-two and nine, and a headquarters staff. Most companies contributed one sergeant each. None of the sergeants were allocated to assist in training the London trained bands as the Society's training efforts were considered to be effective already.

18. *Instructions For Musters And Armes, And the use thereof: By order from the Lords of His Maiesties most Honourable Privy Counsayle* (London, 1623).

19. M. C. Fissel, *The Bishops' Wars: Charles I's campaigns against Scotland 1638–1640* (Cambridge, 1994), pp. 174–214.

20. M. Carasso-Kok, Der Stede Scut, De Schuttersgilden in de Hollandse steden tot het einde der zestiende eeuw, *Schutters in Holland kracht en zenuwen van de stad* (Haarlem, 1988). Schuttersgilden translates as Shooters Guilds. This refers to the origin of the Guilds as shooting clubs. By the late sixteenth and early seventeenth centuries, however, the Guilds were armed and trained as conventional infantry with pikes, calivers and muskets, and Militia Guilds is a more accurate translation.

21. A. G. Chotin, *Histoire de Tournai et du Tournesis* (Tournai, 1840), I, p. 357.

22. *Acts of the Privy Council, 1591–1592*, p. 74.

23. Stowe, *Annales*, pp. 995–6. G. A. Raikes (ed.), *The Ancient Vellum Book of the Honourable Artillery Company being the Roll of Members from 1611 to 1682* (London, 1890).

24. PRO, SP14/70/3. This is printed in full in G. A. Raikes (ed.), *The*

History of the Honourable Artillery Company (London, 1878), app. B, no. 2, pp. 402–3.

25. York Minster Archives, Add MSS 122, f. 2, Marmaduke Rawden, 'Of Militarie Discipline'. I owe this reference to the kindness of Andrew Robertshaw.

26. BL, Birch MS 4122, f. 79, William Waad, 'A Paper of Mr Waad concerning the defence of the Kingdom against Invasions', 18 Nov. 1596. Waad's despairing comment 'I think, if you shall but ask the opinion of three captains how horsemen ought to charge, and so likewise of footmen in their retraicts, the three captains will be therein of two opinions at the least' illustrates the confusion amongst militia officers at this period.

27. PRO, PC2/31, f. 119. Printed in, *Acts of the Privy Council, 1618–1619*, p. 386.

28. Stowe, *Annales*, p. 995.

29. Jacob de Gheyn, *Wapenhandelinghe* (The Hague, 1607). Thomas Cockson, *Postures to the Musketter and to the Pikeman* (London, 1636 edn); the first edition of this work, which has not survived, may date from *c.*1618. The illustrations were copied from Johann Jacobi von Walhausen, *Kriegskunst zu Fuss* (Oppenheim, 1615). *The Orders established, condescended, and agreed by the Societie of Armes, Citizens, and Inhabitants of the Citie of London* (London, 1616), published for the Society of the Artillery Garden, has figures on its frontispiece of a pikeman and musketeer copied from de Gheyn's work. This is the origin of the arms of the Honourable Artillery Company.

30. K. Roberts, 'Lessons in Revolution: The Impact of the London Voluntary Companies', *Cromwelliana* (1992), 35–47.

31. William Barriffe, *Military Discipline, or the Young Artilleryman* (London, 1635), dedications to Captains Ditchfield and Saunders.

32. Stowe, *Annales*, p. 1013.

33. PRO, PC2/31, f. 502, printed in, *Acts of the Privy Council, 1622–1623*, p. 344.

34. J[ohn] C[ruso], *The Art of Warre or Militarie Discourses* (Cambridge, 1639). This is an English translation of the Sieur du Praissac's *Discours Militaires* (Paris, 1612). Cruso was probably a member of the Norwich military company.

35. BL, Royal MSS 18 cxxiii, Edward, Lord Wimbledon, 'Demonstrations of Divers Parts of War'.

36. PRO, PC2/28, f. 489; PC2/31, ff. 64, 502; PC2/32, f. 671; PC2/33, ff. 141, 211, 325, 333; PC2/36, f. 139; PC2/39, ff. 446, 569. Printed in, *Acts of the Privy Council, 1616–1617*, p. 102; *1619–1621*, pp. 406–7; *1621–1623*, p. 344; *1623–1625*, p. 482; *1625–1626*, pp. 211, 309, 464–5, 477–8; *1627–1628*, p. 30; *1629–1630*, pp. 145, 223.

37. Boynton, *Elizabethan Militia*, p. 284.

38. Raikes, *History of the Honourable Artillery Company*, p. 326. The first captain, Robert Keayne, was a London merchant and a former member of the Society of the Artillery Garden. Keayne's will includes a legacy to the Boston 'Artillery Company' and his recommendations for its future conduct are comparable with the views on militia training

expressed by contemporary military authors with a background in the voluntary companies, such as William Barriffe and Richard Elton.

39. There were nine leaders of the Society between 1610 and 1642. The first of these, Philip Hudson, a citizen, only held the rank of Lieutenant. Of the eight officers who held the position of Captain-Leader, six were professional soldiers. These were Edward Panton, John Bingham, 'Colonel' Hackluett, William Taylor, Walter Neale and Philip Skippon. The remaining two, Henry Waller and Marmaduke Rawden, were prominent citizens, members of the Society and Captains in the trained bands. The six professional soldiers were responsible for training in twenty-seven out of the thirty-three years between 1610 and 1642.

40. BL, Harleian MS 5109, 'The List of a Royall Army', ff. 1–22, 23–34.

41. John Bingham, *The Tactiks of Aelian* (London, 1616); Idem, *The Art of Embattailing an Army* (London, 1629, 1631). Barriffe, *Military Discipline*, (first published in 1635, with five further editions by 1661). Nathanael Burt, *Militarie Instructions or the Souldier tried for the use of the Dragon* (London, 1644). Richard Elton, *The Compleat Body of the Art Military* (London, 1650) (there were further editions in 1659 and 1668).

42. William Neade, *The Double-Armed Man* (London, 1625). For debate on Neade's invention see also, PRO, SP16/95/55; SP16/243/70; SP16/356/148.

43. PRO, SP16/398/95.

44. Hessiches Hauptstaatsarchiv, Wiesbaden K924, Offenes Ausschreiben des Grafen Johann von Nassau über die Kriegeschule zu Siegen 24 November 1618, pp. 153–69.

45. William Barriffe, *Mars his Triumph* (London, 1639) (there were further editions in 1645 and 1661). John Roberts, *Great Yarmouths Exercise* (London, 1638).

46. Discussing a comment by the Duke of Alva, Geoffrey Parker notes 'To the duke's mind (and he had a lifetime of experience to draw on) any troops could fight a battle but it required trained veterans to win a skirmish', G. Parker, *The Army of Flanders and the Spanish Road 1567–1659* (Cambridge, 1972), p. 13. In making this comment Alva assumes inexperienced troops have been properly trained, he is not suggesting that untrained men could fight successfully on the battlefield.

47. *A Letter*, p. 582. See below, p. 167.

48. Obadiah Sedgewick, *Military Discipline for the Christian Souldier* (London, 1639). Calybute Downing, *A sermon preached to the renowned Company of the Artillery, 1 September 1640* (London, 1641). The association of another radical preacher, Samuel Kemme, with the suburban 'Martial Garden' in Southwark can be seen in his sermon *The New Fort of true Honour Made impreganable, or The Martialists dignity and duty* (London, 1640). Kemme's sermon on this occasion was not radical in content. All three men served as chaplains to the parliamentary armies, A. Laurence, *Parliamentary Army Chaplains 1642–1651* (Royal Historical Soc. Studies in History, 59, 1990), pp. 12, 141, 172.

49. A fee of 12*d* per infantryman mustered was suggested on 20 October 1638 and although this had been reduced to 6*d* per infantryman by 26 August 1639 the potential fee was still attractive – £150 per annum if all of the 6000 trained band soldiers in the City had paid their individual contributions. Unsuccessful attempts to obtain the post had been made earlier by the personal petition of two of the Captain-Leaders of the Society, Captains Panton and Neale, and by Sir George Calvert, one of the Secretaries of State, who had solicited it for one of his relatives, Captain Mynnes.

50. *Analytical Index to the Series of Records known as Remembrancia preserved amongst the Archives of the City of London* (London, 1878), pp. 536–8.

51. *CSPD, 1641–43*, p. 269.

52. P. S. Seaver, *Wallington's World. A Puritan Artisan in Seventeenth Century London* (London, 1985), pp. 156, 160.

53. See above, pp. 84–5. B. Whitelocke, *Memorials of the English Affairs 1625–1660* (London, 1682), p. 62. Whitelocke recorded in his diary that he personally accompanied Skippon on this march and 'observed his encouragement of his soldiers riding from one Company to another, & saying to them, Come my brave boyes, lett us pray heartily and fight heartily'. R. Spalding (ed.), *The Diary of Bulstrode Whitelocke 1605–1675* (British Academy, Records of Social and Economic History, new series, XIII, 1990), p. 139. As with the rest of his military expertise, Skippon drew his inspiration for these encouraging words from the practice of the Dutch Army, in this case the example of Prince Maurice of Nassau who 'went from troupe to troupe to animate and encourage his souldiers' before the battle of Nieuport on 2 July 1600. Henry Hexham, *A True and Historicall Relation of the Bloody Battell of Nieuport* (Delft, 1641).

54. Clarendon, *History*, III, p. 134.

55. Clarendon, *History*, III, p. 169.

56. Ibid.

57. BL, Thomason Tracts, E669.f.7(33) *An order by the Committee for the Militia for the relief of Gloucester*.

58. BL, Thomason Tracts, E69(15) Henry Foster, *A true Relation of the Marchings of the two Regiments of the Trained-Bands of the City of London for the reliefe of Gloucester from 23 Aug. to Sept.*

59. *Mercurius Aulicus*, 36th week, 3–9 Sept. 1643, pp. 499–500.

60. Clarendon, *History*, III, pp. 174–5.

61. Clarendon, *History*, III, p. 192.

62. HMC, *Thirteenth Report, Portland MSS part I* (1892), p. 154.

63. HMC, *Thirteenth Report . . .*, p. 155.

64. BL, Thomason Tracts, E101(64) Elias Archer, *A true Relation of the trained-bands of Westminster, the Greene Auxiliaries of London, and the Yellow Auxiliaries of the Tower Hamlets; under the command of Sir William Waller; from Munday the 16 of Octob. to Wednesday the 20 of Decemb. 1643.*

65. *CSPD, 1644*, p. 107.

66. *CSPD, 1644*, p. 324.

67. *CSPD, 1644*, p. 301.

68. R. R. Sharpe, *London and the Kingdom* (London, 1894–5), II, pp. 216–17.
69. See above, p. 54.
70. C. H. Firth (ed.), *The Clarke Papers. Selections from the papers of William Clarke* (Camden Soc., new series, I, 1891), pp. 132–3.
71. *Clarke Papers*, I, pp. 141–2.

5

The Lines of Communication: The Civil War Defences of London

Victor Smith and Peter Kelsey

During 1642–3 London, Westminster and Southwark were given the protection of the most extensive defensive circuit built by either side during the English Civil War. This was the eleven-miles-long 'Lines of Communication', as the defences were called, which consisted of a ring of forts or sconces joined by a rampart and ditch.[1] Although not amounting to a city fortress in a continental sense, the lines were among the larger urban defensive enclosures in early modern Europe.

I

London was well away from the fighting for most of the Civil War, yet the need for defences and a security circuit seemed insistent at the time when they were constructed. In the early stages of the war in particular, it must hardly have been possible for parliament and the City's common council to doubt the need to protect London with fortifications. It was their greatest asset and resource, the site of England's principal magazine and armoury in the Tower of London, by far the country's largest city, and its business and trading centre. The wealth generated by its economic leadership made it the chief source of funding for the parliamentary cause, and it was also able to provide large quantities of supplies and manpower for the armies. As the national capital and seat of government, it also had a symbolic significance, giving the parliamentary leadership authority and respectability, both

117

domestically and internationally. Adequate defences would not only protect this major resource, but would also provide security for parliament itself.

An undated memorandum among the State Papers refers to the necessity of fortifications to secure and defend the city from 'any furious and grand assault by day, but especially by night, when bulwarks, unless united by dike and earthen wall, will not serve but may be used against us'.[2] It was no doubt thought necessary to reassure the volatile populace that it was safe from a successful attack by royalist forces. The spectre of the sack of London in the event of its capture by the royalists raised anxieties in the citizens, who were aware of such excesses during the Thirty Years' War in Germany, particularly the sacking and burning of Magdeburg in 1631, the news of which was still a vivid memory in the early 1640s. It was not difficult for parliamentarian pamphleteers to stir up fears that the worst ravages of that war would be inflicted upon the citizenry of London by royalist armies led by Prince Rupert, dubbed Prince Robber, who had served in Germany.

There was not only the need for protection against an external danger, given the uncertainty about the ability of the parliamentary forces to hold their own in the field, but also the real or imagined threat of uprisings or royalist plots to seize control of London. One of the functions of the lines was that they served to discourage plotters by making it unlikely that a royalist force could march in to support a coup. In the context of the discovery of Waller's plot in the spring of 1643 the danger to the parliamentarian cause of royalist elements within London seemed real enough.[3] Indeed, a nervousness about royalist spies and agents permeated 1643 and an Ordinance provided for the arrest of suspicious persons who might be collecting military information. The perceived need for secrecy even extended to the administering of an oath to those living within the lines not to give intelligence of the defences to the enemy or to take part in any unlawful assemblies and tumults. Somewhat cynically, though probably realistically, the Venetian ambassador commented of the forts that 'the shape they take betrays that they are not only for defence against the royal armies, but also against tumults of the citizens and, to ensure a prompt obedience on all occasions'.[4] A defensive line also provided a useful cordon by which to control ingress and egress through its limited number of guarded openings.

This made it feasible to attempt to enforce restrictions against trading with the enemy.

Parliament's need to defend London was mirrored by the king's need to capture it. Indeed, insofar as either side can be said to have had a coherent strategy at the start of the war, Charles's was probably the more clear-cut: to effect the capture, or at least the isolation, of London. This was a recurring aim, but subject to increasing difficulties as the war progressed. Following the battle of Edgehill and the royalist failure at Turnham Green, in November 1642, the king and his commanders were forced to adopt a more gradual approach for ending the war.

As the London defences were under construction, so Oxford, King Charles's headquarters, was being protected by ramparts. The threat which this royalist fortress exerted prompted William Lenthall, the Speaker of the House of Commons, to say that 'the advantage of that place, situate in the heart of the kingdom, hath enabled the enemy to have ill influence upon this city [London] and counties adjoining, and to infest all other parts'.[5] Oxford was closer to more of the action during the war than was London and exerted a considerable influence on the strategy of the war in southern England. It continued to be seen as a danger until its surrender in 1646. Effectively, however, the royalist threat to London was removed by the parliamentarian victories of 1645 and the confrontation at Turnham Green remained the only occasion on which the royalist forces came within striking distance of the capital.[6]

II

The fortification of London was begun in the greatest period of uncertainty about the outcome of the war. A captured royalist document dating from around the time of the advance to Turnham Green and used by parliament for propaganda purposes mentioned the queen's belief that the impending conquest of London would end the war. The impression that this created was furthered by the king's own propaganda, which was designed to create the impression that he planned to launch a spring offensive in 1643 to capture London, also blockading the Thames below the city and occupying both the Essex and Kent shores.[7]

The Thames approaches to London were already protected to

some extent by the small blockhouse forts under parliamentary control at Gravesend and Tilbury. These had originated in Henry VIII's scheme of defence construction in 1539–40.[8] If the king had gained the active support of a continental ally with a fleet strong enough to overcome the parliamentarian navy, an attack up the Thames towards London might have been attempted. This was never a practical possibility, however, and the river forts served out their time as security checkpoints on shipping entering and leaving the Thames.

The main danger to London was from a land assault by the royalist army. The old city wall which had been sufficient to enclose and defend first the Roman and then the medieval city was now inadequate. As the population of London had grown, urban development had steadily spread outside the walls. Not only had the area to be defended expanded, but the vulnerable medieval stone walls, now less complete, were ill-suited to resist an artillery attack. Moreover, the possession of an artillery train by an enemy meant that the Thames was no longer a defence and so Southwark and a stretch of the south bank had to be included within the new defences. It was also unthinkable that Westminster, the seat of government, should be excluded, for the military problems that that would have caused would have been enormous.

Some measures for the protection of London had been undertaken during the months before the onset of hostilities, including the setting of watches at the gates, posterns and landing places and the enforcement of an embargo on strategic materials such as guns and gunpowder being conveyed upriver to the king. A pinnace and wherry were kept above London Bridge 'for guarding and securing the River Thames'. In April 1642 a warrant was issued by the lord mayor to the Company of Painter-Stainers enquiring about the quantities of arms and ammunition it held in readiness for the defence of London. Knowledge of these preparations caused the king to make an abortive attempt on 14 July to frighten the lord mayor, aldermen and sheriffs with a threat to revoke the City's charter if the livery companies persisted in supplying money to be used against him.[9]

No planning of the actual fortification of London appears to have been made until a little after Charles's rejection of the Nineteen Propositions in June 1642. The beginnings may probably be traced to a set of 'Directions for the Defence of London' of 10 August, which contained a provision for the construction of fortifications and for 'a good proportion of horse about the City and 4 or 500 young men trained and exercised in the City'. The Directions also provided for men to go from house to house in London to discover the allegiance of the occupants.[10] About the time of the Edgehill campaign, parliament ordered the trained bands to be in readiness, the passages about the city to be secured with posts and chains, and the building of guardhouses.[11] The Venetian ambassador recorded the existence of these security measures in October and noted the posting of numerous troops to defend the approaches to London. That month it was ordered that rampart and ditch defences should be made in the suburbs to command the most important roads leading in and out of the city.[12] During the initial stages of construction Sir Kenelm Digby was discovered in disguise observing the building of works at Mile End and was arrested. He was not the only royalist to investigate the new defences. As an aid to royalist planning, John Webb, the Deputy Surveyor of Works, managed to take particulars of the fortifications while they were under construction and to send them to the king.[13]

Both the Venetian ambassador and John Rushworth referred to the building of forts and the formation of entrenchments on the outskirts on London during the following months, but did not give detailed locations.[14] In December 1642 John Evelyn visited London to see the 'celebrated line of communication', which implies that at least part of the connecting works then existed, but he left no description of them.[15] In his 1920s study of the defences, N. G. Brett-James referred to 'two distinct fortifications of London, one in 1642, and the other in 1643'. The latter began as a result of an Act of common council of 23 February 1643 and was confirmed by an Order of the Lords and Commons of 7 March.[16] These legislative measures must certainly have marked an intensification of the earlier efforts on the defences. The Order of the Lords and Commons approved that earlier work, which had not been authorised by parliament, and sanctioned the ongoing construction. Both the Act and the Order had been preceded by a resolution of common council which described the works, some of which may already have been started, and their positions.[17]

The resolution referred only to works north of the Thames, but defences to enclose ground south of the river were also begun. Brett-James suggested that the gathering of royalists at Sevenoaks and the king's comment reported by the Venetian ambassador that there was to be an attack on London from the south-east spurred on this extension of the defences.[18]

The new works were to become the main defences of London. However, the city wall, though obsolete, was not disregarded as a second line of defence. The Act of common council also provided for the removal of all buildings erected against the outside of the wall, and it would appear that, in addition, bulwarks for the wall were to be armed. Archaeological investigations carried out by Professor Grimes after the Second World War suggested that at least one section of the remnant of the city ditch may have been recut at this time.[19] Nor should the importance of the Tower as a citadel within the defences be overlooked. Such a citadel was a characteristic feature of early modern urban defences, and possession of the Tower was hotly disputed by the various elements struggling for power in the capital during the 1640s.

According to the Venetian ambassador, the forts of the main defences, which he thought were admirably designed, were complete by May 1643, when the principal ones were being armed with artillery. He added that the construction of the connecting lines (not mentioned in the resolution) was under way and that the whole defensive circuit would be finished within a matter of weeks.[20] The extension of the defences south of the river was already well advanced.

Provision had been made for the ground in front of the forts and connecting lines to be cleared of such obstacles as hedges, trees and buildings which might restrict the field of fire from the defences and provide cover for an enemy approaching them, but it is not known how far this was taken forward.[21] Most references in the State Papers and the letters and journals of the common council from the autumn of 1643 onwards refer less to new construction work and more to maintenance, manning expenditure and the payment of arrears.[22] John Langham, one of the sheriffs, was made Guardian of the Fortifications.[23]

III

The Scottish traveller William Lithgow toured the London defences in April 1643 and made a detailed description of them

which was published in London in the same year.[24] He walked
the length of the defences and recorded the existence of twenty-
eight works, including several with inner and outer elements, and
two outworks covering the Mile End Road. It was impossible to
keep secret the details of such a vast public undertaking. Nevertheless, with the security restrictions in force and the fear of intelligence passing into enemy hands, it seems remarkable that
such a potentially useful document should have been published.
One problem with Lithgow's evidence is that he was notorious
for his apparently imaginative accounts of his adventures abroad,
being popularly known as 'lugless Will' and by some, more brutally, as 'Lying Lithgow'. In this instance it is difficult to see any
motivation for deliberate misrepresentation of the details of the
defences – except perhaps to impress the royalists – but a degree
of exaggeration and superficial observation may have crept in.

Despite the scale of the works, no contemporary map of the
defences appears to exist, although such maps are extant for other
fortified towns, such as Reading, Worcester, Newark, Plymouth
and Liverpool. The earliest known plan was recognised by David
Sturdy in William Stukeley's *British Coins* (1720).[25] This shows a
total of fifteen roughly drawn forts, batteries and hornworks joined
by lines (Fig. 1). Its basis is unknown. A map engraved by George
Vertue, which differs from the Stukeley map in various details,
was first published in Maitland's *History of London* (1739).[26] This
was apparently based on an examination of the ground carried
out by Dr Cromwell Mortimer, a physician. The map is better
executed than Stukeley's and depicts twenty-one works, also connected by lines, plus two outworks in the form of a fort and a
small redoubt at Islington, the fort being joined to the lines by a
spur rampart (Fig. 2). The degree of accuracy of observation and
recording employed in the survey is unclear. There is also a set
of drawings purported to be the work of an eyewitness to the
fortification of London, Captain John Eyre.[27] They appear to be
plausible-looking three-dimensional copies of the Vertue map, but
portray the forts as being of masonry, when they had been largely
earthworks, and contain other inaccuracies. They were regarded
as forgeries as early as 1854, a view supported by Brett-James.[28]
Rocque's map of London of 1746 and its later version of 1769 are
helpful in revealing ground disturbances which might have been
– and sometimes definitely were – traces of the defences, but these
need careful interpretation.[29]

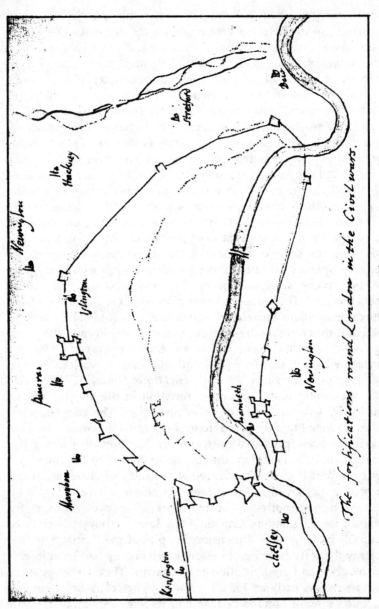

Fig. 1 The Stukeley Plan

The fortifications round London in the Civil wars.

Some of the other pictorial and cartographic evidence is dispersed amongst a miscellany of separate published sources, from illustrations accompanying the contemporary *Malignant's Treacherous and Bloody Plot Against Parliament and Citty of Lo. wch was by God's Providence happily prevented* of 31 May 1643, to a number of maps of parts of London, published at various times during the seventeenth and eighteenth centuries, which, like the Rocque map, reveal actual or apparent traces of the forts and lines. There are, besides, a few perspective drawings which show something of the appearance and condition of several of the works in the eighteenth century.

A range of other written evidence exists in accounts in the State Papers, the records of common council and of the House of Commons, as well as in the correspondence of the Venetian ambassador and the accounts of Rushworth and Bulstrode Whitelocke. This all confirms that the defences consisted of a ring of forts and batteries which were connected by the lines. On the north side of the Thames the general course of the lines was from Wapping, north-west to Shoreditch, then west to Hyde Park and south-east to Tothill Fields. On the south bank, the line resumed at about Vauxhall, and ran north-east to St George's Fields, then east to, or near, the Elephant and Castle and passed north-east to terminate at Rotherhithe. If there were boom defences across the river at Vauxhall and Rotherhithe the details have not come down to us.

Lithgow's account suggests that the lines consisted of a rampart fronted by a ditch, the latter presumably having provided much of the material from which the rampart had been constructed. In referring to the stretch of the line near Islington he commented that the trench dyke was three yards thick 'and on the ditch side twice as high',[30] although he presents a picture of a much more heavily defended northern front to the defences than is suggested in either the Vertue or Stukeley maps.

His description of the fort at Wapping may be representative of the method of construction adopted for the forts. It was '... erected of turffe, sand, watles, and earthen worke, (as all the rest are composed of the like) having nine port holes, and as many cannon; and near the top, round about pallosaded with sharpe wooden stakes, fixt in the bulwarks, right out, and a foot distant from another, which are defensive for sudden scalets, and single ditched below, with a court of guard within'.[31] The illustration of

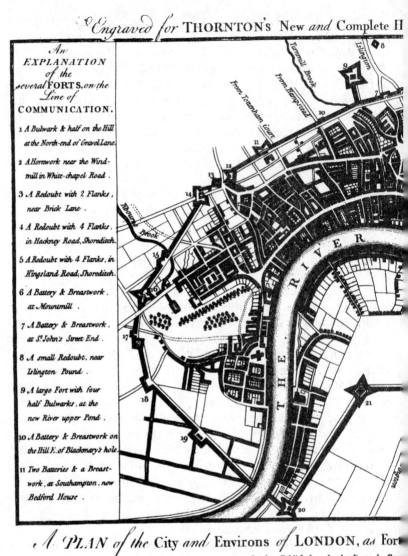

An
EXPLANATION
of the
several FORTS, on the
Line of
COMMUNICATION.

1 A Bulwark & half on the Hill
  at the North-end of Gravel Lane.

2 A Hornwork near the Wind-
  mill in White-chapel Road.

3 A Redoubt with 2 Flanks,
  near Brick Lane.

4 A Redoubt with 4 Flanks,
  in Hackney Road, Shoreditch.

5 A Redoubt with 4 Flanks, in
  Kingsland Road, Shoreditch.

6 A Battery & Breastwork,
  at Mountmill.

7 A Battery & Breastwork,
  at St John's Street End.

8 A small Redoubt, near
  Islington Pound.

9 A large Fort with four
  half Bulwarks, at the
  new River upper Pond.

10 A Battery & Breastwork on
  the Hill E. of Blackmary's hole.

11 Two Batteries & a Breastwork, at Southampton, now
  Bedford House.

A PLAN of the City and Environs of LONDON, as For

London; Published as the Act directs, by Alex

Fig. 2 George Vertue's Plan of the Lines of Communication

12 *A Redoubt with 2 Flanks,
near St. Giles's Pound.*

13 *A small Fort, at the East-
end of Tyburn Road.*

14 *A large Fort with Four
half Bulwarks, across the
Road at Wardour Street.*

15 *A small Bulwark at the place
now call'd Olivers-Mount.*

16 *A large Fort, with Four
Bulwarks, at Hide Park-corner.*

17 *A small Redoubt & Battery,
on Constitution Hill.*

18 *A Court of Guard at
Chelsea Turnpike.*

19 *A Battery & Breastwork
in Tothill Fields.*

20 *A Quadrant Fort with 4.
half-Bulwarks, at Vauxhall.*

21 *A Fort with 4 half Bulwarks, at the Dog & Duck
in St. Georges Fields.*

22 *A large Fort with 4
Bulwarks, near the end
of Blackman Street.*

23 *A Redoubt with 4 Flanks
near the Lock Hospital,
in Kent Street.*

ified *by* Order *of* PARLIAMENT, *in the* Years 1642 *&* 1643.

Hogg, at the Kings Arms, No. 16, Paternoster Row.

another fort, Mount Mill, in 1643 also shows earthen forms and horizontally fixed pointed stakes of the type reported by Lithgow. At least some of the palisades were of fir timber. This approach was typical of the style of fortifications built by both sides during the Civil War. Clearly, though, brick and stone were used to some extent in parts of the fortifications, as there are references in the later accounts of expenditure and arrears of payment to bricklayers and stonemasons. Many carpenters were also employed, constructing courts of guard and probably other internal buildings at the forts and gates.[32]

IV

The Vertue map was reproduced in Colonel W. G. Ross's still-important general discussion of English Civil War fortifications published in 1887,[33] but the first substantive and detailed discussion of the subject was contained in Brett-James's paper in 1928.[34] In 1930 Lieutenant-Colonel J. H. Leslie reproduced a contemporary tract relating to the defences and in the same year the Ordnance Survey published a map showing the line of the defences as then postulated.[35] More recently, David Sturdy's short study, mainly concerned with the siting of the works, appeared in 1974 and Rosemary Weinstein has written on the Camden sector of the defences.[36] The works have also been referred to in a number of general histories of fortification.[37]

The locations of the forts and lines can be related to the features of modern London by comparing the evidence on the Stukeley and Vertue maps and in Lithgow's account with other cartographic evidence, as well as place and street names which seem to perpetuate a memory of the defences. In the years following the Civil War many of the forts were known as Oliver's Castle or Oliver's Mount, although Cromwell had no part in their construction. It cannot be a coincidence that the name Elephant and Castle occurs today on the site of two of these forts, both south of the Thames. Elephant was often spelt Oliphant in the seventeenth century and it is but a short step from Oliver's Castle to Elephant and Castle. Another name that frequently appears on maps close to the location of a fort is Prospect, such as Prospect Street in Rotherhithe. This is confined to south of the river, where the topography is flatter than on the north side, and the remains of the earthworks would no doubt command a good view.

Most of the 'Prospects' shown on eighteenth- and nineteenth-century maps have now disappeared, but some remain. In addition, there is a correlation between the positioning of some later streets and the sites of eighteenth-century toll bars with the route of the lines and the locations of the forts. Evidence has also been detected that subsidence of some later London buildings might have been caused by pre-existing ditches of the Civil War defences. Following Lithgow's approach, and that on the Vertue map, these findings and the numbering of the works are described here in an anti-clockwise direction, beginning on the north side of the Thames at Wapping (Fig. 3).

Whether the rampart line actually began on the riverbank, as shown on the Stukeley and Vertue maps, is uncertain. However, Fort No. 1 was at Wapping, to the south of St George's-in-the-East church. The resolution of the common council provided for a bulwark and a half, with a battery at the north end of Gravel Lane, and this is where Vertue showed it. Lithgow, however, referred to a seven-angled fort and described it as being 'close by the houses and the River Thames'. Rocque's map shows a mound on the generally accepted line of the ramparts at what is now the junction of Watts and Reardon Streets, a location that would accord more closely with Lithgow.

From Wapping the line of the ramparts was traced north by Lithgow and followed Cannon Street Road, past Rampart Street to Fort No. 2 on the south side of Whitechapel Road and close to the site of the present London Hospital, originally built in the 1750s. There was a Mount Street at this point until it was swallowed by a recent extension of the hospital. Lithgow referred to the fort as a nine-angled work, but the resolution of the common council, Vertue and Stukeley described it as a hornwork, an angle of which appears on Christopher Wren's map of West Heath in 1673.[38] The Mount remained an impressive feature until its removal in 1830. Excavations by the Museum of London Archaeology Unit at the corner of New Road and Newark Street, just to the south of the site, may have revealed traces of the ditch of the rampart line which connected from Fort No. 1.[39] Lithgow also mentioned two outlying small forts or redoubts 'towards Myle-end Green', which evidently guarded the road approaches into Whitechapel.

From Whitechapel the rampart line bent north-west to Fort No. 3, near Brick Lane. The resolution proposed that this should be a

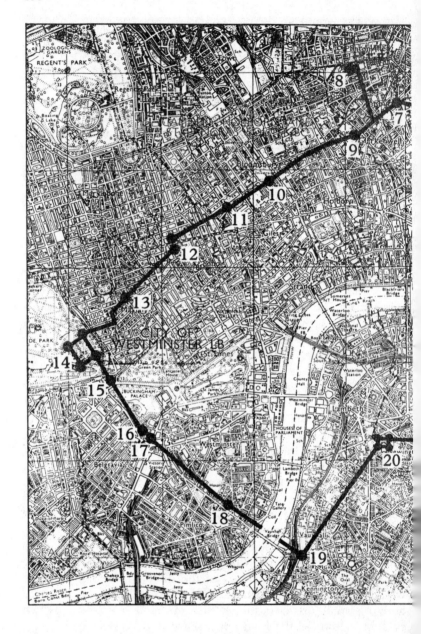

Fig. 3   Lines of Communication Superimposed on a Map
of Modern London

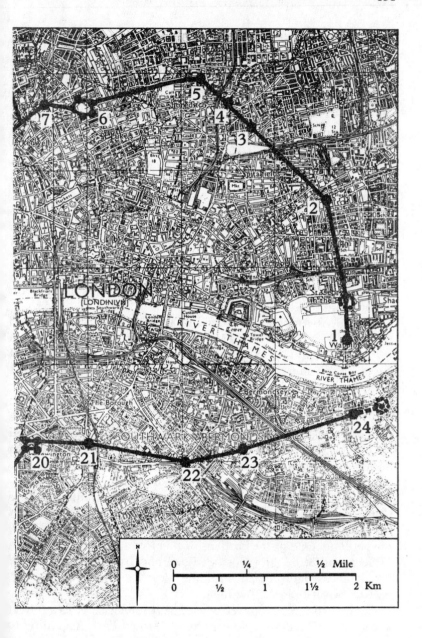

Lines of Communication Superimposed on a Map
of Modern London *cont.*

redoubt and two flankers, while Vertue shows a hornwork and Lithgow recorded a rectangular fort. Until late-Victorian times there was a Mount Street running parallel to the western side of Brick Lane and Rocque's map shows a mound at the south end of that street. There was also a Mount Square just off Mount Street and close to the site of the mound. There is now a Montclare Street in the same area. The site of the mound was at, or close to, the junction of the modern Swanfield and Rhoda Streets.

An extrapolation of the line led to Fort No. 4, which was probably just to the north of Shoreditch Church. The resolution of common council called for two redoubts with flankers and a battery to be formed near the church, but Lithgow described this as another rectangular work. There was an Old Castle Street at this spot until it was renamed Victoria Road in 1884. Lithgow added that 'without which, and at Kingsland (being the old post way for Scotland) there stand two earthen rampires, with two courts du guard'. Kingsland was nearly one-and-a-half miles to the north of the main defence line.

A further extrapolation of the line led to the village of Hoxton and here Lithgow placed Fort No. 5, which he described as a rectangular work. From here the line ran west, probably in a slight curve, which may be suggested on Rocque's map, to follow the alignment of the modern Bevenden Street, before crossing City Road to the site of Mount Mill Fort (No. 6) between Goswell Road and Central Street, just to the north of Seward Street.[40] The resolution referred to this battery and a breastwork. As described by Lithgow it consisted of a central and circular redoubt within a lower and outer fort of five angles. He claimed that it was the first of the forts to have been built. A depiction of this fort in a publication of 1643 is the only contemporary illustration we have of the defences.[41] Rocque's map shows that three large mounds remained in 1746 and they indicate that the fort had a side 300 metres long. One of the bastions of this fort stood at the junction of Sebastian Street and Goswell Road and from here the line of the defences deflected towards the New River waterworks. Sebastian Street follows that line.

The line running from Sebastian Street intersects St John Street at the site of Fort No. 7, known as Waterfield Fort. According to Lithgow it comprised a circular mound armed with nine pieces of artillery, with three more on the point of a counterscarp. Rocque's revised map of 1769 shows a mound and a turnpike here. The rampart line then changed direction again to run west-south-west.

Fort No. 8, a large work called by Lithgow Strawes Fort, was located at Islington Upper Pond, now Claremont Square reservoir. It was described by Lithgow as an eight-angled work and Vertue showed it as a rectangular fort with a demi-bastion at each angle. This fort was outside the main line of defences but evidently was joined to them by a rampart along the line now largely followed by Amwell Street. Maitland referred to the existence of a covered way, the remains of which could still be seen in the early eighteenth century, which ran from the main line of communication to a large bulwark. This appears to have followed the line of a crest of the escarpment facing the valley of the River Fleet.

The main rampart line from Fort No. 7 took a route now followed by Myddelton Street and Exmouth Market to Fort No. 9, the site of the present Mount Pleasant Post Office building. This was named by Lithgow as Pindar of Wakefield Fort. In the resolution of the common council it was referred to as a battery and breastworks on the hill east of Black Mary's Hole. There are two mounds on Rocque's map within the area now covered by the Post Office building and in the eighteenth century there was a building here known as St John's Old Castle, or, as on some maps, Sir John Oldcastle's.

From Mount Pleasant the line continued in the same direction and crossed the River Fleet and Gray's Inn Road, just south of Guildford Street, to a point where Rocque showed ground disturbance either side of Gray's Inn Road and exactly in line with an eighteenth-century turnpike. These mounds may have been the remains of some defences guarding this important road, but, if so, they were not mentioned by Lithgow, or indeed by anyone else. From here the line continued south of Guildford Street to Southampton Fort (No. 10), named after the adjacent Southampton House (later Bedford House). This projected from the main rampart line and consisted of a pair of bastions joined by a curtain with two return curtains to the line. The bastions of this fort are portrayed in a late-seventeenth-century parchment drawing[42] and are clear features on the Rocque map. From this evidence the fort had a front of some 125 metres. The resolution had proposed two batteries and a breastwork on the site.

From Southampton House the line of the defences continued across St Giles Fields to Fort No. 11, which guarded one of the main routes from London to the north. The resolution of the common council called for 'one redoubt with two flankers by St. Jiles in the Fields, another small worke neer the turning'. Vertue referred to a redoubt near St Giles Pound. Lithgow mentioned only one fort in Crabtree Fields. Rocque showed considerable ground disturbance on the east side of Tottenham Court Road, opposite what is now the end of Goodge Street. Nevertheless, a location for this fort so far to the north would be an unlikely departure from the logical line. Assuming that the ramparts continued in a straight line parallel to the north face of Southampton House Fort, which is clearly shown by Rocque, then a location near to the junction of Bayley Street and Tottenham Court Road is more likely. Rocque also shows disturbed ground here and places the Pound at this point. His plan also indicates an S-bend in a ditch, which could represent a diversion around the fort.

The location of Fort No. 12 is also uncertain. The resolution called for 'A quadrant forte with fower halfe bulwarkes cross Tyburne Highway at the second turning towards Westminster'. Wardour Street might fit this description. This is the location given by Vertue and Rocque's map shows ground disturbance on the north side of Oxford Street, opposite the north end of Wardour Street. This is at the eastern end of Eastcastle Street. Lithgow, however, described this fort as the Banqueting House Fortress, composed of 'Two forts upon Taybourne Way and Maribone Fields'. The lord mayor's banqueting house was about 1000 metres to the west, at the junction of Marylebone Lane and Oxford Street. A section of apparent rampart line marked on a map by Desmaretz of 1717 to the south of Mayfair may point to a possible location.[43] If extrapolated north-east this would have passed through Hanover Square to a location at about the junction of Oxford and Great Portland Streets. This was not far from the site of the banqueting house. At either place a fort or forts would have been well placed to guard a main route into London from the west.

From Fort No. 12 the line must have passed south-west to Fort No. 13, which was called Sergeant's Fort and later Oliver's Mount. This was in the Mount Row–Farm Street area. The work was described by Vertue as a bulwark. It was portrayed on the 1717 map as a small rectangular position, perhaps a battery. Its memory is also perpetuated in the name Mount Street.

The line continued, albeit with a local deviation, to the south-west and the region of South Audley Street, and then on to the

Hyde Park Fort (No. 14). The Stukeley map shows this fort as a large irregularly shaped work, but this map is too roughly drawn for a precise location to be established. The resolution referred to a large fort with flankers on all sides and Vertue illustrated a star fort. Previous interpretations of the defences have placed this fort on the east side of Tyburn Lane (now Park Lane), but this seems an unlikely position. The Rocque map shows the outline of a fort within the park at Hyde Park Corner, with an apparent pointed bastion, and at the south-east corner a five-sided earthwork extending from which – parallel to Tyburn Lane – is a long, narrow earthwork which terminates opposite South Street. This is consistent with a very large fort with a flank of some 400 metres. Some of the resulting ground disturbance, including the bastion-like feature, may still be seen today and is marked on the modern Ordnance Survey sheet. Lithgow described this fort as a 'maine great strength, having one fort above and another within another'. He also referred to another fort 'closing the roadway . . . breasting the other two' (No. 15) on the other side of the road, presumably Piccadilly. There was a turnpike at this point into the eighteenth century.

From Fort No. 14 the line of the ramparts turned sharply south-east, crossing Piccadilly and Constitution Hill, to the most likely location for Fort No. 15, which, from Lithgow's description, might have been on a site now within the Hyde Park Corner roundabout.

On a continuation of the line, Forts 16 and 17 would have been at the turnpike on Chelsea Road, now the south corner of the Royal Mews. This is roughly where the resolution described a breastwork and Vertue a court of guard. Lithgow referred to two half-moon works, both sighting Chelsea. Confirming Lithgow, Rocque's plan shows a short curved embankment in what is now Grosvenor Gardens and a second, but less well defined, ground disturbance some 90 metres away from the first. Both of these locations had irregular ponds adjacent to them and both faced Chelsea. These works would have guarded what are now King's Road and Buckingham Palace Road.

Fort No. 18 was in Tothill Fields. Its remains were known as Oliver's Battery for many years after the Civil War. The resolution provided for a battery and breastwork here. According to Lithgow, however, this was a substantial double-ditched fort with nine angles. Stukeley portrayed it as a large irregular work. Contemporary accounts place the fort near the pesthouse, where suspected plague victims were isolated. The islands within a pond shown on the Rocque map, next to a building confirmed by Horwood's survey of 1792 as the pesthouse, are likely to be the remains of this fort. This places the fort on Vauxhall Bridge Road, near the junction with Chapter Street. This is on a direct line between the half-moon works of Forts 16 and 17 and the Vauxhall fort on the south side of the Thames. Both the Stukeley and Vertue maps show the rampart line continuing, to end on the river bank.

If there had been a chain or boom defence guarding the upstream Thames gap in the fortified line it would have been at this point, with its southern end not far from Vauxhall fort (No. 19). This fort can be precisely located, as its outline appears on Desmaretz's map of 1717 and part of it is shown on Rocque's map. The evidence suggests that the work was a rectangular sconce with a demi-bastion on the angles. Defoe made a reference to it in 1724.[44] The remains of the fort were close to Vauxhall Gardens. The Elephant and Castle public house at the side of Nine Elms Station now stands near to its site.

From Vauxhall the line ran north-east, apparently via a small subsidiary redoubt (called a 'counterscarp' by Lithgow) to Fort No. 20 in St George's Fields. As described by Lithgow and shown by Vertue and Stukeley, it was rectangular with corner bastions. This was also known as Fort Royal and Lithgow counted twenty-four cannons royal on its ramparts. According to Defoe, there were remains of the fort and four bastions in 1724,[45] and Rocque's map shows much ground disturbance centred on an inn called the Dog and Duck. The disturbance took the form of irregular-looking ponds and would fit a square fort with a side of 125 metres. In the nineteenth century there was both a Fort Place and a Prospect Place near the site of this fort, but both were subsequently renamed. The Imperial War Museum now stands on this spot.

From Fort No. 20 the line bent sharply east to Forts 21a and 21b at the Elephant and Castle. These were described by Lithgow as redoubts, one either side of the road from London Bridge to Newington, although Vertue shows a single work at this point. There was a toll-gate at the site in the eighteenth century.

From here the line ran to the north of and parallel to what is now New Kent Road until the junction with Old Kent Road, where Fort No. 22 was located (this is now the Bricklayer's Arms interchange). Lithgow noted 'only a circular rampine' at this point, which he described as being at the 'top of Kent Street' and which he evidently regarded as being of small importance. The Rocque map of 1746 indicates a 'Castle Inn' some 300 metres south-east of the Bricklayer's Arms and Brett-James referred to the name 'Oliver Cromwell's Castle' at the end of Kent Street on a map of 1806.[46] At the time of Lithgow's inspection the southern part of the defences was still under construction and it seems certain that in due course a much larger fort was constructed on a continuation of the then line, east of Fort No. 22, which is designated Fort No. 23. Defoe described the remains of what he called 'the great fort' near Bermondsey Church.[47] From his account of the route he took on his tour from Rotherhithe to Vauxhall (which by design or coincidence followed the line of the fortifications) this fort may be placed near the junction of Grange Road and Spa Road, Bermondsey. The Fort Place there has been removed by recent redevelopment, but the Fort public house is still there to mark this spot and a quarter of a mile to the east there is a Fort Road. During the nineteenth century there was a Prospect Road on the site.

The location of the last of the forts, No. 24, at Rotherhithe, is a particularly difficult one to identify. Lithgow simply described the fort as 'at the back of Redrieff' (an alternative name for Rotherhithe) and gave no description. This fort is mentioned only by Lithgow. Rocque's map provides no clear indications of earthworks but does have clues suggesting two possible locations, both within Southwark Park. Coinciding with the modern Prospect Street near the south-west corner of the park, Rocque shows an island or mound within a generally marshy area. The second possible site is close to an irregularly shaped pond near to what is now the north-east corner of the Park, close to the present roundabout near the entrance to the Rotherhithe Tunnel. Southwark Park contains many high ridges and hillocks which are clearly earthworks and of a considerable age, as there are many large and mature trees growing on top of them. Unfortunately, the prospect of extant physical remains of a Civil War fort is dimmed by the knowledge that spoil from the Thames Tunnel (completed in 1843) was dumped in this area. Nevertheless, there is a ridge which extends parallel to Jamaica Road and which points directly to the site of Fort No. 23. The eastern end of this ridge terminates at the second of the alternative locations for Fort No. 24 and may indeed be a surviving trace of the ramparts constructed in 1643.

This description demonstrates the sometimes inconsistent nature of the available evidence and the problems of trying to establish both the number, position and nature of the individual works, and the route of the lines, which cannot be discovered simply by drawing a direct line between the forts. Lithgow's descriptions of the forts are not always sufficient to gain a clear and confident impression of their form and the resolution gave approval for only a proportion of the works actually built. The Stukeley and Vertue maps are significantly different in the way in which they portray the forts and lines, but the Vertue in particular provides a helpful indication of the character of the defences. Further evidence for the form of the forts is available for the Whitechapel, Mount Mill, Southampton and Sergeants forts on the north side of the river and those at Vauxhall and St George's Fields on the south. From such evidence it seems probable that the works which studded the circuit around London comprised a mixture of hornworks, rectangular bastioned forts or sconces, perhaps star forts and irregularly shaped positions and batteries.

V

Fortifications of varying complexity were built by the armies of both sides during the Civil War, enclosing towns, villages, castles and country houses. They ranged from the addition of bastions, bulwarks and ramparts to existing medieval town walls, to completely new circuits with bastions. The finest of the new bastioned *enceintes* were the royalist defences of Oxford. London's fortifications were decidedly unsophisticated by comparison and have been described as 'amateurish'. Indeed, when the inevitable comparison is made with contemporary urban fortifications on the Continent, or even the bastion trace at Oxford, they do appear to be more the work of amateurs than those appropriate for the defence of the greatest city in the land. But of course they were rapidly built as a security circuit in under a year and were very extensive.

A new ring of forts connected by lines such as the London defences was described by Christopher Duffy as being of a 'characteristic English fashion'. Other examples of this form were the parliamentary works at Bristol, with eight works on the line, and Plymouth, where there were five works on the detached northern line and outlying works on the flanks.[48] As well as the complex works at Oxford, the royalists constructed bastioned *enceintes* at Reading and Newark. At Chester the *enceinte* was formed of a line of redans in a suggestion of bastioned fortifications. The parliamentary defences at Liverpool were bastioned, but as an example of the type were naive.[49]

The *enceinte* of the London defences resembled the circumvallation of a besieger. It is difficult to avoid the conclusion that experience of this form in use on the Continent influenced its design. Although there was some French influence in the style of English fortification during this period, both sides largely adopted Dutch methods, and the majority of construction was in earthwork. Robert Ward described the Dutch approach as 'the most absolutest manner that can be invented' and John Cruso commended the use of earthworks for fortifications 'because when they have sufficient thicknesse to make resistance they are not subject to endanger the besieged as those fortifications which are made of masons work, the shivers whereof do much mischief'.[50] In March 1643 the Venetian ambassador commented that the plan of the London defences had been 'commended by experts' but that engineers had been invited from Holland,[51] apparently to help complete the works. It is not known whether such engineers actually arrived and, if they did, what contribution they made.

The known or implied forms of the works, based on the evidence of Lithgow, Stukeley and Vertue, which studded London's Lines of Communication are traceable in Ward's military textbook *The Animadversions of Warre*, published in England in 1639, as well as in other manuals of this period, and had been described earlier by Paul Ive.[52] Although referred to as forts in contemporary accounts of the London defences, in textbook terms they were sconces. These forms would have been familiar to anyone with experience of siege warfare on the Continent and were used conventionally at the sieges of such places as Colchester, Newark and Pontefract Castle. The ability to design and construct fortifications during the Civil War was limited to a small number of specialists, most of whom had served abroad. Some Irish towns had been protected with bastioned defences earlier in the seventeenth century, but most engineers who had experience in urban fortification were those who had served in the contemporary continental conflicts, where siege warfare was an almost endemic condition.

A number of British soldiers who had served in Germany and the Netherlands joined the military establishments of both sides during the Civil War and experts from the Continent were recruited as advisers. The Dutchmen John Dalbier and Peter Manteau Van Dalem were employed by parliament, for example, and the royalist experts included the Walloon Bernard de Gomme and the Swede Diderich Beckmann.[53] Continental methods of warfare were also known from the dozen or so textbooks on military matters that included coverage of fortification which had appeared in English between 1622 and 1642. These were largely based on continental experience or practice; some were by foreign authors and others were by English writers but were derivative works.

Ward specially cited the siegeworks of the Spanish general Spinola at Breda in 1624. The forts which Spinola had constructed, although for attack rather than defence, were joined by a line and were close in design to those implied by Vertue's map. A siege-work form of this kind could equally well be used for a defensive purpose. It had also been used as a contravallation and its long lines were effective as a barrier. Philip Skippon, who commanded the London trained bands until November 1642, was at the siege of Breda. It is probable that he was closely involved with the preparatory designs for the London defences before he left the capital to serve as a Major-General in the parliamentarian field army. Skippon was a practitioner as well as an observer and he had gained first-hand experience of siege warfare during his twenty-four years of service in foreign armies. He had, for example, been involved in the construction of fortifications during the recapture of Breda in 1637 and had earlier served under the command of Lord Vere at the sieges of Bois le Duc and Maastricht in 1629.[54]

VI

Compared with the closely placed bastions of the Oxford fortress, the London defences presented long lines of vulnerable rampart and ditch between the forts. Once penetrated by an enemy in one place, the line could have been turned. Lithgow stated that the forts could command their intervals. On the northern front the forts were about 500 metres apart, but those of the western front were 700–800 metres apart, on the southern front they were

600–900 metres apart and, worst of all, on the eastern front the intervals were 1000–1500 metres. Unfortunately, we do not know enough of the detailed design of the forts and, more especially, of the positioning of the guns within them to say more about the extent to which interval defence was an intended feature, but the distances between forts appear to have been far from ideal for this purpose. All of the intervals were, of course, too long for enfilade firing by musketry along their fronts.

Each member of the militia was required to mount guard at the forts in a cycle of day- and night-time watches. The operational plans for fighting the defences are unknown. The Venetian ambassador twice commented upon the difficulty in manning the entire line,[55] but this was probably never the intention. As long as all the forts were manned, mobile troops could move on interior lines to defend a threatened sector. There were enough suitable buildings, such as churches, to provide high observation points from which to spot the movements of an attacking force.

The artillery armament seems to have been restricted to mounting in the forts and batteries along the line. An Order of the Commons of 5 April 1643 provided for guns to be borrowed for the defences from the East India Company, or requisitioned from them if they refused.[56] Lithgow's account suggests that at the time of his visit there were 212 guns mounted. The guns he described were in the upper weight-range of artillery: cannons royal, whole cannons, demi-cannons, culverins and demi-culverins. The cannon royal was the heaviest gun then in service, while the demi-culverin (the lightest referred to) was only half-way down the scale of calibres then in use. Extreme ranges for all these guns was well over a mile, but effective ranges were shorter than this.[57] It is possible that Lithgow was unreliable in this respect, however, either noting only the heavier pieces or exaggerating both the numbers and the calibres. It is likely that the armament included many guns that were smaller than demi-culverins. Later financial accounts refer to 94 guns mounted on the defences.[58]

So far as a land attack was concerned, the enclosure of London by siegeworks would have been wholly impracticable. A more likely royalist strategy would have been a bold and penetrative attack in one or two places along the most vulnerable parts of the rampart line which joined the forts. Such a strategy would not have been possible unless the parliamentarian field armies in southern England had first been defeated and in that event prolonged resistance would have been questionable. Indeed, the defences do not seem to have been seriously designed to resist a regular siege. Many forts were positioned to control road communications to and from the enclosed area and the lines joined the forts together to produce a restricted zone. These functions seem to have been at least as important as the military-defensive ones in the design of the works.

VII

Only a city as wealthy as London could afford such extensive defences.[59] Nevertheless, the collection of sufficient money to fund the Lines of Communication was not achieved without difficulty. The common council received a less than enthusiastic response when it asked the suburbs to contribute to the great cost of building the defences. The City was forced to advance six sums of £2000 per month out of its own funds between March and July 1643, but it was successful in negotiating a remission of £3000 per month from the weekly assessment for defence purposes.[60] In September 1643 an Ordinance of parliament imposed £5482 monthly upon the City in an attempt to secure payment of the charges of the defences, including the growing arrears.[61] Further measures were needed nevertheless. In 1644 the common council requested that money from sequestrations within the Lines of Communication be used towards the maintenance of the defences and an Ordinance of December of that year provided for the raising of further money for that purpose.[62] In 1644–5 arrears were due to victuallers, gunners and matrosses, timber merchants, bricklayers, masons, carpenters and other tradesmen, and for gunpowder.[63]

The people of London themselves, with the assistance of the militia, and on one occasion at least of sailors, provided the unskilled labour. Several writers painted a picture of the enthusiastic willingness amongst Londoners to take part in this work. Lithgow reported that 100 000 citizens worked on the defences, although the Venetian ambassador, more realistically, stated that 20 000 were working daily without pay and commented that the people 'do not even cease to work on Sunday, which is so strictly observed by the Puritans'.[64] According to Lithgow 'all sorts of Londoners' marched to the works 'with great alacritie'. Even those of high social rank were said to have forsaken the comfort of their homes to toil at the trenches, including 'a great company of the Common Council and diverse other chiefe men of the citty'.[65] The Londoners were evidently not deterred by the conditions, which were neither easy nor pleasant. The autumn of 1642 was cold with early frosts and there was snow in December, while the following months appear to have been very wet, with some flooding.[66] This had implications for the process of labour, as well as the integrity of the earthen structures being built. The royalists gave the impression of being amused by this frenetic activity and celebrated it with a song incorporating the words 'Round headed cuckolds come dig'.[67]

How far commentators' perception of enthusiasm among the people of London to labour at the defences reflected a genuine sentiment, and how long lasting such apparent enthusiasm was, is unclear. Rushworth thought that it was the 'terror of the citizens which made such a prodigious number of persons of all ranks, ages and sex offer themselves to work by unfeigned application in digging, carrying of earth and other materials'.[68] The churches and the livery companies played an important role in calling upon their congregations and memberships to volunteer. There must also have been social pressures to participate. In October 1642 parliament ordered people in London and Westminster to shut up their shops and cease trading so that 'they may with greater diligence attend the defence' of London.[69] Tradesmen and merchants had a vested interest in their protection, but even from these groups there were petitions to the common council about the damage to trade of their constantly having to attend at the fortifications.[70] The works damaged farm land and caused hardship among those whose livelihoods depended upon agriculture. Cultivated land was covered with works or became hard of access, grazing land was rendered unusable for several years by the extensive stripping of turves for building and facing ramparts, some areas were spoiled by deliberate flooding and at least two windmills were enclosed within the *enceintes* of forts. In addition, some buildings were destroyed to make way for the fortifications.[71]

VIII

The occupation of London by Fairfax in 1647 has been seen as, in a sense, a sign of the ultimate failure of the defences.[72] However, political divisions within the City prevented any prospect of offering a united front to the army. In particular, the Southwark trained bands disapproved of the Presbyterian takeover and offered no resistance to Rainsborough's forces.[73]

Following the occupation it was ordered that the fortifications were to be 'forthwith slighted and demolished to ease the charge of maintaining and keeping them'.[74] In reality this was perhaps as much to prevent their possible use by factions hostile to the army trying to seize control of London.[75] An Ordinance was passed to enable the militias of London and Westminster to pull down the guardhouses and lines and sell the timber, and the citizens were invited to send their servants to assist in this work.[76] Demolition appears to have started by the end of September and was being rapidly undertaken in October. The guns were taken to the Tower under the army's direction.[77] It is uncertain how far the 'demolition and slighting' was taken. Slighting did not normally mean complete levelling, but rather the destruction of parapets, emplacements, magazines and barracks so that they could not be restored without a great deal of labour and new construction. Tantalisingly, at the same date the Venetian ambassador reported that 'Now that the fortifications of London are demolished, Fairfax . . . is laying the foundations of three forts in different places which will be three citadels to bridle the city and all the people'.[78]

London was again threatened with attack during the second Civil War and on 29 August 1648 the Committee of Both Houses suggested to Fairfax that now his troops that had been besieging Colchester were free they could be deployed around London for its defence.[79] Were some of the defences re-occupied and refurbished during this period? Certainly the posts and chains were again set up around the City.[80] There is also evidence that an artillery battery was built around 1650 to defend Whitehall.[81] In 1651 the Militia Commissioners laid an assessment for the charge of the fortifications and two years later the Council of State ordered that all guns at Leadenhall 'and other places in and about London' should be taken into the Tower.[82]

The Lines of Communication served not only as fortifications, but as a convenient definition of London during the 1640s and

1650s.[83] Sir William Petty had both administrative and defensive functions in mind when, during the decades after the Restoration, he drew up proposals to enclose London, Westminster and Southwark with a 'wall'. In his early schemes this was to be over twelve miles long, but in his later ones was nineteen miles in extent.[84] The defence of London was a recurring problem. During the Jacobite Rebellion of 1745 it was suggested that the original Civil War scheme should be used as a model for new works, with small bastions or redans 'at proper distances' along the lines.[85] There were also schemes to protect London during the Napoloeonic Wars and again later in the nineteenth century.[86] It is clear from maps and records that traces of the forts and lines were still visible in the eighteenth century and some survived into the nineteenth century, until they succumbed to erosion and were covered by the outward spread of the capital.

The lines were short-lived and did not make a lasting contribution to London's topography in the way that the fortifications of many continental cities did, yet not until well into the nineteenth century were many of the remaining traces obliterated. Even today there are still remains in Hyde Park and there are many street names that perpetuate the memory of the fortifications. Yet the defences have not made a lasting impression on the consciousness of historians of London. Not only have they received comparatively little attention, but they have also been misinterpreted. As recently as 1990 the Mount Fort at Whitechapel was described as a Saxon fortification, for example. Walter Besant denied the existence of the lines between the forts on the apparently rational, although in fact erroneous, basis that not enough labour was available to construct such long works in such a short time.[87] These were indeed the longest continuous defence lines constructed during the period in Britain and they were noteworthy even in continental terms, despite their unsophisticated nature. The achievement was impressive in terms of the speed of construction, the mobilisation of labour to build them and the organisation that was involved. The Lines of Communication should be seen as one of the major achievements of the parliamentarian war effort.

Notes

1. This distance has been calculated by the authors. William Lithgow mentioned that the fortifications were 'eighteen Kentish myles' long and this was reported by Brett-James as though these were statute miles. William Lithgow, *The Present Surveigh of London and England's State* (London, 1643), reprinted in W. Scott (ed.), *Lord Somers Tracts*, IV (London, 1810), p. 541. N. G. Brett-James, 'The Fortification of London in 1642–3', *London Topographical Record*, 14 (1928), 1–35, reprinted as 'The Fortifications of London During the Civil War', in *The Growth of Stuart London* (London, 1935), pp. 268–95. A connecting rampart provided a covered route between the forts and this must have given rise to the name 'Lines of Communication'.
2. *CSPD*, 1644–45, p. 214. This document is misdated to 1644 in the calendar.
3. Edward Husband (ed.), *A Collection of all the publicke Orders, Ordinances, and Declarations of both Houses of Parliament . . . March 1642 until December 1646* (London, 1646), f. 199.
4. Husband, *Orders*, f. 289. *CSPVen*, 1642–43, p. 257.
5. A. Kemp, 'The fortification of Oxford during the Civil War', *Oxoniensia*, 42 (1977), 237–46.
6. Quoted by F. J. Varley, *The Siege of Oxford* (Oxford, 1932), p. 131.
7. *CSPVen*, 1642–43, p. 231.
8. V. T. C. Smith, 'The Artillery Defences at Gravesend', *Archaeologia Cantiana*, LXXXIX (1974), 153–4.
9. *CSPD*, 1641–43, pp. 306, 369.
10. *CSPD*, 1641–43, p. 369.
11. B. Whitelocke, *Memorials of the English Affairs 1625–1660* (Oxford, 1853), I, p. 184.
12. *CSPVen*, 1642–43, pp. 175–6.
13. H. M. Colvin, D. R. Ransome and J. Summerson (eds), *History of the King's Works*, III, *1485–1660*, Part 1 (London, 1975), p. 158. Brett-James, *Growth of Stuart London*, p. 293.
14. *CSPVen*, 1642–43, pp. 192, 198.
15. E. S. de Beer (ed.), *The Diary of John Evelyn* (Oxford, 1955), II, p. 80.
16. Brett-James, *Growth of Stuart London*, p. 269.
17. CLRO, Journals of Common Council, XL, 1641–49, f. 52. See R. R. Sharpe, *London and the Kingdom* (London, 1894–5), III, pp. 431–2, and Brett-James, *Growth of Stuart London*, pp. 271–2.
18. Brett-James, *Growth of Stuart London*, p. 275. *CSPVen*, 1642–43, p. 257.
19. W. F. Grimes, *The Excavation of Roman and Medieval London* (London, 1968), pp. 83–8.
20. *CSPVen*, 1642–43, p. 273.
21. CLRO, Letter Book of the Common Council of the City of London, QQ, f. 99b.
22. CLRO, Letter Book . . ., QQ, ff. 125b, 130, 145 *et seq.*
23. Brett-James, *Growth of Stuart London*, p. 276.
24. Lithgow, *Present Surveigh*, pp. 534–45. *CSPVen*, 1642–43, pp. 304–6.

25. Corpus Christi College, Cambridge, MS 613.
26. William Maitland, *History of London* (London, 1739), I, p. 369, reprinted in *The Gentleman's Magazine*, June 1749, p. 251.
27. GL, A.52, no. 33.
28. Brett-James, *Growth of Stuart London*, pp. 285–6.
29. Rocque's Map of London, 1746, published as *The A to Z of Georgian London*, London Topographical Soc., 126 (1982).
30. Lithgow, *Present Surveigh*, p. 540.
31. Lithgow, *Present Surveigh*, p. 539.
32. *CSPD*, 1645, pp. 380–1.
33. W. G. Ross, 'Military Engineering during the Civil War, 1642–9', *Professional Papers of the Corps of Royal Engineers ... Occasional Papers*, XIII (Chatham, 1887).
34. Brett-James, *Growth of Stuart London*, pp. 268–95.
35. J. H. Leslie, 'The defences of London in 1643', *Journal of the Soc. of Army Historical Research*, X (1930), 109–20. Ordnance Survey, *A Map of Seventeenth-Century England*, 1930.
36. D. Sturdy, 'The Civil War Defences of London', *The London Archaeologist*, 2 (1975), 334–8. R. Weinstein, 'Camden at War – Civil War Fortifications in Camden', *Camden History Soc. Review*, 5 (1977), 21–3; Idem, 'Southampton House and the Civil War', in Joanna Bird, Hugh Chapman and John Clark (eds), *Collectanea Londiniensia* (London and Middlesex Archaeological Soc., Special Papers, 2, 1978), pp. 329–45.
37. B. H. St.J. O'Neil, *Castles and Cannon* (Oxford, 1960), p. 92. C. Duffy, *Siege Warfare: The Fortress in the Early Modern World* (London, 1979), p. 158. A. Saunders, *Fortress Britain* (Liphook, 1989), p. 76.
38. H. Llewellyn Smith, *History of East London* (London, 1939), p. 59.
39. Museum of London Archaeology Service report, *London Hospital Medical College – Newark Building: An Archaeological Evaluation* (Nov. 1992).
40. Maitland, *History of London*, p. 1370.
41. BL, King's Library, single sheets, f. 669, f. 8 no. 22.
42. Weinstein, 'Southampton House'.
43. PRO, MPH 258.
44. Daniel Defoe, *A tour Thro' the Whole Island of Great Britain* (4th edn, London, 1748), I, p. 277.
45. Defoe, *Tour*, I, p. 277.
46. Brett-James, *Growth of Stuart London*, p. 283.
47. Defoe, *Tour*, I, p. 277.
48. Duffy, *Siege Warfare*, p. 157.
49. Saunders, *Fortress Britain*, pp. 75–6.
50. Duffy, *Siege Warfare*, p. 157.
51. John Cruso, *The Complete Captain* (Cambridge, 1640).
52. R. Ward, *The Animadversions of Warre* (London, 1639). Paul Ive, *The Practice of Fortification* (London, 1589).
53. Saunders, *Fortress Britain*, p. 74.
54. *DNB*, and information kindly supplied by Keith Roberts.
55. *CSPVen*, 1642–43, p. 256.

56. *CJ*, III, p. 30.
57. R. Norton, *The Gunner* (London, 1628).
58. *CSPD*, 1644–45, pp. 380–1.
59. I. Roy, 'England Turned Germany? The Aftermath of the Civil War in its European Context', *Trans. of the Royal Historical Soc.*, 5th series, 28 (1978), 132.
60. CLRO, Journals of Common Council, XL, ff. 56, 59 *et seq.* Sharpe, *London and the Kingdom*, II, p. 184.
61. CLRO, Letter Book . . ., QQ, f. 149a.
62. CLRO, Letter Book . . ., QQ, f. 145.
63. *CSPD*, 1645–47, pp. 380–1.
64. Lithgow, *Present Surveigh*, p. 538. *CSPVen*, 1642–43, p. 274.
65. *A Perfect Diurnall*, May 1643, ff. 47–8, 50–1.
66. We owe the information about the weather conditions to the kindness of Professor H. H. Lamb and Mr John Kington of the Climatic Research Unit of the University of East Anglia.
67. Brett-James, *Growth of Stuart London*, p. 292.
68. J. Rushworth (ed.), *Historical Collections [of Private Passages of State . . .]* (1721), III, p. 2.
69. Brett-James, *Growth of Stuart London*, p. 292.
70. CLRO, Letter Book . . ., QQ, f. 148b.
71. S. Porter, 'Property destruction in Civil War London', *Trans. of the London and Middlesex Archaeological Soc.*, 35 (1984), 59–62.
72. Sturdy, 'Civil War Defences of London', 338.
73. Whitelocke, *Memorials*, II, pp. 190–2.
74. Whitelocke, *Memorials*, II, p. 203. *A & O*, I, p. 1008.
75. *CSPVen*, 1647–52, p. 18.
76. Whitelocke, *Memorials*, II, p. 206.
77. *CSPVen*, 1647–52, pp. 18–20.
78. *CSPVen*, 1647–52, p. 23.
79. *CSPD*, 1648–49, p. 154.
80. Whitelocke, *Memorials*, p. 305.
81. O. F. G. Hogg, 'The Office of Master Gunner of Whitehall and of St. James Park', *Journal of the Royal Artillery*, CV, no. 2 (1978), 86.
82. *CSPD*, 1653–54, pp. 260, 269.
83. Brett-James, *Growth of Stuart London*, p. 291.
84. The Marquis of Lansdown (ed.), *The Petty Papers* (London, 1927), I, pp. 30–7.
85. PRO, SP41/37.
86. PRO, MR 1200. V. T. C. Smith, 'Chatham and London – the changing face of English Land Fortification, 1870–1914', *Post Medieval Archaeology*, 19 (1985), 105–49.
87. *The London Hospital Illustrated: 250 Years* (London, 1990), p. 36. W. Besant, *London in the time of the Stuarts* (London, 1903), pp. 43–4.

6

'This Proud Unthankefull City': A Cavalier View of London in the Civil War

Ian Roy

Relations between the king and his capital before the Civil War had never been easy. The great city had grown in importance with the permanent residence there of the kings of England; London housed the centre of government, the law courts and the Inns of Court, and the great town houses of those nobles, leading politicians, office-holders and courtiers, who needed to be close to the sovereign. The presence of the king's palace at Whitehall, close to such a centre of population – the London metropolitan area contained at least a third of a million inhabitants on the eve of the Civil War – presented peculiar problems, of which the king and his entourage were acutely aware.

The unplanned growth of London, seemingly so inexorable for over a century, was a challenge to those in authority. The fact that the palace of Westminster was but a mile from the gates at Temple Bar, that the Middlesex suburbs – to the north and west, as well as more notoriously to the east – contained a high proportion of the disorderly poor, was one which no Stuart government could overlook. The expansion of the city threatened to overwhelm the local forces of law and order. The large number of apprentices and other migrants – young, poor, male and single – meant that turbulence was endemic; the rallying cry 'prentices and clubs' often rang through the crowded streets.[1]

The government of Charles I's personal rule, like several of its predecessors, attempted to call a halt to this undesirable and dangerous development. The problems generated by uninhibited expansion, the difficulty of maintaining social control, religious conformity and political obedience were uppermost in the minds of Caroline politicians. The king himself, however, had a vision of his capital which went far beyond the age-old concerns of his predecessors. Charles had grandiose schemes for London, as for so much else, based on his passion for decency and order in the realm. They found expression in the proclamations he issued in the late 1620s and early 1630s to regulate new building, enforce the use of better materials and impose some semblance of social control through town planning. He wished to rebuild and beautify both his palace at Whitehall and the great cathedral, St Paul's, now so tumbledown and given up to profane activities that it was unworthy of a capital city. If these schemes led to the demolition of existing buildings, so much the better, for London's jerry-built medieval housing stock urgently required replacement.[2]

An ordered society was the wider expression of a strictly regulated royal court and household, centred on the family of the uxorious king himself. London must be brought to reflect the same ideals, and provide a noble and appropriate setting for the activities of the court and government, and the practice of the reformed religion. As the sovereign acted, so must his chief supporters, and Charles deplored the unnecessary residence in the city of those who should be setting an example, in conscientious administration, impartial magistracy and old-fashioned hospitality, to their localities. The gentry were strictly prohibited from neglecting, by their residence in London, their estates in the country and the duties they should be performing there.[3]

The ideals cherished by the king were not designed to please the leading members of the corporation, however, nor were they packaged with much political skill, or regard for their concerns and interests. The result was that in the 1630s the government clashed with the corporation on several grounds; the attempted incorporation of the suburbs, the Londonderry Plantation and the claims of the church, such as tithe payments and Laud's aim to renew and beautify St Paul's. The major problem, however, was financial, for where in the past the English crown had raised loans on the Continent, particularly the Netherlands, by the reign of Charles I it had come increasingly to rely on the London money market. But the king's worsening financial situation placed ever heavier burdens on those who were his creditors and their reluctance in the crisis of 1640 – when the royal forces' defeat in war coincided with a widespread refusal to pay outstanding taxation

– to continue providing credit for the government, brought Charles's house of cards tumbling down. Several of the richest men in the City were ruined in his fall, and the existing authorities were reluctant to rescue him. The action of the king over the bullion deposited at the Mint in the Tower, and over the stock of East India Company pepper, which he threatened to seize, further worsened relations between them. Strafford was reported as remarking that the king would get no satisfaction from the City until a few aldermen were hanged at their own front doors.[4]

It could be said, by way of summary of these relations in the decade before the crisis of 1640–1, that the government of Charles I had bullied and threatened the City, and shown an astonishing lack of tact in its dealings with a proud and essentially loyal body of men, the lord mayor and the court of aldermen. The successful resistance of the Scots to the king's policies changed all that, however: from a stance of authoritarian disdain the Privy Council had now to defer to those who held the purse strings. A temporary rapprochement followed in 1641, when those sympathetic to the court gained ascendancy in the ruling élite, and a potential royalist was elected lord mayor. But this was negated by the council elections of December, when radicals won seats on the common council and, ahead of their official recognition, seized the key positions in the City government.[5]

The political struggle was only a part of the king's problems with his capital, however, for the seething discontent of London, especially at the popular level, had in a sense been augmented, given a broad target to aim at, and the means of release, in the difficulties faced by the crown in 1640–1. There had been a long tradition, which the king himself recognised, deplored, and was active in suppressing, of popular puritan sentiment, anti-Catholic and anti-court prejudice, which was expressed in the cheaper, open-air theatres of the time, and the illicit printing of subversive literature. Radical dissent of all kinds existed just below the surface in Caroline London, repressed by Archbishop Laud and his agents, but ready to manifest itself when the time was ripe. John Lilburne had been whipped at the cart's tail for publishing an attack on the bishops in 1637. There had been separated congregations in the less-well-regulated 'Liberties' outside the City's jurisdiction, even, it was rumoured, homosexual cells on the south bank.[6]

Following the elections and popular demonstrations in December 1641, a battle ensued for the heart of the capital, almost as important as the conflict at Westminster. The king responded to the riots around his palace and the roughing up of his supporters in parliament by attempting to arrest the five Members. They fled to the City, and when Charles came in person to demand their surrender, the common council offered them protection. As he left, popular hostility boiled over. He and the royal family abandoned Whitehall, fearing that they could no longer live there in safety. Nor was the Tower, which had been a royal palace, and was in part designed to be, as Clarendon said, 'a bridle to the city',[7] long to remain as a stronghold of royal power once the court had fled. In the English Revolution it played a part scarcely less dramatic, though much less well known, than the Bastille in the French Revolution. By February 1642, a month after the king had left his capital, the fortress passed under the control of the City authorities, and the garrison was provided by the trained bands of the eastern suburbs, the Tower Hamletters. London was securely in the hands thereafter – until a new set of political developments arose – of the leaders of the parliamentarian-puritans, with the backing, so far as can be judged, of the great majority of the populace.[8]

These events formed a watershed in the relations between the court and the City. In seeking an explanation of the growing division of the nation, and the slide to civil war, those around the king immediately blamed the tumults in London which had forced him to flee. On the subject of his capital the mind of the king and his supporters was divided. The royal ideals still embraced the city which had been his home. The leading merchants, whose families supplied a succession of lord mayors and aldermen, had, despite the problems already mentioned, more to lose than to gain from any breach with the government of the day. Many were closely tied to the court by the royal grant of patents, offices and other concessions. The chief officers of the City, such as the Recorder, were often royal appointees. Sir Thomas Gardiner, the Recorder in 1640, had been the king's choice as Speaker of the Commons, but had failed to get elected.

The most prominent courtiers and government servants were usually Londoners themselves and domiciled there. The citizens they knew best, and had dealings with, were the richest merchant-princes, mainly sympathetic to the royal cause: such men regretted his departure, which had potentially disastrous economic consequences, and deplored the growing influence of popular nonconformity, puritan schism in the national church, disorder and iconoclasm. In their view the political radicals and the dissenters and image-breakers were only a small minority, their importance exaggerated because of the sheer size of London, where so many groups could operate undetected by the authorities, and even a minority faction could recruit thousands. London's élite had been loyal, led by Sir Richard Gurney, elected lord mayor in 1641, and Gardiner; some at least of her greatest merchants willing to lend to the government even in hopeless circumstances. The royalists were enabled, from their own local knowledge, to keep alive a hope that the great city would once again turn to the king.[9]

That a body of respectable, wealthy and conformist citizens remained opposed to the recent radical takeover, and was not yet afraid to express its views publicly, was clear from the circulation of a petition in the name of the leading City merchant Sir George Bynion. He had been knighted in December 1641, but had lost his council seat in the elections of that month. He now organised a protest against the takeover of the militia by the new councillors, which was presented to parliament in February 1642. Most of the 351 citizens who subscribed were wealthier and more politically experienced than those supporting the popular petitions of the day. They were the 'Grandees of the Metropolis', representative of the old order in the City which had dominated the pre-war court of aldermen, the leading livery companies and the great overseas trading monopolies. As substantial creditors of individual MPs and peers, as well as of the king and his courtiers, many, like Bynion himself, no doubt regarded the political activities of their debtors at Westminster, in their view increasingly subversive and populist, with a mixture of cynicism, distaste and alarm.[10]

The reaction of the ruling party in the corporation and their allies in parliament to this weighty protest reflected the alarm they must have felt at such a substantial challenge to their new authority; and possibly the lingering doubts they had concerning their reception among the broad mass of Londoners. Bynion and Gardiner were impeached, their houses searched and their goods eventually impounded. Their harsh treatment was comparable to that meted out to the petitioners from Kent, who included a wealthy, well-connected London citizen, Sir George Strode. When, in June 1642, Gurney attempted to proclaim the commission of

array, the device used by the king to muster armed support –
and London's was the first issued – and in the following month
oppose the radical takeover of the City government, he was
arrested. He, too, was impeached, and imprisoned in the Tower,
where, some years later, he died. The grip of the king's opponents on the capital was almost complete.[11]

As the royalists contemplated the disastrous division of the nation
in the summer of 1642, and the gathering war clouds threatening
their anointed king, there could be little doubt about who was
responsible. The leaders of the 'popular party' at Westminster
had so manipulated the 'fears and jealousies' – as the common
phrase was, and which we would now express as 'anxiety and
distrust' – of the people of London, and encouraged their riotous
demonstrations, that they had overawed the majority of MPs,
otherwise basically loyal to the old order, and forced the king
and his family into exile. They had emptied the capital's pulpits
of loyal clergy and filled them with radical preachers, who took
their cue from well-known puritan divines, now in positions of
power, like Edmund Calamy. They had encouraged the weekly
press to print diatribes against the court. In this conspiracy the
wicked intentions and crafty plotting of Pym, Lord Saye and
Hampden were matched by the political activities of the leading
puritan-parliamentarians in the City, especially Alderman Isaac
Pennington and his fellow MPs, John Venn and Samuel Vassall.

Pennington, a wealthy merchant and brewer, had fallen foul of
the church authorities, and some prominent courtiers, before the
war. He was blamed by royalists for organising one of the first
political demonstrations aimed at the Long Parliament, the city's
Root and Branch Petition, which called for the radical reformation of the church. It had been presented to the House of Commons by a thousand well-to-do citizens, and reputedly signed by
15 000 ordinary Londoners. At his house, in that 'stronghold of
London Puritanism and revolution', St Stephen's, Coleman Street,
the five Members had probably taken refuge in January 1642.[12]
When the political revolution culminated in the following summer in the displacement of Mayor Gurney, it was Alderman
Pennington who succeeded him. He was at the centre of the moves
in the City to assist the nascent war effort of parliament during
the first months of the war itself.

The essence of a conspiracy, however, is that it is the work of
a dedicated minority. It was a touchstone of royalist belief

articulated by those charged with the propaganda issued in the king's name during the paper war which accompanied the slide into open hostility, and later argued by the great royalist historian, Clarendon (in fact, often the same person), that the people of England remained basically loyal to the king, though grievously misled by their temporary political masters. If they could hear, in impartial circumstances, the royal point of view, they would respond positively to it. According to this theory most Londoners were untainted with the puritan beliefs of a Pennington or the political outlook of a Venn. There remained, even after the outbreak of the war, a wide measure of support for the king. In the political calculations made by the royalists in the first year or so of the armed conflict this basic fact was never lost sight of, and, as we shall see, influenced the kind of propaganda the king's men produced.[13]

There was some reality behind this belief. As we have seen, many of the 'grandees' of the city remained loyal in spite of the political success of the opposite party. And further to that, in the summer of 1642 there had been a remarkable shift in public opinion in favour of the king. In the provinces the royal declarations began to be well received, once they could be printed and circulated – itself an indication of the failure of parliament to close down debate. The defection of so many office-holders, MPs and peers, and the recruitment of the king's first army, was the best indicator of his new-found popularity. Such a change of attitude must have affected London as well as the regions from which the royalists now drew their support. We know that several prominent Londoners sent help to the king at York and later Oxford. Who else is 'P.P.', credited in the earliest pages of the accounts of the royal Treasurer-at-War with sending £5000, other than Sir Paul Pindar, the City financier and, as a leading customs farmer, one of the chief pre-war lenders to the king? Sir Nicholas Crispe, another prominent courtier-merchant, customs farmer, African slaver, Master of the East India Company and a member of the Society of the Artillery Garden, sent cash to Oxford before he arrived there himself early in 1643. He was related by marriage to, and a close associate of, Sir George Strode. As we shall see, he continued active in London politics even while he helped organise cavalry recruitment and (later) the royalists' new navy. These men were more important in City politics before the war than Alderman Pennington.[14]

A steady stream of refugees fled London as the war measures taken there began to bite. Most had lost their homes, livelihoods and possessions; some left their families behind. At Oxford they formed a band of embittered political exiles, a veritable Greek chorus demanding vengeance on the rebellious city, the punishment of their persecutors, and the restoration of their fortunes. The stream of royalist pamphlets and orders directed to the capital testifies to their influence: the king and his advisers were never likely to forget their plight. By 1643 it was possible to form two regiments of horse for the royalist army from, in part, London citizens, and later the garrison of Basing House in Hampshire was notable as a refuge for displaced actors (the London playhouses had been closed down by the City authorities in September 1642), artists, print-sellers and other members of the cultivated élite of the capital. Inigo Jones was captured there when it fell to Cromwell at the end of the war.[15]

In assessing the military and political situation in the new royal capital, Oxford, following the drawn first campaign of the war, the position of his old capital would be among the matters uppermost in the minds of the king's advisers. Charles had been driven out of London by his enemies, who were now busy transforming it into what John Milton well described as 'the shop of war'. The citizens, led by Pennington, Venn and the other prominent figures on the common council and at Westminster, and inspired by the fiery preaching of Hugh Peter and the several puritan ministers who now occupied London pulpits, flocked to the Guildhall to lend their silver and gold, ornaments and jewelry, to pay for the first army sent into the field to oppose the king.

Commanded by the earl of Essex, popular in the capital, where his great house stood just outside Temple Bar, and where his family was viewed sympathetically as the innocent victims, over three generations, of a corrupt and vengeful court, this army was largely recruited in London. The citizens willingly brought in thousands of horses – even their coach-horses – for this first campaign. When the royal army marched on the capital, in November 1642, they had massed at Turnham Green to resist it, giving timely support to the trained bands of the City and the battered residue of the original regular forces. They had rebuffed the king's advances and were now preparing for a long war by submitting to the legislative measures which the parliament imposed on London first, as a model for the rest of England to follow, to pay for the supply of men and munitions. They also engaged, with some enthusiasm, in building the enormous defensive system round London to keep the cavaliers at bay, and prevent them again threatening the city with invasion.[16]

There was no doubt, therefore, that London was the main prop of the king's opponents in the war, just as it could be accused of being primarily responsible for the war itself. The new radical regime was, as the months passed, tightening its grip on City government. Pennington became Lieutenant of the Tower, as well as lord mayor. But, as has been argued above, in the eyes of the cavaliers it was not, in political terms, by any means a wholly lost cause. The contacts between the capital and Oxford, in spite of the military frontier which now separated them, and parliament's ban on trade with royalist quarters, remained good. While many had fled to the king, their families, friends and business associates remained in the City, a substantial body of sympathy and potential support for the royal cause. Opposition to the new regime had still to be harshly suppressed; in October 1642 over fifty rich citizens had been imprisoned for refusing to pay taxes, and many more were distrained for non-payment later. In addition, widespread dismay at the continuation of the war, after Turnham Green, surfaced in the capital, 'many thousands', according to Clarendon, subscribing to a City petition for peace in December.[17]

The royalists took every opportunity to appeal to this source of latent support, in both official declarations and unofficial approaches. Messengers, scouts and spies, and 'certain adventurous women', concealing secret despatches in their voluminous skirts, passed to and fro, often using High Wycombe as their base. As we have seen, money could be sent, in a clandestine manner, to the king. The opportunity was taken to send messages to London which aimed to weaken the hold on the ordinary citizens enjoyed by their radical leadership, by distinguishing between them. In August 1642 the king had declared the parliamentary leaders guilty of high treason, and, blaming again the tumults in the capital for the breach in the nation, had added to their number Pennington and Venn. When, in October, the promise of royal pardon was made to his erring subjects if they would lay down their arms, the first was directed to London: but Alderman Fowke and the leading militia commander Randall Mainwaring (as well as those named previously) were excepted. It was couched in the language a kindly parent might use to wayward offspring, in the spirit of the royalist belief in the underlying loyalty of the king's subjects.[18]

When the clamour for peace in London forced parliament to send a delegation from the corporation to Oxford, in January 1643, Alderman Sir George Garrett presented proposals directly to the king. They expressed dismay that Charles should harbour any doubts about the loyalty of the City; begged his majesty to return to parliament; and promised to defend the royal family 'from all tumults, affronts and violence'. While the king listened politely to these disingenuous sentiments his courtiers could not restrain their titters. Nevertheless, when the delegation returned to London, there went with it a young courtier, Henry Heron, who was to prepare the ground for further negotiations. Charles had been reminded that the government of the capital rested on a popular basis, Common Hall, and that could this body of opinion be reached, and his case made impartially, the machinations of the ruling élite might be circumvented.

The Venetian envoy in London caught the gist of the rumours which were circulating about Heron's mission at this time. The king still viewed his capital with forgiving eyes; it had been led astray by wicked men; but it could still return to the fold, by putting pressure on parliament's representatives in the forthcoming treaty, when Charles, ever merciful, would be making generous concessions. But the king's velvet glove, so to speak, contained an iron fist. If the city was so sunk in its depravity as to reject these terms, and give continuing support to the enemies of the king, then a terrible vengeance would be exacted. It would be noted, Heron's message apparently implied, that the royal forces sat astride the main supply routes to the capital, the greatest concentration of population in the land.

Few of the inhabitants grew their own food; most were utterly dependent on the produce of the surrounding countryside. Those engaged in industrial production – and London was of course the greatest centre of industry in the country – were equally reliant on the supply of raw materials to the capital from the provinces. Commerce too – and London commanded at least two-thirds of the nation's overseas trade – depended on access to the markets in the city and the quayside facilities along the Thames, for the export and internal redistribution of goods from the rest of England. What if the royalists, in their righteous anger at the obduracy of the city, prevented these commodities reaching their destination? The king, unlike parliament, had not yet decided to cut off trade between royalist and enemy quarters, but the threat was in all probability common currency among the royal councillors at Oxford, and may well have been transmitted to London as part of the political softening-up campaign that preceded the Treaty of Oxford in March 1643.[19]

None of this was made public by the king in the negotiations at Oxford, but his agents there were clearly bargaining from a position of actual military strength: the royalists were making gains in several regions, and the cessation of arms which was proposed during the negotiations drew attention to the significance of their hold on the area to the west of London. Potentially his situation was even stronger. Charles had no hesitation in mentally rejecting the terms offered by his enemies, but was sufficiently confident to go through with the peace process as part of his plan 'to undeceive the people' and explain that it was not he, but the parliamentarians, who were responsible for the continuation of the war. When he decided, in mid-April, that it was time to break off negotiations he blamed Londoners particularly for driving MPs from Westminster by their 'tumultuary petitioning', deplored their seditious preaching and printing, and proposed that parliament be reconvened to a place of safety at least twenty miles from the city. This demand was of course completely unacceptable to parliament: not only did it enable the king to end the treaty but it allowed his public declarations to stress the responsibility of London for the breach.[20]

As well as the propaganda opportunities presented by the peacemaking, abortive though in the end it was bound to be, the king had, as he explained to the queen, newly landed in Yorkshire with fresh supplies from the Netherlands, bought with the royal jewels, 'many fine designs' which would exploit 'the distractions of the rebels'. One of these sprang directly from the belief that a substantial proportion of Londoners was ready to throw off its allegiance to his enemies, perhaps especially after the failure of the peacemaking and the supposed success of his propaganda campaign. As well as the many wealthy tax defaulters under penalty since the previous year, seven aldermen, according to the royalist newspaper, had been committed to prison for their non-co-operation with the ruling authorities, and there appeared to be growing resistance to puritan iconoclasm, increasingly heavy taxation and parliament's proposals for more of the same.[21]

One of the king's fine designs had been launched even before the arrival of the peace commissioners at Oxford. In mid-March he took the first steps to authorise named London royalists to organise an armed uprising there, designed to overthrow those who traitorously were waging war against their liege lord. Letters patent were drawn up, very secretly, and addressed to seventeen prominent citizens, which gave them extraordinary powers to raise forces, appoint officers and spend money. The names of Recorder Gardiner (now the king's Solicitor), Crispe, Strode and Bynion, all active in royalist administration or actually in the field with their commands, headed the commission. It was witnessed by the king alone, few, even high in Oxford counsels, can have known of its existence, and for the moment it remained unused.[22]

But by the beginning of May – after the failure of the peace negotiations, cavalier successes in the field, and with Essex's army, devastated by typhus, wasting away – the time seemed ripe to activate the commission. It was entrusted to Lady D'Aubigny, the widow of one of the glamorous and valiant Stuart brothers, cousins of the king himself, who had been killed at Edgehill, and taken to London to give official backing to the activities of the chief conspirators. They were instructed to make secret contact with like-minded members of both Houses of Parliament and begin active preparations for a royalist rising. At the same time public messages sent by the king to the City reiterated the propaganda points made earlier, adding that, a good part of the reinforcements brought by the queen having now arrived at Oxford, the king was even better placed to punish those who rejected his overtures for peace.[23]

For a month the plot thickened. At its centre, linking London and Westminster with Oxford, was the wealthy MP-poet, Edmund Waller. A parliamentary commissioner at the recent treaty, he had many contacts with the leaders of the 'Peace Party' at Westminster: and, inevitably, later, his presence at Oxford during the negotiations of the spring appeared suspicious. Before the war he had been one of the Great Tew circle, which had gathered at Lord Falkland's house in Oxfordshire; this meant that, by 1643, he could count on the friendship of one of the royal secretaries of state and a group of now highly placed royalist intellectuals. If his verse, much admired at the time, was shallow, his purse was deep: as well as a town house, at Holborn, he had inherited a fine estate at Beaconsfield. Its strategic position between Oxford and the capital no doubt facilitated his work, which exploited the deep disillusionment with the war felt at London. In the Lords he drew in the earl of Northumberland, Viscount Conway and Lord Portland; he also sounded out prominent MPs thought to be sympathetic, such as John Selden, Symonds D'Ewes and Bulstrode Whitelocke. In this work Waller's two chief helpers were his brother-in-law and neighbour, Nathaniel Tompkins, and the prominent linen-draper, Richard Challoner. They categorised those they approached under one of three headings: 'right' to the cause, 'averse' or 'moderate'. Unfortunately this poll of élite opinion in the capital, at a crucial juncture of the war, does not survive.[24]

But the propaganda directed at London backfired on the plotters. The boastful messages sent from the king had caused alarm, and soon aroused suspicion. It was in a hostile atmosphere that the House of Commons began the impeachment of the queen for assisting the king with weapons of war. Fearful and angry, the House suborned some of the servants of suspected persons to act as spies on their masters, and eventually, their suspicions confirmed, authorised searches of their houses. It was rewarded on 31 May when, with the finding of the commission itself in Tompkins's cellar, the plot was revealed.

Our knowledge of it remains, however, after the passage of the years, severely restricted. The cavaliers' secrecy, though far from complete, was matched by the discretion observed by the parliamentary and City authorities, who did not want the full implications of the plot – that a substantial number of MPs, peers and citizens were in communication with the enemy – broadcast to the world. That a broad sentiment for peace in London concealed a good deal of clandestine activity subversive of the parliamentary war effort is obvious. But it is not clear whether all those named, in the commission, or the purported confessions of the principal participants, or the diarists of the day, worked as a group, under Oxford's direction. None of the leading commissioners was in London; there is no sign of the royalist troop movements around the capital promised the plotters. Challoner denied any foreknowledge of the commission itself, and it may be that his circle of prominent merchants in the wealthy central area of the City, which had recently sent money to the king's war chest but was probably doing little more than testing opinion, can be distinguished from the group centred on Tompkins. He had been a royal servant for over twenty years, was connected to the queen's household and Catholics abroad, and was well known to the royalist high command. It was probably his network which stored arms, contacted leading cavaliers (including a militarily experienced old Army Plotter) in City prisons, never very secure places, received money from Oxford and made most of the active preparations for a rising.[25]

As in the past, when the king had appeared to treat with his enemies while actually planning the next round of the war, the exposure of his duplicity, in the sending of messages of peace (admittedly with the threats described) while encouraging an armed uprising in the city, did him great harm. Already prepared to arraign the queen for her military intervention, before the plot's discovery, the parliamentary leadership was quick to seize the initiative. A day of thanksgiving was ordered, to praise the Lord and His mercies to embattled London (now miraculously preserved from imminent destruction), and Pym at last was able to gain acceptance for his long-wished-for scheme to impose a binding, and divinely sanctioned, loyalty oath upon his followers. In June a vow and covenant was made law, by which all men could dedicate themselves anew to the cause of parliament.[26]

Harsh measures followed. The royal peace messengers, whose incautious boasts had alerted the authorities in the first place, were arrested and died in prison. The chief conspirators, Tompkins and Challoner, were tried and executed; such was the popular clamour against them, a reflection no doubt of the fear they had inspired among ordinary citizens, that they were hanged close to their own front doors and their bodies exposed to the public gaze. The houses and goods of those citizens named in the commission were seized. Political expediency, however, required more lenient treatment of MPs and peers. Waller was permitted to bribe his way out of trouble, and pay a huge fine, and the peers to flee to Oxford. During the summer of 1643, after further royalist victories, other prominent waverers and secret sympathisers followed them to the king's quarters. A series of risings in parliament-controlled areas, including Kent and Norfolk, troubled the authorities there. As several leading officers of their forces in the field had also deserted the cause at this time it seemed as though, despite the failure of Waller's plot, the king's star was in the ascendant.[27]

No doubt influenced by the imminent presence of his queen,

as well as by his strong military position, Charles responded to the events in London of June with a further pronouncement which struck a more pessimistic note than some earlier. The hope that – in the cant phrase employed by royal propaganda since the start of the war – his 'good subjects' might desert their wicked leaders, was balanced by genuine anger at the proceedings in parliament against his queen and the plotters. As the London disorders had rendered the parliament unfree, its proceedings were declared null and void. Treason had been committed at Westminster, as also at Bristol: Charles was furious with the authorities there for hanging two citizens for plotting – like those at London – to surrender the city. While the king could not dissolve the two Houses at Westminster, having consented, two years before, to their continuance, he offered pardon again to those who would desert their sitting. In any case the queen, rapidly approaching the royal headquarters with substantial reinforcements and preconceived ideas of how to deal with rebels, was in high spirits and no mood to compromise. She headed her own forces, kept control of the supplies she brought, and was no longer the largely ineffective figure of the pre-war court.[28]

The following weeks were, as it turned out, the high point of royalist fortunes in the Civil War. The queen was welcomed to Oxford, guarded by troops provided by the royal commander in the North. Her train of arms and ammunition was a magnificent addition to the king's strength. In the West the cavaliers won a series of victories over Sir William Waller – the battle of Roundway Down was won on the day of the public thanksgiving at London – which culminated in the capture by Rupert of Bristol itself. Much of the South West, including the ports through which the king could expect further supplies from the Continent, passed into royalist hands. At this juncture, favourable to the king, another royal proclamation took stock of the situation of the capital, this time with respect to its trade.

Since the beginning of the war the king had permitted commerce with London. This was consonant with his view of the citizens as 'formerly Famous for their loyalty, and love to their Soveraignes'. But now, he declared, 'above all other parts of this Our Kingdom, a prevalent faction of that Citty (which over-rules the whole) hath so farre joyned with and in that horrid Rebellion', that it 'is now become the head of that Traiterous faction, and the receptacle of all such as are disaffected to Our Government,

and the Lawes of the Kingdom'. The same faction had recently
opposed all ways to peace. Condign punishment was now required:
the right to trade with London and other enemy-controlled areas
was withdrawn. The Oxford Privy Council, advising the king,
no doubt decided that more harm would be done as a result
to parliament's economic base than to his; and that trade could
now be directed exclusively through the recently won ports and
markets.[29]

The response of parliament and its friends in the City to these
measures, and failures in the field, was a radical upsurge. The
'Peace Party' was compromised by the revelations of the Waller
plot, and the desertions to Oxford which ensued. The king's military
success, combined with the discovery that the Waller Plot had
involved some of the cavaliers held in London prisons, led to
fears of an enemy within, a Fifth Column which was ready to
open the gates to the invader. In August, if only temporarily,
royalist captives, including several divines and academics, were
sent to the hulks in the Thames. 'Delinquency', which led to for-
feiture of property, was redefined to include the Waller plotters.
Renewed attempts were made to galvanise the war effort by creating a new army with a fresh commander; and military control
of London was transferred from Essex to lord mayor Pennington
and the common council, now dominated by those willing to prosecute the war more heartily. It was at this time that a key post in
the defence of the metropolitan area, the Lieutenancy of the Tower,
fell to Pennington.[30]

The displeasure of the king, however, expressed in his recent
orders, did not prevent a further attempt at reconciliation. While
his forces pursued their victories in the West by the investing of
Gloucester, the capture of which would clear their lines to the
major recruiting areas of the West Midlands and South Wales,
another political initiative was begun at Oxford. It could not now
be argued by friend or foe that the king was dealing from a position of weakness when he again offered to treat. His next declaration, of 30 July, restated the principles he was fighting for, as
they had originally been set out in his now celebrated speech at
Wellington in Shropshire at the beginning of the war. The defence of the privileges of parliament, the laws of England and
the true protestant religion was his only aim; this was the legend
inscribed on his coinage, medals and military banners – and in
the commission to London of March – so long as the conflict

lasted. As he had done earlier the king offered pardon to those
who would now lay down their arms, embrace these principles
and repudiate rebellion. It was still not too late for those, previously misled by his enemies, to become 'good subjects' once again.

Clarendon, the probable author of the July declaration, later
believed, when he came to write his *History*, that it had the desired effect, recollecting that a week later hundreds of women
mobbed Westminster, clamouring for peace. But those who received their petition were in fact divided on the political and
military situation. While several peers grasped every opportunity
to promote a policy of near surrender to the king's demands,
Pym and the majority in the Commons backed the efforts of Essex
to ready his forces for the relief of Gloucester. Pennington and
the City authorities gave crucial support, encouraging counter-
demonstrations at Westminster and exhortation from the press
and pulpit. As importantly, they provided six regiments of the
London trained bands for Essex's expedition, thus substantially
reinforcing his infantry.[31]

It was at this juncture, the point of the great conflict at which
key decisions were made by both sides which would affect its
outcome, that a more considered and literary contribution to royal
propaganda, directed at London, first appeared. Published at
Oxford in mid-August, and quickly reprinted in the capital, it
was not, like the 30 July Declaration, a statement of official policy.
It is, however, the fullest exposition of the royalist case against
the capital up to this time, based on a detailed narrative of events,
both before and during the war, seen and interpreted from a hostile
point of view. Among the best examples of sustained political
invective produced by the English Civil War, it is the most lively,
knowing and effective lampoon of their opponents the cavaliers
achieved.

Entitled *A Letter from Mercurius Civicus to Mercurius Rusticus*, it
purported to be the confession of an erstwhile London supporter
of parliament, to a friend in the country, of the responsibility of
the capital for the disaster which had overtaken the nation. The
comedy of the piece derives from the impersonation of a repent-
ant citizen, and the delicate irony with which the pious language
and sententious moralising of the godly party are turned against
it. Dated 5 August, the point at which the rival factions in London were pressing for peace or war, the letter-writer looked back
on the recent history of the city. He wrote as an insider, claiming

to have been present at some of the crucial incidents there in 1641 and 1642. So knowledgeable, accurate, and entertaining are the author's descriptions of key events and personalities in London that historians have made ample use of his work.[32]

Not only is *A Letter* written with great journalistic skill, it is as up-to-date as that week's newspaper, taking an informed and opinionated stance, as it did, on contemporary issues. Only one other royal production can match it and that is *Mercurius Aulicus*, the official royalist newsbook. It is not surprising therefore that historians have suggested that the editor of the one is the anonymous author of the other. John Berkenhead, Oxford academic and protégé of Laud, possessed an inimitable style characteristic of both newspaper and pamphlet, and by the summer of 1643 he had produced twenty-six issues of *Mercurius*. That week's paper speaks of London as 'that prodigall and licentious City', language borrowed from the royal proclamation of 17 July 1643 which prohibited trade with enemy quarters: it was used again in *A Letter*. Berkenhead handed over the editorship of the paper to Peter Heylin, another of Laud's followers, during the time the pamphlet was written.

He was qualified for the task by more than a facile pen and some experience of weekly journalism. A fellow of All Souls, he had been one of the circle of rising young academics in the 1630s, patronised by Laud as Chancellor of the University. He had also been a member of the set of talented young men gathered round William Cartwright, another Oxford fellow, and this gave him access to the 'tribe of Ben' Jonson, the poets of the 1630s who had been influenced by the greatest versifier of the age. Berkenhead had been at Lambeth in the last years before the war, as the archbishop's amanuensis, and must have gained insights into the London literary scene, as well as the politics of the City. He no doubt became acquainted with those youthful exponents of the graceful and courtly style, such as Sir John Suckling, Sir John Denham and Edmund Waller, which later generations would see as characteristic of the school of cavalier poets.[33]

From this vantage point Berkenhead rehearses the means by which discontent with the king's government before the war was fostered, especially in the capital, uncovering the conspiracy which for most royalists caused the rebellion. He provides the earliest and now classic statement of the connection between pre-war puritan patronage in the church and colonising activities overseas, and the rebellion. It was first hatched at Banbury (the home of Lord Saye), he writes, and fostered by small groups of Providence Island merchants. Lecturers were placed by puritan feoffees in corporations – 'those nurseries of schisme and rebellion' – to rival the orthodox parish clergy; certain Oxford and Cambridge colleges were taken over; and in London several key pulpits. The Society of the Artillery Garden had a special role to play: According to Berkenhead puritans had at first scorned to engage in such a prophane recreation as training in arms: 'but, at last, when it was instill'd into them that the blessed reformation intended could not be effected but by the sword, these places were instantly filled with few or none but men of that faction'. It was at the Artillery Garden, during the Scots Wars, he continues, that their preacher, Calybute Downing, first asserted 'that for defence of religion, and reformation of the church, it was lawful to take up armes against the king'.[34]

Berkenhead depicts 'the puritan faction' in the City working busily in these years to gain a common council of its own mind. Poorer men, even non-Londoners, were assisted to aldermanic seats by the creation of a common purse to defray their expenses. He cites the case of Thomas Atkins of Norwich, advanced in this way. When the great crisis of 1641–2 divided the City it captured the council's key committees in the way already described. The old guard was routed by the new radical candidates: Alderman Fowke, Ryley 'the squeeking bodyes-maker', Atkins, Towse and a host of tailors, cutlers, dyers, wine-coopers, whom it was easy for a royalist satirist to contrast unfavourably with 'the grave, discreet, well-affected citizens' like Sir George Bynion, whom they replaced. Then it was ready to heighten the 'fears and jealousies' of the ordinary citizens. On the night of 6–7 January 1642, when the five Members had taken refuge in the capital, the faction raised a false alarm that the cavaliers would surprise the city. The author claimed to have been with the lord mayor and seen the frantic preparations made to resist, which included the women providing hot water, 'besides what they sprinkled for feare', to throw on the invaders.[35]

Thereafter, the author asserts, it only remained to co-ordinate the efforts of the leaders in parliament and their supporters in the City, to drive the nation to open warfare. So closely did they work together that "twas a question, which was the parliament, that at Westminster, or this at Guild-Hall'. Crucial to their plan was the tuning of the City pulpits and the control of the London press. It was not divine inspiration which caused the same texts to be preached in every church on a Sunday, but the instructions received from the leaders of the faction by Edmund Calamy and 'the junto that meet at his house'. It had long been the royalist lament that the puritan takeover had erected a Tower of Babel in London, where many voices preached blasphemy and treason, and a thousand lying pamphlets and sermons inflamed the giddy multitude. *A Letter* gave memorable expression to that view.[36]

This led Berkenhead, in his closing peroration, to dilate on the catastrophic consequences of the rebellion, no less for the authors of it as for the nation as a whole. 'There is but one rebell, and that is London.' Without the backing of its citizens parliament's cause could not have survived. 'They have supplyed the treasury of the rebels with no lesse than three millions of money, and their army with threescore thousand men.' All the ancient, time-honoured obligations of religion, nature and the known laws having been set aside, sons are arrayed against parents, apprentices and servants against masters. Many parents, sending their sons to London in the hopes of their rising to be lord mayor, are now wringing their hands as they are flung into battle against the Lord's anointed. Not only are their bodies imperilled, but their precious souls too, argues Berkenhead, for they are dying or being maimed in a sinful cause, that of rebellion. Although the king has treated Londoners 'like an indulgent father of rebellious children', they have cast dirt in his face, slighted his offers of peace, supported his enemies and persecuted his friends. He concludes with a ringing condemnation, which echoes some of the sentiments, already quoted, in the recent royal proclamations:

If, therefore, posterity shall aske who broke downe the bounds to those streames of blood that have stained this earth; if they aske who made liberty captive, truth criminall, rapine just, tyranny and oppression lawful; who blanched rebellion with the specious pretence of the defence of lawes and liberties, warre with the desire of an established peace, sacriledge and prophanation with the shew of zeale and reformation; lastly, if they aske who would have pulled the crown from the king's head, taken the government off the hinges, dissolved monarchy, inslaved the lawes, and ruined their countrey, – say, 'twas the proud, unthankefull, schismaticall, rebellious, bloody city of London; so that what they wanted of devouring this kingdome by cheating and cozening, they meane to finish by the sword.[37]

The denunciation of the capital employed the ancient Horatian and Virgilian contrast between the corrupt city and the ideal country-side, which was newly fashionable among the poets of Charles I's reign, whose work Berkenhead knew. As we have seen, the city was viewed by the rest of England as a monopolising centre, which drained, by sharp practices and usurious dealing, the wealth of the nation, the better to sustain, in unnatural luxury, the commercial élite of its swollen population. It was, for the cavaliers and their like, 'that prodigall and licentious city'. The only consolation was that its cheating merchants were themselves cheated by their wives, a scurrilous accusation the king's men never tired of making, in print, on banners and in song.

These sentiments were echoed by a much weightier apologist for the royal cause, Sir John Spelman, whose well-known tract, *The Case of our Affaires in Law, Religion*, must have been written at about this time. He, too, blamed 'our great Metropolis' for the ills of the kingdom, and condemned its sins in the language of the Old Testament. Like the biblical city which harboured a murderer and was faced with divine punishment, London had a choice; to yield the culprit to justice, or perish at the hands of avenging Israel. The blood of Tompkins and Challoner demanded atonement.

For both Spelman and Berkenhead it seemed that, by the high summer of 1643, the capital had chosen continued defiance. The tone of both pamphlets, in spite of Berkenhead's natural sprightliness, is pessimistic. They follow the lead of the earlier proclamation, which cut off trade with London, rather than the more recent royal declaration with its renewed offer of pardon. Spelman could foresee, just before his own death of typhus at Oxford in July, that the city was too hardened in sin to avoid 'God's determined Visitation upon the Land'. Incalculable sorrow would be the reward of the nation which could not expunge the wickedness of the great city, and was rather inclined to follow its unnatural and sacrilegious example. London, wrote Berkenhead, would spread its cancer of rebellion to the otherwise healthy parts of the body politic, 'dissolve the nerves, and luxate the sinewes of this admirable composed government'. The only solution was a drastic one; 'reducing this stubborne city either to obedience or ashes'.[38]

Of course the capital would not be destroyed either by Berkenhead's delicate use of irony or the blunt instrument of Old Testament censure, wielded by Spelman. The cavaliers had rung the changes in their approaches to the city, offering olive branches at propitious moments, but also dire warnings of future punishment. They had encouraged those whom they thought sympathetic to the royal cause to persuade their fellow citizens to come out of their trance-like state and throw off their temporarily usurping masters – 'the puritan faction'. At the same time, no doubt deafened at Oxford by the Greek chorus of exiles, they had authorised more direct action. When that failed the king had roundly condemned the shedding of the blood of the Waller plotters, whose public execution had been turned into a political spectacle. He had cut off trade with the city and stepped up the propaganda campaign against the place he held primarily responsible for the outbreak of rebellion and the continuation of the war. The longer-term economic and political consequences of these royalist initiatives were unclear: but it was quickly evident that, in spite of the great hardships suffered by much of the population, the decisive response of parliament and City had the support of the majority of the citizens. Little more could be hoped for, as the city trained bands played a decisive part at the battle of Newbury in September 1643, and received a heroes' welcome on their return, from obdurate Londoners. The closure of this phase in the relations between the monarch and his capital was the ringing denunciation which ended the lampoon of the character and actions of 'the proud, unthankefull . . . city of London', at the hands of John Berkenhead. It would not be the end of the story – there were other conspiracies, nipped in the bud, and further hopes, equally blasted, to come – but it was a fitting climax.

Notes

1. V. Pearl, *London and the Outbreak of the Puritan Revolution* (London, 1961), pp. 37–40. K. J. Lindley, 'Riot Prevention and Control in Early Stuart London', *Trans. of the Royal Historical Soc.*, fifth series, 33 (1983), 109–26.
2. K. Sharpe, *The Personal Rule of Charles I* (New Haven and London, 1992), pp. 403–12.
3. Sharpe, *Personal Rule*, pp. 414–18.
4. Pearl, *London and the Outbreak*, pp. 100–1. R. Ashton, *The Crown and*

the *Money Market, 1603–1640* (Oxford, 1960); Idem, *The City and the Court, 1603–1643* (Cambridge, 1979), p. 199.

5. Pearl, *London and the Outbreak, passim*, especially chap. IV.

6. B. S. Manning, *The English People and the English Revolution* (London, 1976), Chapter 2. M. Butler, *Theatre and Crisis 1632–1642* (Cambridge, 1987), Chapter 8. M. Heinemann, *Puritanism and Theatre*, (Cambridge, 1982), Chapter 12. M. Tolmie, *The Triumph of the Saints. The Separate Churches of London 1616–1649* (Cambridge, 1977), Chapters 1–2.

7. W. D. Macray (ed.), Edward, Earl of Clarendon, *The History of the Rebellion and Civil Wars in England* (London, 1888), I, p. 448.

8. 'London rehearsed all this [the fall of the Bastille] but distantly and as in a play that was never performed', Pearl, *London and the Outbreak*, p. 143. See also, Manning, *English People*, Chapter 4.

9. E. Walker, *Historical Discourses upon Several Occasions* (London, 1705), pp. 238–9. Walker, the king's secretary-at-war, is a reliable witness to Charles's state of mind. Ashton, *The City and the Court, passim*. R. Brenner, *Merchants and Revolution. Commercial Change, Political Conflict, and London's Overseas Traders, 1550–1653* (Cambridge, 1993), pp. 306–7. Pearl, *London and the Outbreak*, pp. 66–7.

10. Pearl, *London and the Outbreak*, pp. 148–51. K. J. Lindley, 'London's Citizenry in the English Revolution', in R. C. Richardson (ed.), *Town and Countryside in the English Revolution* (Manchester, 1992), pp. 21 *et seq.*

11. Pearl, *London and the Outbreak*, pp. 136–7, 149–57. T. Woods, *Prelude to Civil War 1642. Mr Justice Malet and the Kentish Petitions* (Wilton, 1980). I. Roy (ed.), *The Royalist Ordnance Papers, 1642–1646* (Oxfordshire Record Soc., 42, 1964), pp. 17–18.

12. Pearl, *London and the Outbreak*, pp. 176–93.

13. A good example of this argument is that contained in the royal proclamation of July 1643, J. F. Larkin (ed.), *Stuart Royal Proclamations Volume II: Royal Proclamations of King Charles I 1625–1646* (Oxford, 1983), pp. 932–4, discussed below. Hyde was so pleased with his 'fine writing' (as one, less literary, royalist described it), in the war of words which preceded the Civil War, and accompanied its early stages, that he included all of it in his later 'History' (Clarendon, *History*, II, book v). The king's subjects were sometimes spoken of as temporarily 'infatuated', *Mercurius Aulicus*, p. 385.

14. *A Narrative by John Ashburnham* (London, 1830), II, Appendix, pp. vi, viii, xiv. Other contributing customs farmers may be concealed by their initials, on p. viii (A.P. may be Alderman Sir Henry Pratt). *CSPD, 1641–43*, p. 491. Roy (ed.), *Royalist Ordnance Papers*, pp. 18, 41–2, 468. See also, *Calendar of the Committee for the Advance of Money*, pp. 511, 999, 1096; PRO, SP20/6, ff. 15–16. It was alleged that money was sent to Oxford hidden in soap barrels, Walker, *Historical Discourses*, p. 238.

15. I. Roy, 'The Libraries of Edward, 2nd Viscount Conway, and Others: an Inventory and Valuation of 1643', *Bulletin of the Institute of Historical Research*, XLI (1968), 35–46. *CJ*, III, p. 149. *Calendar of the Committee*

for Compounding with Delinquents, pp. 858–9, 1559, 1651. Nearly 300 citizens suffered sequestration of their property in 1643, PRO, SP20/ 6. Crispe's and Sir Horatio Cary's regiments of horse were officered by London citizens, as was the foot regiment, stationed at Basing, of the leading Spanish trader Sir Marmaduke Rawden, Dr Williams's Library, MS Modern F 7, ff. 130–1. BL, Harleian MS 986, ff. 86, 91. Roy (ed.) *Royalist Ordnance Papers*, pp. 441, 487.

16. Pearl, *London and the Outbreak*, pp. 209–10, 232, 237–75. *A & O*, I, pp. 6–9, 26–7, 38–40, 85–100. PRO, SP28/131, parts 3–5. Essex was described as 'the most popular man in the kingdom' in 1642. Peter became famous in royalist lampoons for urging the citizens' wives to lend their silver thimbles and bodkins to the cause, and 'hug' their husbands into rebellion, *A Letter from Mercurius Civicus to Mercurius Rusticus* (Oxford, 1643), reprinted in W. Scott (ed.), *Lord Somers Tracts*, IV (London, 1810), p. 588. The major military tax, the weekly assessment, levied twice as much from the London conurbation as the size of its population warranted.

17. HMC, *Portland MSS*, I, p. 86. Pearl, *London and the Outbreak*, p. 274. Lindley, 'London's Citizenry', 33. Roy, 'Libraries of Edward, 2nd Viscount Conway, and Others', 37, 42, 44–6. Several aldermen and other leading citizens were still in prison in the summer of 1643, though some of those mentioned by Dr Pearl were at Oxford by this time, Pearl, *London and the Outbreak*, p. 266. Clarendon, *History*, II, p. 430.

18. P. Barwick, *The Life of . . . the Reverend Dr. John Barwick* (London, 1724), pp. 61–2. Proclamation, 27 Oct. 1642, Larkin (ed.), *Proclamations*, II, pp. 806–8. Clarendon, *History*, II, pp. 275–81.

19. Clarendon, *History*, II, pp. 431–8. HMC, *Portland MSS*, I, p. 85. *CSPD*, 1641–43, p. 439. J. Rushworth (ed.), *Historical Collections [of Private Passages of State . . .]* (1721), III pt ii, pp. 113–16. S. R. Gardiner, *History of the Great Civil War, 1642–1649* (London, 1910), I, pp. 82–3, 95, 99, 135. C. V. Wedgwood, *The King's War 1641–1647* (London, 1966 edn), p. 157. Free passage of goods to London had been promised by the king in December 1642, Larkin (ed.), *Proclamations*, II, pp. 825–6.

20. Gardiner, *Great Civil War*, I, p. 95. R. Spalding (ed.), *The Diary of Bulstrode Whitelocke 1605–1675* (British Academy, Records of Social and Economic History, new series, XIII, 1990), pp. 145–6. *The Proceedings in the Late Treaty of Peace* (London, 1643), pp. 47–8, 76.

21. The king's letter to the queen was intercepted and published, *The Proceedings*, p. 76. Pearl, *London and the Outbreak*, pp. 257, 262. Clarendon, *History*, III, pp. 33–4.

22. The commission, dated 16 March 1643, was found and later printed by parliament, T. B. Howell (ed.), *A Complete Collection of State Trials* (London, 1816), IV, cols 628–30.

23. The king's message brought with Alexander Hampden, 19 May 1643, Clarendon, *History*, III, pp. 35–6. Hampden, like Heron and other royal messengers, already enjoyed good contacts with London: he had paid secret subsidies from royalist sympathisers there into the

king's war chest, *Narrative by Ashburnham*, II, Appendix, pp. iii, vii.

24. *State Trials*, IV, cols 626–51. *Diary of Bulstrode Whitelocke*, p. 147. Rushworth, *Historical Collections*, V, pp. 322–30. J. Sanford, *Studies and Illustrations of the Great Rebellion* (London, 1858), pp. 560–4.

25. Crispe, referred to by Clarendon, may have had a leading role, and another commissioner, Captain Marmaduke Rawdon, jnr, the son of the Spanish trader and governor of Basing, Sir Marmaduke, was passing between Oxford, Basing and London at this time with 'Barbary gold' brought from the Canaries. Clarendon, *History*, III, p. 50. R. Davies (ed.), *The Life of Marmaduke Rawdon of York* (Camden Soc., 85, 1863), pp. 32–3. *Narrative by Ashburnham*, II, Appendix, pp. v, vii, xxvii–iii. *Calendar of the Committee for Compounding with Delinquents*, pp. 893, 1474, 1686–8. *Mercurius Aulicus*, pp. 292, 300, 315–16, 355–6, 372, 386.

26. *A & O*, I, pp. 175–6. Clarendon, *History*, III, pp. 47–50.

27. Clarendon, *History*, III, pp. 38–53. *State Trials*, IV, col. 628. *Mercurius Civicus*, p. 597. PRO, SP20/6, where the goods of eleven plotters are valued. R. R. Sharpe, *London and the Kingdom* (London, 1894–5), II, p. 190. *CJ*, III, p. 181.

28. Larkin (ed.), *Proclamations*, II, pp. 911–18. *Mercurius Aulicus*, pp. 291–2, 295–6, 324–6, 417.

29. Larkin (ed.), *Proclamations*, II, pp. 825–6, 932–4 (December 1642 and 17 June 1643). *Mercurius Aulicus*, pp. 398–400. I. Roy, 'England Turned Germany? The aftermath of the English Civil War in its European Context', *Trans. of the Royal Historical Soc.*, 28 (1978), 138.

30. *CJ*, III, pp. 197, 205, 229. Sanford, *Studies*, pp. 560–1. Pearl, *London and the Outbreak*, p. 274. *A & O*, I, pp. 254–60. Gardiner, *Great Civil War*, I, pp. 180–8.

31. Gardiner, *Great Civil War*, I, pp. 180–8. Clarendon, *History*, III, pp. 118, 135, 139. *Mercurius Aulicus*, pp. 415–16. *Mercurius Civicus*, pp. 596–8. See above, Chapters 4 and 5, for the construction of the defences and the contribution of the London trained bands.

32. *A Letter* is F. Madan (ed.), *Oxford Books* (Oxford, 1895–1931), II, no. 1441. Both *Mercurius Civicus* and *Mercurius Rusticus* were existing newsbook titles.

33. *A Letter* was composed in July and published in August, P. W. Thomas, *Sir John Berkenhead 1617–1679. A Royalist Career in Politics and Polemics* (Oxford, 1969), pp. 107–11. Its authorship is also discussed in Pearl, *London and the Outbreak*, p. 133 and note. For the literary scene see H. Maclean (ed.), *Ben Jonson and the Cavalier Poets* (New York, 1974), and T. Clayton (ed.), *Cavalier Poets* (Oxford, 1978), especially, in both, 'The Wits (A Session of the Poets)', by Suckling.

34. *A Letter*, pp. 582–4. This well-known interpretation was given modern form by A. P. Newton, *The Colonising Activities of the Puritans* (London, 1920), and, more recently, Brenner, *Merchants and Revolution* (on the American trades), and (on the feoffees' patronage) P. S. Seaver, *The Puritan Lectureships. The Politics of Religious Dissent 1560–1662* (Stanford, Cal., 1970), where Downing's sermon is discussed on pp. 367–8. It should be noted that while there is some evidence

of the godly penetrating the voluntary companies of the City's artillery gardens, both Crispe and Rawdon, snr., were prominent members of the Society of the Artillery Garden before the war.

35. *A Letter*, pp. 587–91.
36. *A Letter*, pp. 592, 595.
37. *A Letter*, pp. 582, 595–8.
38. *The Case of our Affaires, in Law, Religion,* ... is anonymous, published at Oxford in January 1644, but written by Spelman just before his death. It was printed with the last pages of *A Letter* as an addendum. It is Madan (ed.), *Oxford Books*, 1516, D. Wing, *Short-title Catalogue of Books Printed* ... *1641–1700* (2nd edn, New York, 1988), III, S 4935, and see Pearl, *London and the Outbreak*, p. 133 n. 107. The Biblical references are to Judges 20, and II Samuel 20, v. 16; *The Case*, pp. 31–2. *A Letter*, pp. 581, 598.

7

The Economic and Social Impact of the Civil War upon London

Stephen Porter

As the centre of the largest concentration of population, wealth and economic activity in England, London's crucial economic role in determining the outcome of the Civil War is unquestionable and has long been acknowledged.[1] The royalist chronicler Sir Philip Warwick was in no doubt of parliament's advantage in controlling London, which he described as 'an inexhaustible fountain',[2] and historians have not challenged that view. Yet there has been less interest in the other side of the question, that is, the impact of the war upon London, rather than its effect upon the war. The mood of the citizens as reflected in their petitions and the occasional tumult – and as reported by the Venetian envoy – has been adduced as evidence of the capital's problems during the war years.[3] As part of a more searching and wider-ranging study, Margaret James concluded that because of London's role in the national economy it was adversely affected by the disruption caused by the war, although it has also been recognised that there were compensations for London's economy to offset the losses.[4]

One way of attempting to assess the effect of the first Civil War upon the metropolis is to assemble a rough balance-sheet of the gains and losses, and endeavour to give some idea of the relative values of the various elements. The creation of a simple model of this kind is clearly an imperfect methodology, given the size of the city, the complexity of its economy, the coarseness of the evidence and the doubtful accuracy of some of the values. Moreover, the confusion and changes brought about by the war

175

adversely affected the compilation and survival of some of the sources which provide such statistical information as exists for the mid-seventeenth century. Nevertheless, there is sufficient evidence to make the balance-sheet at least partially complete and allow some tentative conclusions to be drawn from it.

An obvious, but important, factor was that London was only ever held by one side and was never besieged, and passage along the Thames downstream of the capital was not cut or threatened. After the confrontation at Turnham Green, London was not even approached by a royalist army, and from the early summer of 1643 it was protected by its encircling defences. The extensive fortifications were built partly to reassure the citizens that the capital was safe from a surprise attack and they were constructed so far away from the built-up area on most sides that the city could not be subjected to an artillery bombardment if the royalists did manage to mount a siege.[5] But another of the reasons given to justify the enormous effort involved in constructing the lines was an economic one; that they would provide something of a sanctuary from the war and so 'encourage our friends to frequent her, and to come with their estates to inhabit in her by multitudes, whereby she will grow mighty, famous, and rich even in time of wars'.[6] When that happened there would be an increase in the sums that could be levied by taxation and from the customs, as trade from the port increased. The Dutch example during the Eighty Years' War was cited in support of this argument. It seems that the capital did become a place of refuge to some extent. Sir William Petty later wrote that between 1642 and 1650, 'Men came out of the Countrey to London, to shelter themselves from the Outrages of the Civil Wars'.[7] The merchants from ports where trade was locked up by the war may have moved to London in order to be able to continue trading and maintain their contacts, and some of the gentry brought their families there for safety.

Sir Thomas Barrington was an Essex gentleman who moved to London, bringing his family and servants with him. He was an MP and, once it became apparent that parliament was going to be sitting for a long time, he gave up his temporary lodgings and took a substantial house in the West End. His accounts show that in the first year of the Long Parliament he spent £500 in London.[8] Not all Members were as wealthy as Barrington and many of them were at Westminster only intermittently, or did not bring their families with them, and so spent less than he did, but the presence of parliament throughout the war years undoubtedly brought some business to the capital.

In 1625 the collective expenses of MPs during a parliamentary session was put by one of their number at £7000 a week, which may have been something of an exaggeration, for the statement was designed to illustrate how expensive it was to keep parliament in session. Nevertheless, taken at face value it suggests that the outlay was equivalent to roughly £350 000 per annum if the Houses sat for the whole year.[9] During the Civil War the Westminster Parliament was much reduced in numbers, for most of the peerage and roughly one-third of the House of Commons joined the king, and other MPs must have been away for some of the time, on military service, or looking after their estates. The numbers attending the Commons barely exceeded 200, even when major issues were being discussed, and probably no more than one-quarter of the lay peers continued to sit in the Lords.[10] A few of the Members may already have had accommodation in London, and not all of the others took a house, as Barrington did, but simply stayed in lodgings. Halving the 1625 figure to £175 000 still seems high in the context of the 1640s, when it was incumbent on MPs to show some austerity, but nevertheless may be taken as an indication of the scale of the annual input to London's economy that came from parliament's continuing in session.

The religious counterpart to the Houses of Parliament was the Westminster Assembly, which began work in July 1643 and laboured slowly thereafter in search of a religious settlement. It had 150 members, of whom 30 were lay members, including a number of peers and MPs, who would presumably have been in London even if they had not been nominated to the Assembly, as indeed would some of its clerical members.[11] They were paid the not inconsiderable sum of £3 per day, and although we may assume that many of its members still had less spending power than the Members of Parliament, nevertheless their presence should be counted on the positive side of London's wartime account.

A more obvious benefit to London during the war was its role as the headquarters of the parliamentarian administration, which was, virtually from the beginning of the war, well organised and comparatively efficient, much of its success being due to the involvement of the City merchants and the application of their business acumen and organisational skills to the problem of financing the war effort. The size of the administration is uncertain, but it expanded during the war to meet the growing demands of the armies. The introduction of the excise in 1643 required the creation of a wholly new section, for example. The intention of centralising all of parliament's military finance was impractical and was not successful, but much of it did pass through London nevertheless.[12]

A large part of the wartime revenue was used to purchase clothing and equipment to fit out the armies, with a great deal of it ordered from or through London tradesmen. The orders for harness, belts, bandoliers, clothing, tools, vehicles, weapons and ammunition must have provided a great deal of business for the armourers, leatherworkers, shoemakers, clothiers, cutlers, gunmakers, blacksmiths, carpenters and other tradesmen. The total cost of supplying the armies is uncertain, but in the first year of the New Model's existence, in 1645–6, the expenditure on the army from the central treasury for equipment, but not for food and quarters, was £117 000, most of it accounted for in contracts given to approximately 200 suppliers based in and around London, who were paid promptly and in full.[13] The New Model was not entirely typical of the parliamentarian armies, however. The earlier ones would initially have had comparatively little equipment and so may have ordered more than did the New Model, which also captured large quantities of weapons on campaign, but on the other hand they may not have been as thoroughly provided for as it was, and their supplies may not have come from London to the extent that the New Model's did. The equipment obtained from the metropolis for the militia and parliamentarian garrisons also has to be taken into account, as well as the relatively small orders from individuals and organisations such as the livery companies. In 1643, for example, the Haberdashers' Company strengthened its armoury by the purchase of 150 swords and belts and 100 muskets and bandoliers, at a cost of £178.[14]

Multiplying the figure for the New Model for 1645–6 by four to cover the years of the first Civil War, and rounding it up to take account of the needs of the garrisons and other purchasers, provides an estimate that the London tradesmen received orders worth a minimum of £500 000 between 1642 and 1646. This figure provides some sort of benchmark for the scale of business which military orders brought to the capital. Some of the most expensive items ordered for the armies were not from London however. Much of the ordnance was acquired from the Wealden ironmasters and, later in the war, from those in the Severn valley,[15] and horses were obtained while the armies were on campaign as well as through the half-dozen dealers who were based on Smithfield and adapted their already well-established businesses to supplying horses for the parliamentarian forces.[16] Other supplies came from elsewhere, including Birmingham, Northampton and Coventry, which provided swords, shoes and hosiery respectively, and the Continent. Indeed, the number of tradesmen in London was limited and they were unable to respond quickly enough to meet the needs of the parliamentary armies, which had to obtain weapons from abroad, as the king had been forced to do during the Bishops' wars.[17]

In addition to such direct military expenditure, the creation and maintenance of the armies also generated a great deal of incidental employment in the capital, in administrative work and the movement of supplies, for example.[18] Some creditors had to wait a long time for payment, however. The claims of the bricklayers, carpenters and other workmen for labour and materials valued at almost £7500 for the construction of the fortifications in 1643 had not been fully settled by the corporation three years later.[19]

London must also have received some of its financial contributions back again, from the pay and booty received by the soldiers and militia. It was common for soldiers to desert after a successful siege or battle, returning home in order to deposit the plunder which they had acquired. Much of the pay received on campaign was probably spent more or less straight away, and little brought back, but some may have been remitted and the pay received by soldiers in London, either while they were serving there or when they came to collect their arrears, went into the metropolitan economy. The officers in particular passed the winters in the capital, trying to get the resources to fit out their units for the coming campaign, lobbying for a command, or simply avoiding the unpleasantness of being in quarters. They obviously had more spending power than the common soldiers, but were not always welcome nevertheless. In the spring of 1645 a complaint was made that many of Sir Thomas Fairfax's officers spent their time in London 'in idlenesse and prophanesse' and some of them had been involved in a drunken brawl in Covent Garden.[20]

One factor which may have deterred soldiers from visiting London or from staying for very long was the possibility that they would be arrested and imprisoned for debt, either for a personal obligation or for money owing for quarters or military supplies. This was the experience of both common soldiers and officers, regardless of the importance of their current responsibilities. Captain Cornelius Vandenboome, who was the engineer to the Newport Pagnell garrison, was out walking in the city with a companion one evening when he was arrested by the watch and imprisoned, and an application had to be made to the lord mayor for his release.[21]

The profit that accrued to the capital from its own soldiers was limited by the number of Londoners serving with the armies, at least with the successful ones. The armies which Essex commanded on the Edgehill campaign in 1642 and during the march to relieve Gloucester in the following year had a high proportion of Londoners, as did Waller's armies.[22] These were generally campaigns which produced little booty, however, with no notable sackings of towns other than that of Winchester by Waller's troops in 1642, or the plundering of large contingents of royalists, except at Reading in 1643,[23] while both Essex's and Waller's campaigns in 1644 ended in the virtual disintegration of their armies. The soldiers of the London militia were singled out for criticism by Waller for their mutinous behaviour, and a search was instituted in London for deserters from his army, while those returning from Essex's campaign that ended at Lostwithiel were said to have been in 'a very naked and miserable condition'.[24]

By the spring of 1644, when the time came to find recruits for the summer campaigns, something of a shortage of soldiers had developed in London because of the reluctance of its citizens to serve in the armies, and conscripts had to be found among the prison population or from non-residents who were then staying in the city. Indeed, complaints were voiced respecting the proportion of recruits being taken from London, and increasingly it was the outer areas of Tower Hamlets, Southwark and Westminster from which the armies' manpower was drawn.[25] The willingness with which money was offered to set out the New Model is in marked contrast to the reluctance with which recruits were enlisted. None had arrived by the deadline at the end of March 1645 and soon afterwards it was objected that 'Scotsmen and other foreigners' were being impressed, whereas it should only have been 'those who are inhabitants' of London who were enlisted in its quota for the army.[26]

Things were even worse when the second impressment for the New Model was ordered in the early autumn. The average shortfall in the numbers of recruits sent in from eastern and south-eastern England was 50 per cent, from London it was 96 per cent, the capital having sent only 57 out of the 1469 men required from it. Presumably because of this experience, the quota of recruits allotted to London in January 1646 was reduced, only 700 being required from the capital.[27] The New Model's campaigns did produce plunder, especially from the royalist foot captured at Naseby, which in turn had come from the sack of Leicester by the king's army two weeks earlier (as many as 6500 of the army's soldiers went absent after Naseby in order to secure their booty),[28] but the evidence regarding recruitment suggests that little of this bounty was taken to London.

Some of the unwillingness to serve was caused by the disruptive effects of the absence of men, particularly of apprentices, for they still played a crucial part in London's economic organisation in the early seventeenth century and constituted a significant proportion of its population at the time of the Civil War.[29] Their temporary absence was encouraged by parliament to stimulate recruitment by ordering that their masters should take them back into their service when their time with the forces was completed, indemnifying those who had stood surety for the apprentices' good behaviour against any action taken against them by their masters. It also offered compensation for masters who could demonstrate that they had made a loss because their apprentices had been away on service.[30]

It was not only the apprentices who enrolled, for on such special occasions as the royalist threat to the city in the autumn of 1642 which ended at Turnham Green, and Essex's march to relieve Gloucester in August 1643, parliament ordered that the shops should be closed, so that no tradesman who had gone with the army should feel that his business rivals who had stayed at home were taking advantage of his absence. The trained bands, which contained a mixture of householders and apprentices, took part in a number of campaigns away from London during 1643 and 1644.[31] The result was that in November 1643 the Committee of the Militia objected to the practice, pointing out to the House of Commons that the 'City Forces were raised for the Guard of the City, and are Tradesmen; and when they are abroad, their Plough lieth still at home; and, besides, they lose their Employment; and you cannot be ignorant that, if the Course be continued, it will be a great Wasting of Men'.[32]

The absence of the apprentices with the armies was not made up by new enrolments. Indeed, it seems that the supply of young labour diminished during the war years, with fewer apprentices reaching London than in normal times. A survey of eight livery companies shows that only one of them, the Cordwainers' Company, enrolled more apprentices during the war years than its average for the period from 1630 to 1660, and that was a marginal increase of only 6 per cent, while the other seven experienced a fall in enrolments averaging 23 per cent. There was also a change in the place of origin of apprentices, with those coming from London and the nearby counties forming a much greater proportion than in peacetime, as the movement of youths to the capital from areas under royalist control was reduced.[33]

Nevertheless, it was presumably the absence of the established apprentices which was more crucial for tradesmen than the lack of new ones, for the skills of the more senior apprentices were needed in order to expand output and so take advantage of the increased orders for the armies. In a skilled trade, such as gun-making, the artisan's output was limited by the time which he had available and the flow of components from his suppliers, for each piece had to be hand-crafted and then assembled by the gunsmith.[34] In this trade, as in others, output could be raised if some tasks were given to the more experienced apprentices, but they were the ones who, if only because of their age and maturity, were likely to be away at the wars. Those masters who were in the habit of entrusting their cash to their servants and senior apprentices, and even allowing them to manage their businesses when they were away, were further inconvenienced, for they had to make alternative arrangements and probably spend their time running a business which they had normally been able to leave in the hands of their apprentices.[35]

As well as a reduced flow of labour, supplies of food, cloth and fuel were also reaching the capital in diminished quantities. In December 1642 the king had issued a proclamation that trade with London should not be interrupted, although Clarendon exaggerated the position when he claimed that in the summer of 1643 the citizens 'hitherto felt not the miseries of the war, having the same ease and the same plenty which they had formerly enjoyed'.[36] This policy was completely reversed in July 1643 with a proclamation prohibiting trade to London except under licence, and that was followed by a second one in October that extended the ban to the movement of goods from the capital.[37] The change of tactics was carefully debated before it was implemented, and it was designed not only to deprive London of trade and supplies but also to divert them to towns held by the royalists, so that they would be able to tax the wealth generated.[38] Parliament had a similar policy, regulating traffic between London and royalist areas.[39]

Some carriers were apparently able to circumvent these measures by travelling from Oxford to High Wycombe with a royalist pass and then completing their journeys to London with a parliamentarian one, incidentally making High Wycombe a prosperous place during the war,[40] but it is clear from the petitions which were sent to the royalist authorities from various parts of the country under their control that the proclamations were enforced and did interrupt the flow of both food supplies and manufactured goods to the capital.[41] Indeed, for much of the war the royalists were in a position to cut routes to London from the Midlands and the West because their garrisons controlled an arc of territory from Banbury in the north to Basing and Winchester in the south.[42]

By the early seventeenth century London's food supplies were drawn from a wide area extending well beyond its immediate environs, East Anglia, Kent, and other areas which remained under parliamentarian control. Grain was brought from the south Midlands down the Thames from Berkshire, Oxfordshire and Buckinghamshire via Oxford, Abingdon, Reading, and, above all, Henley, while livestock were driven from a much wider area that included Wales and northern and western England, to be fattened in the Midlands and finished on pastures closer to London.[43] The royalists were able to dislocate much of this trade, for many of the areas of supply were in their hands and they were also able to intercept trade passing through their territory. They also carried out raids in the Chilterns and mid-Buckinghamshire, driving off livestock which might have found its way into the London market. They held Reading and Abingdon for part of the war and Henley was on the frontier of the areas controlled by the two sides. The inhabitants of North Wales petitioned in 1643 that the stop to the cattle trade threatened to ruin those who were dependent on it,[44] and the farmers in the south Midlands told the royalists that they had no money with which to pay their taxes because their inability to sell their corn had reduced their incomes. It was reported that those who were taking food to London were harshly treated by the royalists.[45]

As early as August 1643 food shortages in London were so bad that they had attracted the concern of parliament, and the royalist capture of Newport Pagnell a few months later was aimed at further disrupting supplies, producing fears that a garrison there would be able to cut off provisions from a wide area.[46] In fact the royalists failed to secure their hold on the town, which was quickly occupied by parliamentarian forces, provoking Prince Rupert's anger and disgust at the missed opportunity.[47] The worst of the food shortages may have been temporary, until London switched to alternative areas for its supplies of grain, perhaps by increasing the amounts brought in by the coastal trade and importing more from northern Europe, although it must have been less easy to find alternatives for its livestock supplies. Even so, the interruptions to the movement of goods along the Thames were still being felt in July 1644, when the parliamentarians, having captured Greenlands House, near Henley, then destroyed it, 'that it should no more prove a hinderance to the Barges that laden with fuell and provision were to come up to London by it'.[48] Nor was such disruption confined to inland communications, for in the following winter concern was expressed that the royalist privateers attacking shipping bringing food from the East Anglian ports might cause such disruption to the coastal trade that they would 'cause a great want' in London, especially of fish, butter and cheese.[49]

The interruption of trade also had a serious effect on the cloth industry, for most English cloth passed through London and much of it was finished there. Indeed, clothing was the capital's largest single industry, occupying roughly one-fifth of its workforce, and cloth was by far the biggest item of London's exports.[50] Cloth valued at roughly £1 150 000 was exported from London in 1640, three-quarters of the national total, and that was a poor trading year.[51] The royalists disrupted the movement of cloth, by attempting to divert it to ports under their control and by raiding the clothiers' convoys heading for London, confiscating the cloth or taking tolls before they would allow it through.

The organisation of the cloth trade made it susceptible to control. The shipment of cloth from North Wales to London was largely channelled through the Shrewsbury drapers, and cloth manufacture in Worcestershire was concentrated in five towns, particularly Worcester itself. Both Shrewsbury and Worcester were in royalist hands for most of the war.[52] Although it may be that trade was never completely disrupted for more than a few months, supplies reaching London were much reduced. The 'Hallage' receipts show that the sums received from payments on cloth reaching Blackwell Hall in 1643–5 were two-thirds of the average for 1638–42, and that for the year ending August 1644 (the first year after the royalist prohibition on trade) they were only 45 per cent of the 1638–42 average. Only in 1646 did the receipts return to their pre-war level.[53] Part of the explanation may lie in a reduction in cloth production in those areas disrupted by the war, and the supply of wool for cloth-making generally fell because of the number of sheep killed by the soldiers.[54]

Clothiers may also have been reluctant to move their cloth, particularly in large batches, given the uncertainty engendered by the risk of confiscation, of tolls, and even of just being turned back. The clothiers in Worcester complained bitterly about the effects that the royalist embargo on trade with areas under parliamentary control was having on their city and, like the farmers, insisted that they would be unable to pay their assessments if they could not sell their cloth. The city's common council tried to negotiate 'for freedom of trade for the cytie to London' and in June 1644 the ban was apparently relaxed, only for a convoy to be robbed by royalist troops, who took all the horses and cloth. Nor was it only the royalists who interfered with the trade, for a safe passage had to be negotiated through the parliamentarian areas and a substantial fee paid for the privilege.[55]

Some of the north-country clothiers, such as Thomas Priestley from near Halifax and the Rodes family partnership from Rochdale, were able to continue to supply cloth to London during the war, although sometimes having to move it along very indirect routes.[56] Similarly, the West Country clothiers were able to move cloth to London for much of the war, although rarely without some risk. Nevertheless, the uncertainties of travel, the actual confiscation of goods and perhaps, too, the delays in payment, which had hitherto been made promptly, substantially reduced the flow of cloth to London. This must have added to the recession in the industry, which was already a serious one before the outbreak of the war.[57]

Reductions in the supply of cloth presumably reduced the level of goods shipped overseas from London, for it had accounted for 80 to 90 per cent of the capital's exports before the war. Imports were also affected, particularly by the reduced demand for luxury items. Indeed, overseas trade generally was depressed during the war years, because of the disruption caused by the Civil War (including the depredations of royalist privateers), exacerbated by Dutch interloping, particularly in the colonial trades, and the difficulties of trading with the Baltic during the war between Denmark and Sweden from May 1643 to August 1645.[58] The conclusion of one pamphleteer, writing in 1644, that 'there is no greater enemy to trade than war, be it in what country it will', reflects the trading conditions of the time.[59] The problems in overseas trade had an major impact on London, for in the early seventeenth century between two-thirds and three-quarters of national exports were shipped from the capital.[60]

The coastal trade to London was also affected, particularly by parliament's own naval blockade of the north-east coast which prevented coal from reaching London. The blockade was very effective: in a normal, pre-war, year over 3000 vessels entered the Tyne, but in 1644 only 188 did so, and in the year ending Michaelmas 1644 fewer than 3000 tons of coal left Newcastle, compared with the annual pre-war figure of up to 450 000 tons.[61] This caused a major shortage in London, indeed the decline in coal consumption was such that, according to Evelyn, orchards and gardens in the middle of London bore 'plentiful and infinite quantities of Fruits' because of the consequent reduction in air pollution.[62] Alternative sources of coal were found – some was brought from Scotland and South Wales[63] – but nowhere near enough to match the pre-war levels of supply.

The fuel shortages produced hardship because the scarcity of coal and the switch to wood as the main domestic fuel caused a dramatic increase in the price of wood, and virtually any source of supply within a practical distance of London was drawn upon.[64] In October 1643 parliament authorised the cutting of wood from crown, church and royalist delinquents' estates within sixty miles of the capital, partly to improve supplies and partly to regulate the process.[65] In the following summer, anticipating unrest and possibly riots during the coming winter because of the fuel situation,[66] a committee of the House of Commons began to consider the possibility of bringing peat on a large scale from the Egham area and from the Fens of the Isle of Ely.[67] The shortages and high prices affected not only the householders, especially the poor,[68] but also those tradesmen who used large amounts of fuel, such as the brewers, bakers, dyers, maltsters, soapmakers and blacksmiths.

Glassmaking provides an example of a relatively small industry which was particularly disrupted because of its fuel requirements. In the early seventeenth century it had overcome the technical difficulties of switching from wood to coal, and the London glassmakers had changed from Scottish to Newcastle coal in the early 1620s to take advantage of its lower price. The shortages must have severely restricted their activity during the first two years of the war, for one glass furnace had a yearly consumption of approximately 450 tons of coal, and many other consumers were competing for supplies.[69] Even such a crucial military industry as the manufacture of firearms was interrupted in 1643 by the coal shortage.[70] Only after the Scottish army captured Newcastle in October 1644 and agreed to release the coal could the coastwise trade from the Tyne to London resume, bringing the price of fuel back to something like normal levels. The citizens' patience was not, therefore, stretched to the limit, which might well have been reached had the fuel crisis continued into the winter of 1645–6, which included an intensely cold spell during which the Thames above London Bridge was completely frozen over and brought added discomfort to the war years.[71]

The reduced levels of activity in both the coastal trade, of which the carriage of coal formed a major part, and of overseas commerce, may have caused a cutback in activity in the shipbuilding and ship-repairing yards along the Thames and also have affected the victualling trades. There seems to have been a decline in the building of East Indiamen, for example, and Lithgow's comment, made in 1643, that the river was full of merchant shipping suggests that many vessels were laid up.[72] Some compensation was provided by the maintenance of the ships of the earl of Warwick's fleet, but an added problem was the interruption in naval supplies coming from the Baltic during the war between Sweden and Denmark.

In addition to a decline in industrial activity, there was a reduction in the service sectors of London's economy, such as the law. The Inns of Court attracted fewer students than normal, with admissions in 1643, 1644 and 1645 only 30 per cent of those in the years preceding the wars; in absolute terms, this was a shortfall

of almost 600 students.[73] These were not poverty-stricken schol-
ars, for the sons of peers, esquires and gentlemen made up 90
per cent of admissions to the Inns,[74] which were used not only to
train for the law, but effectively as a third university, with young
gentlemen attending them, typically for no more than two years,
to study the common law and as part of their general social and
intellectual education. The absence of the students therefore represented a considerable loss of spending power within the metropolitan economy, probably equivalent to something over £10 000
a year.[75]

The legal profession itself was suffering from a loss of business.[76] This was partly because fewer courts were operating, with
Star Chamber and the High Commission Court having been abolished in 1641 and the Court of Requests having apparently ceased
to function. It was partly, too, because fewer cases were being
heard in the surviving courts than in peacetime. John Greene, a
barrister of Lincoln's Inn, noted that there was 'but small store
of business' during the Easter Term of 1644.[77] One reason for the
reduced business was that litigants from many parts of the country either could not make the journey to London or were reluctant to do so, or they simply could not afford to pursue their
legal actions at a time when their other expenditure was high
and their revenues were uncertain. The scriveners eventually did
brisk business with the sales of the lands of royalist delinquents,
the church and the crown, but these did not take place until the
late 1640s and the 1650s, and the land market was stagnant during the war years.[78]

The losses discussed so far were serious enough, but were modest
compared to the major loss, which was the absence of the royal
household and the court. The crown revenue before the war was
over £1 000 000 and much of this must have found its way into
London's economy. The household itself was enormous, with between 1850 and 2600 members and, if their dependants are also
included, it alone represented one of the largest communities in
England, bigger than all but the largest provincial towns.[79] In the
early 1630s it had cost just over a £250 000 each year, and although
there had been some subsequent attempts to reduce expenditure
as Charles's income faltered, costs increased as separate households were established for the royal children. By the end of the
1630s the queen and the royal children had almost 400 servants.[80]

The members of the court also had expensive tastes. Courtiers had to live and dress in an appropriate style and maintain a household consonant with their rank, and they naturally vied with each other in the luxuriousness of their furnishings and outfits. The court entertainments give some idea of the costs of court life; the average outlay on a masque was over £1300 and several such masques were performed each year, while 368 plays were presented at court during the first fifteen years of Charles's reign.[81] When Rubens arrived in London in 1629 on a diplomatic mission he found that, 'All the leading nobles live on a sumptuous scale and spend money lavishly, so that the majority of them are hopelessly in debt... splendour and liberality are the first considerations at this Court'.[82]

George Villiers, duke of Buckingham, was the most powerful commoner in the kingdom in the early years of Charles's reign and his expenditure was unavoidably high; in the years just before his death in 1628 it was £23 000 per annum, and he died with debts of £70 000.[83] Another of the really big spenders was James Hay, earl of Carlisle, who was said to have spent more than £400 000 during his thirty years at the English court, lavishing £2000 or £3000 on an especially important banquet. According to his biographer, 'Grandeur and debt were the two themes that consistently ran through Hay's life'. He owed £34 000 when he died in 1636, although this was not especially high for one of his rank, for the average indebtedness of roughly a half of the peerage at the time of the Civil War was £25 000.[84] A more typical Caroline courtier was Endymion Porter, whose annual income was almost £3000 in 1628 and was probably considerably higher than that during the 1630s. A great deal of his expenditure was in London, where he had a house in the Strand, and he and his wife evidently lived in some luxury.[85]

The numbers drawn to the court are uncertain, although it exerted a powerful attraction and when a survey was taken in 1632 roughly one in four of the peerage and one in six of the baronetage and knightage were living in London, despite the recent royal proclamation to the contrary. The attempts made during the 1630s to reduce the size of the court did have some success, but could not deter those who, out of ambition or sheer necessity, hung around Whitehall in the hope of gaining some position or privilege, and even those without any office had to spend at least £1000 per annum in order to maintain themselves in a suitable style and get themselves noticed.[86]

Of course, not all of the royal and court expenditure passed through London. The royal family had other palaces besides Whitehall, and periodically went on progresses, and not all of the courtiers were in London all of the time. Nevertheless, much of their outgoings entered the metropolitan economy and the total and sudden withdrawal of their business must have been devastating for those tradesmen who had supplied it, ruining their market and their credit, and have had a much wider impact as their spending power was reduced in turn. It was not only the suppliers of food, such as poulterers and fishmongers, that were affected, but also those engaged in the luxury trades, providing furnishings, jewellery, saddlery, footwear and clothing. In 1647 William Perkins, a tailor, found himself imprisoned for debt, yet having at least £12 000 owing to him. In that year he sent the marquess of Ormonde two suits, taking the opportunity to request payment of £226 for clothes delivered to the marquess in 1641, and adding that 'our trade is so spoiled that no man now will give any credit'.[87]

The merchants were unable to switch their sales to the courtiers at Oxford, chiefly because of the restraint on trade with the royalist headquarters, but also because many of their former customers, both within the royalist areas and those held by parliament, were living on reduced incomes. Some of the gentry, such as Sir Ralph Verney and John Evelyn, chose to go abroad for the duration of the war. Even those living in the regions free of military activity felt that in all other respects they were not much better off than their counterparts whose estates were under royalist control, as they had to pay taxation, accept lower rents from their tenants, quarter troops who were being mustered or were in winter quarters, provide poor relief for those who returned wounded, and manage with less labour than was usually available to them because of the demands of the armies.[88] Most imported luxury goods were brought in through London, the centre for the trade in such goods, and so those distributing them suffered the double blow of losing their market among the courtiers and much of that in the provinces.[89]

The impression is that Westminster, St Martin's and Covent Garden were distinctly under-populated during the war.[90] There had been a considerable exodus of royalists and their dependants in the months leading up to the outbreak of the conflict, and the outflow continued until the spring of 1643, until movement in and out of the capital was controlled by the issue of passes.[91] It was said that most of the tenants in Covent Garden managed to persuade their landlords to agree to a halving of their rents[92] and even then the landlords found that their rent arrears accumulated and houses stood empty because they could not attract tenants.[93] The owner of one house in Covent Garden claimed that he received little or no income from it during the 'troubles'.[94] Those who pleaded for a reduced rent or more time to pay cited the 'decay of trade' in London.[95]

Evidence that shopkeepers found that their trade was sluggish during the war years comes both from the testimony of individuals and from petitions to that effect from the corporation. The reduction in the number of customers was partly because of the uncertainty engendered by the war and the consequent difficulty of obtaining credit. It was indicative of the general lack of confidence when Edward Bynion reported to Sir Samuel Luke in February 1645 that a draper had been unwilling to part with cloth except for ready money. Bynion concluded that 'here is nothing to be done without money'.[96] Nehemiah Wallington, a wood turner in Eastcheap, in the City, wrote in the same year that 'workmen are gone and trading is dead and customers hard [to come by]'.[97] Admittedly Wallington was by no means a model businessman, being more concerned for the fate of his soul and his collection of devotional reading matter than caring for his business, but his statement is supported by others. Anne Segar complained that her shop just off the Strand had been closed for four years during the Civil War because of the 'want of trade'.[98]

In March 1643 it was reported that many houses were empty, some of the shops were closed and those that remained open had few goods to sell, and later that year the Committee for the Militia petitioned the House of Commons that: 'Our rich Men are gone, because the City is the Place of Taxes and Burdens; Trade is decayed, and Shops shut up in a great measure; Our Poor do much increase'.[99] In 1644 the royalist newspaper *Mercurius Aulicus* claimed that as many as 12 000 houses and shops in the city were empty. The point was repeated in 1647, when it was said that many inhabitants and their families had left London.[100] With the over-capacity of housing that occurred during the war, building activity, a good indicator of economic well-being, came more or less to a halt.[101]

The poor referred to by the Committee for the Militia included soldiers and the widows of soldiers, who came to London hoping to collect their pay arrears or to get work, and those who had been wounded. The hospitals came under increasing pressure at a time when their income was reduced by the effects of the war. In November 1644 St Bartholomew's, St Thomas's, Bethlehem and Bridewell were exempted from taxation because of the 'great numbers of sick, wounded, and other Soldiers' that they had treated since the spring of the previous year. The Savoy Hospital was taken over as a military hospital and was so full by 1645 that an overflow of 1500 soldiers and widows had to be accommodated elsewhere.[102] After the battle of Naseby it was pointed out that wounded soldiers got most of their assistance from collections taken in London and Westminster 'and the counties are no ways sharers therein, although they have been equal sharers in the mercy'.[103]

Prisoners were also brought to the capital, some of them well-to-do and able to pay for their keep. Among the prisoners lodged in Ely House, for example, were Richard Williams, the town clerk of Chichester, George Lowe, MP for Calne, Hugh Henn, Page of the Back Stairs to the king, John Herbert, the High Sheriff of the County of Brecknock, and Dr William Fuller, Chaplain in Ordinary to the king.[104] Others were pretty well destitute, however, and dependent on allowance being made by parliament for their upkeep and on charity. The resentment engendered by prisoners was increased by the influx of more than 4000 royalists captured at Naseby, which prompted the remark that they were like 'buzzle-bees, which eat up the honey without doing any service'.[105] Because many volunteered for service in Ireland, two collections were ordered for them in London to maintain them until they could be moved.[106]

The more typical poor were also affected, and the numbers requiring relief rose during the war because of the interruptions to trade.[107] With the general dislocation caused by the war, those charities financed by the rents of properties outside London had their incomes reduced or interrupted, because the rents could not be collected or it was impossible to send them, or, in the worst cases, the properties from which they were drawn had been destroyed. By 1645 King James's Hospital at the Charterhouse had an annual deficit of £1500 when its expenditure was roughly £4500. No rent had been received from its tenants in Devon, Wiltshire and Yorkshire since 1642, and those in the parliamentarian areas were in difficulties because of the high tax burden.[108] The level of charitable giving within London was much lower than it had been in the preceding decades, with the annual average figure for such donations during the 1640s being only 44 per cent of those for the 1620s and 1630s. In 1644 it was claimed that the gifts and legacies to the hospitals were 'much decreased, and very small'.[109] The funds raised by the parishes for poor relief also fell. In St Dunstan's in the West, a comparatively wealthy parish, income from the poor rate was down by over 20 per cent during the war years and had to be made up by further collections among the parishioners.[110]

Plague victims also had to be provided for. Plague was endemic in early seventeenth-century London but, except in years of epidemic, was not a major killer and between the epidemics of 1625 and 1636 it was responsible for under 2 per cent of deaths. Unfortunately, as with so many series of statistics, the Bills of Mortality are incomplete for the war years, but they do show that the proportion of deaths caused by plague was rising, and was between 14 and 17 per cent of the recorded deaths in the Bills in 1644, 1645 and 1646.[111] This was enough to cause alarm in the summer months, for in August and September 1645 one-third of recorded deaths were from plague and a year later the proportion reached almost 37 per cent. John Greene was surprised that Bartholomew Fair was allowed to go ahead in 1646, the plague was so bad.[112] The apprehension which outbreaks of plague produced also had the damaging effect of causing the wealthier citizens and the country gentry to leave the capital until conditions had improved. This was a feature of early modern epidemics, as was the disruption of the afflicted community's economy, and there is no reason to suppose that these aspects were any different because of the war.[113]

The better-off citizens also left London to escape the high levels of taxation.[114] Not only were local rates increased, but the forced loans and, by pre-war standards, massive taxation to pay for the war, imposed a considerable burden on what was already a rather depressed economy even before the start of the conflict. We have seen that some of the money collected in London was absorbed into its economy through the orders for military equipment and that part of their pay that soldiers spent there, but much of it was taken to the armies in convoys and spent elsewhere.[115] It was objected that London bore an unduly large proportion of the wartime taxation. When the monthly cost of supporting the New Model was apportioned London and Middlesex were allotted one-sixth of the total, for example, and the capital contributed between one-quarter and one-third of all the sums collected on the assessments and 70 per cent of those received from the customs.[116] Its own commercial community played an important part in instituting and administering parliament's finances,[117] so that to some extent the tax collectors were also the tax payers, which had implications regarding the opportunities for evasion, although those who attempted to avoid payment were likely to find their goods distrained by armed soldiers.[118] London did at least escape the fate of paying double taxation, because it was only ever taxed by one side, but its share of the tax burden was certainly high.

A royalist pamphleteer writing in 1647 purported to have assessed the cost to London of supporting the parliamentarian war effort at £3 378 100 per annum.[119] The figures are notional and absurdly high, but point to the various taxes levied from the citizens during the war years; the loans, the monthly and weekly assessments, the payments on the weekly fast days, the excise on a range of goods, and the taxes levied to provide pay for the members of the militia and the navy. The conclusion that the level of taxes constituted 'the largest that this City ever was put to' was surely correct.

The sudden surge of impositions after 1642 had a dramatic impact on the finances of some of the livery companies. The Vintners' Company had to borrow money and sell its plate to make up its share of the loans and assessments. Its debt rose from very little at the start of the war to £10 000 by October 1645, and by then its interest charges were almost as high as its rental income.[120] The larger companies had to find even more. By 1645 the Drapers' Company had lent £150 000 within the previous five years, not including the monthly assessments, had received only £425 in interest and was £14 000 in debt. The Merchant Tailors' Company had lent £26 000 by 1647, and the Haberdashers' Company was forced to borrow to such an extent that it was paying interest charges of over £1200 per annum from late 1643 and £1500 by 1650; the loans that it had made were never repaid.[121] Of course, as the common council reminded the House of Commons, the tax burden did not fall on the corporation and the companies, whose main contribution came from their plate and through their creditworthiness, but upon the individual members, who also had to pay the taxation levied directly from them.[122] A half of the Vintners' share of £5000 towards the loan levied in 1642 was paid by twenty-eight of its members and £1500 more by the remainder of the membership, but still leaving £1000 which had to be borrowed.[123]

Many citizens must have found the high taxation a hardship, but there were beneficiaries, whose incomes rose because of the wartime redistribution of wealth which was the effect of taxation, to a point where it more than offset the extra cost of their taxes. Wallington's view was that at a time of high taxes business was difficult but 'trading is good with those that make things for the wars, and those that have places and offices do not want, but enrich themselves'. His own brother John was a military contractor, adapting his trade as a wood turner and supplying shovels and spades to the forces. He seems to have done well from this and within a year of his death in 1653 his widow married into the gentry.[124] Among the other individuals who benefited and have come to our attention was Katherine Chidley, who was able to take advantage of the increased demand for stockings for the troops, securing two substantial contracts to supply the army campaigning in Ireland. Her son Samuel was also a successful haberdasher, as well as a pamphleteer and propagandist, who profited from his contacts among the parliamentarian leadership and, from 1649, his involvement in the sales of the crown lands. By the mid-1650s Samuel was describing himself as a gentleman.[125]

Despite the difficulties and costs of playing such a prominent part in maintaining the parliamentarian war effort, the City was able and willing to finance the outfitting of the New Model Army in 1645 and its support for the parliamentarian cause seems still to have been undiminished at that stage. This may have been due to the influence and accumulated wealth of those, such as the colonial merchants, who had prospered during the 1620s and 1630s,[126] and the earnings of the contractors who were supplying the military. It was also partly a result of the profits which accrued to the merchant community from the entrepôt trade based on Dover.

England's neutrality during the 1630s had permitted the growth of a carrying trade in her ships in both commodities and silver, and although the commodity trade was in decline in the early 1640s, that in Spanish silver, based upon an agreement made in

1632, remained strong throughout the first Civil War. From 1632 two-thirds, and from 1638 one-third, of the silver was coined at the Mint and was used by Spanish agents to buy bills of exchange redeemable in Flanders, resulting in a huge increase of silver in circulation in England. In 1647 it was reported that since 1643 'many millions' of Spanish silver had been imported, but none re-exported because of 'the height of the Exchange'. This trade undoubtedly contributed to the prosperity of the merchant community and thus to the financing of the war effort.[127] On the other hand, the inherent problems of the city's economy in the pre-war years had been exacerbated by the uncertainty produced by the political crisis of 1641, followed by the economic disruption caused by the war itself.[128] In this context, the unwillingness of Londoners to serve in the New Model suggests that a certain war-weariness had developed.

The rough balance sheet of the war's impact on the metropolitan economy indicates that the net effect was a negative one, that the scale of the business gained did not equal that which was lost or compensate for the various charges levied to finance the war. The writer of the memorandum who in 1643 had argued that the new defences would bring prosperity to London must have been a disappointed man by 1646, for the disruption caused by the conflict surely outweighed the gains.

Some sections of the community were seriously affected, such as the luxury tradesmen who had made a living supplying the court or distributing their goods to customers around the country, and the inhabitants of the Tower Hamlets and Southwark, who provided a disproportionately large share of recruits for the armies. Yet some of the war's more damaging effects, such as the interruptions to food, coal and cloth supplies, lasted for a relatively short time. The coal trade was restored by the end of 1644 and the royalist garrisons along the main lines of communication were gradually eliminated. Basing House was captured in October 1645, for example, and Donnington Castle was surrendered on 1 April 1646.

Most importantly, perhaps, the outcome of the battle of Naseby in June 1645 signalled that parliament would win the war, and that uninterrupted internal trade would be restored in the comparatively near future. Furthermore, wartime conditions provided scope for the expansion of existing enterprises and for the development of others. Those tradesmen, such as the cutlers and gunmakers, who could readily adapt their production to military needs could hardly fail to benefit, and others were able to profit by modifying their output or by opening up new lines of supply for provisions for the capital to supplement those disturbed by military intervention.

Some of the more positive aspects of the war persisted beyond 1646. Military expenditure was maintained at a high level, for example, providing a potential benefit to the capital in the longer term; many of those who had been drawn to the capital during the war, either as a refuge or as a place of opportunity, stayed on; and the solutions to the short-term problems of supply produced new patterns of trade which endured after normal conditions were restored. Indeed, although the Civil War had a deleterious effect that should not be under-estimated, it was also a stimulus for adaptation and change, redistributing wealth and bringing opportunities as well as problems for London and that large sector of the national economy that was inextricably bound up with it.

Notes

1. I am very grateful to Dr Joan Thirsk, Dr Ian Roy, Dr Ann Robey and Ben Coates for their comments on an earlier draft of this chapter.
2. Philip Warwick, *Memoirs of the Reign of King Charles the First* (Edinburgh, 1813), pp. 298–9. In his fictional narrative of the war seen through the eyes of a royalist, Defoe wrote that 'The City of London was their inexhaustible Support and Magazine, both for Men, Money, and all things necessary', J. T. Boulton (ed.), *Daniel Defoe, Memoirs of a Cavalier* (Oxford, 1991), p. 179.
3. C. V. Wedgwood, *The Great Rebellion: The King's War 1641–1647* (London, 1958), pp. 154–5, 161, 237, 242–3, 284–5. According to Reginald Sharpe, in 1644 the trade and commerce of the city were in 'a deplorable condition', R. R. Sharpe, *London and the Kingdom* (London, 1894–5), II, p. 213.
4. M. James, *Social Problems and Policy during the Puritan Revolution: 1640–1660* (London, 1930), p. 46. A. L. Beier and R. Finlay (eds), *London 1500–1700: The making of the metropolis* (London, 1986), p. 26.
5. For the effects of artillery, especially mortar, fire see S. Porter, *Destruction in the English Civil Wars* (Stroud, 1994), pp. 23–4.
6. CSPD, 1644–45, p. 214, where the unattributed and undated document is erroneously placed with items relating to 1644.
7. C. H. Hull (ed.), *The Economic Writings of Sir William Petty* (Cambridge, 1899), II, p. 469.

8. A. Searle, 'Sir Thomas Barrington in London, 1640–1644: 1. Setting up House' and '2. Life at Queen Street', *Essex Journal*, II (1967), 38–40, 63–8.

9. S. R. Gardiner (ed.), *Debates in the House of Commons in 1625* (Camden Soc., new series, VI, 1873), p. 114.

10. S. R. Gardiner, *History of the Great Civil War 1642–1649* (reprinted, Moreton-in-Marsh, 1987), I, pp. 184, 235, 300; II, pp. 89, 119. The Recruiter elections, which increased the numbers of MPs, did not begin until 1645.

11. *A & O*, I, pp. 181–2.

12. D. H. Pennington, 'The Accounts of the Kingdom 1642–1649', in F. J. Fisher (ed.), *Essays in the Economic and Social History of Tudor and Stuart England* (Cambridge, 1961), pp. 184–5, 191.

13. G. I. Mungeam, 'Contracts for the supply of equipment to the "New Model" Army in 1645', *Journal of the Arms and Armour Soc.*, VI (1968–70), 60–115. I. Gentles, *The New Model Army in England, Ireland and Scotland, 1645–1653* (Oxford, 1992), pp. 41, 457.

14. I. W. Archer, *The History of the Haberdashers' Company* (Chichester, 1991), p. 147.

15. D. Blackmore, *Arms & Armour of the English Civil Wars* (London, 1990), pp. 6, 85–6. The mortar shells bought from William Quinton of Highley, Shropshire, in February 1646 are an example of relatively high-value purchases from the Severn valley, PRO, SP28/36, f. 405. Gunfounding in the Tower of London seems to have fallen into abeyance by the early years of Charles I's reign, H. L. Blackmore, *The Armouries of the Tower of London: I Ordnance* (London, 1976), pp. 13–14.

16. P. R. Edwards, 'The supply of horses to the parliamentarian and royalist armies in the English Civil War', *Historical Research*, LXVIII (1995), 63–5.

17. Blackmore, *Arms and Armour*, p. 6. M. C. Fissel, *The Bishops' Wars: Charles I's campaigns against Scotland, 1638–1640* (Cambridge, 1994), pp. 98–106.

18. C. H. Firth, *Cromwell's Army* (London, 1992), pp. 213–14.

19. CLRO, Journals of Common Council, XL, 1641–49, ff. 80v, 91v–2, 167v, 173v.

20. R. Ollard, *Cromwell's Earl: A Life of Edward Mountagu, 1st Earl of Sandwich* (London, 1994), p. 24. BL, Thomason Tracts, E260(29) *A Perfect Diurnall of Some Passages in Parliament*, 28 April–5 May 1645, p. 729.

21. H. G. Tibbutt (ed.), *The Letter Books 1644–45 of Sir Samuel Luke* (London, 1963), p. 382.

22. At least 6000 of Essex's army raised in the summer of 1642 were recruited in London, A. Fletcher, *The Outbreak of the English Civil War* (London, 1981), pp. 338–9.

23. J. Adair, *Roundhead General. A Military Biography of Sir William Waller* (London, 1969), p. 51. W. D. Macray (ed.), Edward, Earl of Clarendon, *The History of the Rebellion and Civil Wars in England* (Oxford, 1888), III, p. 25.

24. *CSPD*, 1644, p. 301. Wedgwood, *Great Rebellion*, p. 285. CLRO, Journals of Common Council, XL, f. 120.
25. *LJ*, VIII, p. 170.
26. *CSPD*, 1644–45, p. 396.
27. *CJ*, IV, p. 299. *CSPD*, 1645–47, p. 319.
28. Gentles, *New Model Army*, p. 37.
29. Finlay puts the proportion of apprentices at *c*.15 per cent of the total population at the beginning of the seventeenth century and *c*.4 per cent at the end, R. Finlay, *Population and Metropolis. The Demography of London 1580–1650* (Cambridge, 1981), p. 19.
30. *A & O*, I, p. 37.
31. See above, pp. 104–9.
32. *CJ*, III, p. 316.
33. S. R. Smith, 'The Social and Geographical Origins of the London Apprentices, 1630–1660', *The Guildhall Miscellany*, IV (1973), 203–4.
34. Only with the introduction of machine tools in the mid-nineteenth century could the parts be standardised to such a degree of accuracy that production could be rapidly expanded in response to increased demand, D. S. Landes, *The Unbound Prometheus. Technological change and industrial development in Western Europe from 1750 to the present* (Cambridge, 1969), pp. 307–8.
35. This point was made in a memoir of 1676 cited in E. Kerridge, *Trade and Banking in Early Modern England* (Manchester, 1988), p. 69. See also P. Earle, *The Making of the English Middle Class. Business, Society and Family Life in London, 1660–1730* (London, 1989), pp. 97–8.
36. Clarendon, *History*, III, p. 291.
37. J. F. Larkin (ed.), *Stuart Royal Proclamations Volume II: Royal Proclamations of King Charles I 1625–1646* (Oxford, 1983), pp. 825–6, 932–5, 961–4.
38. Clarendon, *History*, III, pp. 290–2.
39. Larkin, *Proclamations*, pp. 932–3. CLRO, Journals of Common Council, XL, ff. 112–14.
40. Wedgwood, *Great Rebellion*, p. 209.
41. Clarendon thought that the policy was not as effective as it should have been because some royalist governors allowed goods through on payment of a toll, which they kept, although that was of course itself a disincentive to the movement of goods, Clarendon, *History*, III, p. 292.
42. I. Roy, 'England Turned Germany? The Aftermath of the Civil War in its European Context', *Trans. of the Royal Historical Soc.*, 5th series, 28 (1978), 134.
43. F. J. Fisher, 'The Development of the London Food Market', *Economic History Review*, V (1935), reprinted in P. J. Corfield and N. B. Harte (eds), *London and the English Economy, 1500–1700* (London, 1990), pp. 61–79.
44. The petition also referred to the lack of sale of their Welsh cottons (woollen cloth). C. Skeel, 'The Welsh Woollen Industry in the Sixteenth and Seventeenth Centuries', *Archaeologia*, LXXVII (1922), 249–50.

45. *CSPVen*, 1643–47, pp. 6–7.

46. *CSPVen*, 1643–47, pp. 6–7, 36.

47. Wedgwood, *Great Rebellion*, pp. 264, 266–7.

48. BL, Thomason Tracts, E254(3) *A Diary, or an Exact Journall*, 11–19 July 1644, p. 60. The Common Council was willing to send London troops to capture Greenlands because its garrison had interrupted passage along the Thames: CLRO, Journals of Common Council, XL, f. 99v.

49. CLRO, Journals of Common Council, XL, ff. 120, 122. See also, J. H. Ohlmeyer, 'Irish Privateers during the Civil War, 1642–1650', *The Mariner's Mirror*, 76 (1990), 119–33, and R. A. Stradling, *The Armada of Flanders: Spanish Maritime Policy and European War, 1568–1668* (Cambridge, 1992), pp. 137–8, 226.

50. A. L. Beier, 'Engine of manufacture: the trades of London', in Beier and Finlay (eds), *London 1500–1700*, pp. 147–9. J. L. Archer, 'The Industrial History of London 1603–1640', unpublished M.A. thesis, University of London, 1934, pp. 9–11, 23–5. F. J. Fisher, 'London's Export Trade in the Early Seventeenth Century', *Economic History Review*, 2nd series, III (1950), reprinted in Corfield and Harte, *London and the English Economy*, pp. 121–2.

51. That is, New Draperies worth £515 000 and 87 000 'shortcloths' valued at a notional £7 6s 8d each, the mid-point between the low of £6 13s 4d and high of £8 discussed by Gould and Stephens, J. D. Gould, 'Cloth Exports 1600–42' and W. B. Stephens, 'Further Observations on English Cloth Exports', *Economic History Review*, 2nd series, XXIV (1971), 249–52, 253–7. B. Supple, *Commercial Crisis and Change in England 1600–1642* (Cambridge, 1959), pp. 128–9, 258.

52. T. C. Mendenhall, *The Shrewsbury Drapers and the Welsh Wool Trade in the XVI and XVII Centuries* (London, 1953), pp. 38, 45–7 and *passim*; A. D. Dyer, *The City of Worcester in the sixteenth century* (Leicester, 1973), pp. 113, 117–18.

53. Although these data do not constitute an ideal series of statistics, there is no reason to suppose that those for 1638–47 are not comparable, D. W. Jones, 'The "Hallage" Receipts of the London Cloth Markets, 1562–c.1720', *Economic History Review*, 2nd series, XXV (1972), 567–87, the figures for 1638–47 are on p. 569. The receipts do not include cloth from Norwich and Norfolk, and it is possible that some of the shortfall could have been made up from there, although the New Draperies from that region were not direct substitutes for West Country cloth.

54. E. Kerridge, *Textile manufacture in early modern England* (Manchester, 1985), p. 151. In one night in June 1645 the New Model Army's soldiers killed more than 210 sheep in a single parish in Northamptonshire, PRO, SP28/173 unfol., Returns of the parish of Guilsborough. The problem became so serious that in 1649 Henry Robinson called for a prohibition on the killing of sheep 'for some few years', Henry Robinson, *Briefe Considerations concerning the Advancement of Trade and Navigation* (1649), printed in J. Thirsk and

J. P. Cooper (eds), *Seventeenth-Century Economic Documents* (Oxford, 1972), p. 54.

55. P. Styles, *Studies in Seventeenth Century West Midlands History* (Kineton, 1978), pp. 231–2.

56. J. Priestley, 'Some Memoirs Concerning the Family of the Priestleys', *Surtees Soc.*, LXXVII (1886), p. 23. T. S. Willan, *The inland trade* (Manchester, 1976), pp. 107–21.

57. J. de L. Mann, *The Cloth Industry in the West of England from 1640 to 1880* (Oxford, 1971), pp. 3, 70. See also, G. D. Ramsay, *The Wiltshire Woollen Industry in the Sixteenth and Seventeenth Centuries* (2nd edn, London, 1965), pp. 108–9, 111–12.

58. Kepler's analysis of the yield of the customs provides a corrective to the impression given by Ashley's figures for customs revenues, J. S. Kepler, *The Exchange of Christendom: The international entrepôt at Dover 1622–1651* (Leicester, 1976), pp. 114, 152; M. Ashley, *Financial and Commercial Policy under the Cromwellian Protectorate* (2nd edn, London, 1962), pp. 57, 133.

59. J. B., *The Merchant's Remonstrance*, cited in Ashley, *Financial and Commercial Policy*, p. 4.

60. Fisher, p. 120. Supple, *Commercial Crisis*, pp. 4, 128.

61. J. U. Nef, *The Rise of the British Coal Industry* (London, 1932), I, p. 25; II, pp. 69, 287, 380–1.

62. John Evelyn, *Fumifugium* (1661, reprinted, Exeter, 1976), p. 7.

63. CLRO, Journals of Common Council, XL, ff. 60, 101v.

64. The price was fixed at 17s.–19s. per chaldron in 1637–40, but Scottish coal was selling in London and Cambridge at 30s. or 40s. per chaldron in 1643 and 1644, Nef, *Coal Industry*, II, p. 81. In January 1643 coal was said to be selling at 'intolerable prices', *CSPVen*, 1642–43, p. 235.

65. *A & O*, I, pp. 303–5.

66. *CSPVen*, 1643–47, pp. 30, 106, 116.

67. *CJ*, III, p. 551.

68. *A & O*, I, p. 171.

69. E. S. Godfrey, *The Development of English Glassmaking 1560–1640* (Oxford, 1975), pp. 105, 131, 134, 194–6.

70. Blackmore, *Arms and Armour*, p. 6.

71. E. M. Symonds, 'The Diary of John Greene (1635–57)', *English Historical Review*, XLIV (1929), 106–7.

72. R. Davis, *The Rise of the English Shipping Industry in the Seventeenth and Eighteenth Centuries* (Newton Abbot, 1972), p. 259. William Lithgow, 'The Present Surveigh of London and England's State', reprinted in W. Scott (ed.), *Lord Somers Tracts*, IV (1810), p. 536.

73. The annual mean number of admissions for 1630–41 was 274, and the total number for 1643–5 was 238, W. R. Prest, *The Inns of Court under Elizabeth I and the Early Stuarts 1590–1640* (London, 1972), p. 245.

74. Prest, *Inns of Court*, p. 30.

75. Based upon a shortfall of 200 students per annum and an average annual expenditure of £50 per student. This probably errs on the

conservative side, Prest puts the minimum per student at £40 per year for the period 1558–1640, Prest, *Inns of Court*, pp. 27–8.

76. W. R. Prest, *The Rise of the Barristers. A Social History of the English Bar 1590–1640* (Oxford, 1986), pp. 73, 82.

77. E. M. Symonds, 'The Diary of John Greene (1635–57)', *English Historical Review*, XLIII (1928), 599.

78. H. J. Habbakuk, 'Landowners and the Civil War', *Economic History Review*, 2nd series, XVIII (1965), 130–51. I. Gentles, 'The sales of the bishops' lands in the English Revolution, 1646–1660', *English Historical Review*, XCV (1980), 573–96; Idem, 'The Sales of Crown Lands during the English Revolution', *Economic History Review*, 2nd series, XXVI (1973), 614–35.

79. G. E. Aylmer, *The King's Servants: The Civil Service of Charles I 1625–1642* (London, 1961), pp. 26–32, 472–5. C. Carlton, *Charles I: The Personal Monarch* (London, 1983), p. 125.

80. Aylmer, *King's Servants*, pp. 27, 474–5; Idem, 'Attempts at Administrative Reform, 1625–40', *English Historical Review*, LXXII (1957), 246–59.

81. Carlton, *Charles I*, pp. 149–50.

82. C. V. Wedgwood, *The Political Career of Peter Paul Rubens* (London, 1975), p. 47.

83. R. Lockyer, *Buckingham: The Life and Political Career of George Villiers, First Duke of Buckingham 1592–1628* (London, 1981), pp. 212–13, 412–14, 460.

84. R. E. Schreiber, *The First Carlisle: Sir James Hay, First Earl of Carlisle as Courtier, Diplomat and Entrepeneur, 1580–1636* (Trans. of the American Philosophical Soc., vol. 74, pt 7, 1984), pp. 5–6, 11. L. Stone, *The Crisis of the Aristocracy 1558–1641* (Oxford, 1965), pp. 779–81.

85. G. Huxley, *Endymion Porter. The Life of a Courtier 1587–1649* (London, 1959), pp. 220–4.

86. J. Rushworth (ed.), *Historical Collections [of Private Passages of State . . .]* (1721), II, pp. 288–92. L. Stone, 'The Residential Development of the West End of London in the Seventeenth Century', in B. C. Malament (ed.), *After the Reformation: essays in honor of J. H. Hexter* (Manchester, 1980), p. 175; Idem, *Crisis of the Aristocracy*, pp. 385–98, 450, 464.

87. HMC, *Calendar of the Manuscripts of the Marquess of Ormonde*, new series, I (1902), pp. 114–15.

88. J. T. Cliffe, *Puritans in Conflict: the Puritan Gentry during and after the Civil Wars* (London, 1988), pp. 88–91. J. Broad, 'Gentry Finances and the Civil War: The Case of the Buckinghamshire Verneys', *Economic History Review*, 2nd series, XXXII (1979), 185–7.

89. F. J. Fisher, 'The Development of London as a centre of Conspicuous Consumption in the Sixteenth and Seventeenth Centuries', *Trans. of the Royal Historical Soc.*, 4th series, XXX (1948), reprinted in Corfield and Harte, *London and the English Economy*, pp. 105–18.

90. According to Clarendon, the inhabitants of these areas 'always underwent the imputation of being well affected to the King', Clarendon, *History*, II, p. 430.

91. *CSPVen*, 1642–43, pp. 252, 277–8, 280.
92. PRO, C3/453/33.
93. F. H. W. Sheppard (ed.), *The Survey of London*, XXXVI (London, 1970), p. 7.
94. PRO, C7/441/90.
95. PRO, C10/46/45; C3/453/33.
96. Tibutt, *Letter Book of Samuel Luke*, p. 438.
97. P. S. Seaver, *Wallington's World: A Puritan Artisan in Seventeenth-Century London* (London, 1985), p. 117.
98. HMC, *Calendar of the Manuscripts of the Most Honourable the Marquess of Salisbury, Part XXIV Addenda 1605–1688* (1976), p. 281.
99. *CSPVen*, 1642–43, p. 252. *CJ*, III, p. 316.
100. *Mercurius Aulicus*, 15 July 1644, p. 1088. HMC, *Sixth Report: House of Lords MSS* (1877), p. 195.
101. N. G. Brett-James, *The Growth of Stuart London* (London, 1935), p. 119.
102. *A & O*, I, p. 570. Firth, *Cromwell's Army*, p. 260. *CJ*, IV, p. 153.
103. *CJ*, IV, p. 185.
104. *Calendar of the Committee for Compounding with Delinquents*, pp. 838, 959, 1240, 1359, 1565.
105. BL, Thomason Tracts, E289(1) *The Exchange Intelligencer*, 18–24 June 1645, p. 44. CLRO, Journals of Common Council, XL, ff. 141, 146.
106. *CJ*, IV, pp. 187, 218.
107. CLRO, Journals of Common Council, XL, ff. 118, 145v.
108. Sutton's Hospital at Charterhouse, Assembly Order Book B, 1637–58, ff. 57, 60–2.
109. W. K. Jordan, *The Charities of London 1480–1660: The Aspirations and the Achievements of the Urban Society* (London, 1960), pp. 25, 423. *A & O*, I, p. 570.
110. R. W. Herlan, 'Poor Relief in the London Parish of Dunstan in the West during the English Revolution', *Guildhall Studies in London History*, III (1977), 20–5, 31–2.
111. Finlay, *Population and Metropolis*, pp. 156–7.
112. John Bell, *London's Remembrancer* (1665), unpaged, tables for 1644–5, 1645–6. Symonds, 'Diary of John Greene', 1928, 604; 1929, 107.
113. P. Slack, *The Impact of Plague in Tudor and Stuart England* (London, 1985), pp. 124–5, 166–9, 188–90.
114. *CSPVen*, 1642–43, p. 280.
115. Gentles, *New Model Army*, p. 48.
116. *CSPD*, 1644–45, pp. 232–3. J. Morrill (ed.), *Reactions to the English Civil War 1642–1649* (London, 1982), p. 19.
117. V. Pearl, *London and the Outbreak of the Puritan Revolution* (Oxford, 1961), p. 210. Fletcher, *Outbreak*, p. 344.
118. *CSPVen*, 1642–43, pp. 237, 252.
119. A further one million pounds was added for the crown revenue lost to London's economy, *London's Account: Or, A Calculation of the Arbitrary and Tyrannicall Exactions ... within the Lines of Communication* (1647), pp. 9–12.
120. A. Crawford, *A History of the Vintners' Company* (London, 1977),

pp. 129–31.

121. T. Girtin, *The Triple Crowns: A narrative history of the Drapers' Company 1364–1964* (London, 1964), p. 237. G. Unwin, *The Gilds & Companies of London* (London, 1938), p. 240. Archer, *Haberdashers' Company*, p. 89.

122. HMC, *Sixth Report: House of Lords MSS* (1877), p. 195.

123. Crawford, *Vintners' Company*, p. 129.

124. Seaver, *Wallington's World*, pp. 118, 235.

125. I. Gentles, 'London Levellers in the English Revolution: the Chidleys and their circle', *Journal of Ecclesiastical History*, XXIX (1978), 297–303.

126. R. Brenner, *Merchants and Revolution: Commercial Change, Political Conflict, and London's Overseas Traders, 1550–1653* (Cambridge, 1993), pp. 113–93.

127. This topic is fully dealt with in Kepler, *The Exchange of Christendom, passim*, esp. pp. 85, 114.

128. Wedgwood, *Great Rebellion*, pp. 36–7. Fletcher, *Outbreak*, pp. 223, 258.

8

Political Funerals during the English Revolution

Ian Gentles

As the seat of government, and by far the largest concentration of population in the kingdom, the combined cities of London and Westminster were the natural stage for national political spectacles and displays of state power during the early modern period. In the hundred years between 1550 and 1650 London's population had leapt from 120 000 to 375 000 inhabitants.[1] A great port and entrepôt for international trade, London also boasted extensive manufacturing of luxury goods, a developed hotel industry, and a strikingly diversified artistic and intellectual culture. These multifarious functions, as well as its role as the venue of the royal court, made the metropolis an ever more powerful magnet for England's landed class. Every great courtier maintained his own household near Whitehall (most often in the Strand), each a miniature court in its own right, which functioned as the nerve centre for its own affinity. In addition, parliament, the law courts, speciality shopping and the allure of the budding London 'season', drew increasing numbers of gentlemen to build town houses in Westminster and its environs.[2]

Since the late fifteenth century or earlier, London had provided the audience for displays of political power in the shape of civic pageants – royal entries, coronations, lord mayor's shows, openings of parliament, and royal funerals.[3] A royal entry was a particularly lavish and urban form of the 'progress', such as occurred whenever a monarch or any other great figure travelled along a public road. The idioms of the progress and the funeral were similar: heraldic banners to proclaim the great man's ancestry, trumpeters to announce his coming, an entourage of mounted gentlemen and a foot guard of liveried yeomen. Whatever the occasion, these lavish processions functioned both as vehicles of the charisma of Tudor and early Stuart monarchy, and as a test of the public's esteem for the monarch or other great personage. The acclamation of the crowd, reinforcing as it did the aura of legitimacy, was an essential element in these spectacles.

> An entry publicly celebrated the Christian love that united ruler and ruled in a well-governed commonwealth. It reflected the medieval conviction that, however unequal people may be in this world, they are both equal and interdependent in God's eyes. For all his grandeur a King belonged to a Christian community of fallible men and women. The English expected his public conduct to show an awareness of this fact.[4]

Thus, Henry VII, after his victory on Bosworth field, rode to London, where the mayor, aldermen, magistrates and people crowded around to salute him and celebrate his conquest of the tyrant Richard III. Mary, too, drew critical support from the London crowd when she fought for her throne against Northumberland in 1553 and Wyatt in 1554. Elizabeth was treated to warm displays of public affection, notably at her coronation and after the defeat of the Armada. During her entry in 1558 she witnessed pageants which alluded to her adherence to the Reformation. In Fleet Street, for example, she encountered a representation of Deborah, 'the judge and restorer of the house of Israel', and a transparent symbol for Elizabeth herself. Equally, James received warm vocal support at his royal entry after the Gunpowder Plot in 1605. The story, however, was not always one of acclamation. Anne Boleyn was given a sullen reception at her coronation entry in 1533, while during the 1620s the crowds openly expressed their hatred of Spain and the duke of Buckingham.

Under the Stuarts public royal ceremonies became less frequent and less magnificent until in the 1630s Charles I virtually withdrew from his people's gaze. One of the least theatrical of English kings, Charles almost never appeared in the streets of his capital. The consequence was fatally to weaken royal charisma in such a way that the king was unable to control London on the eve of, and during, the Civil War. The one exception to this pattern of royal neglect of public ceremonial only serves to prove the rule: Charles's entry into London in November 1641. In spite of the evidently genuine acclamations that greeted the royal family as they processed to Guildhall, it was too late to repair the neglect of sixteen years.

In the course of the 1640s London provided the stage for four significant funerals, each of which exploited the familiar idioms of civic pageantry for the purpose of forwarding a political agenda. While all four men were rebels, two of their funerals – those of John Pym and Robert Devereux, third earl of Essex – were officially sanctioned by the state, while the other two – those of Colonel Thomas Rainborowe and Private Robert Lockyer – were unofficial, revolutionary pageants. The contrasting character of these two sets of funerals is instructive. By imitating the extravagance and pomp of the traditional royal or heraldic funeral, the Long Parliament was attempting to proclaim the greatness of its leaders, and, by implication, the greatness, wealth and power of the cause which had produced them. More broadly, their funerals were affirmations that despite the loss of a great individual, and in the face of the apparent triumph of evil, life continues, death is *not* victorious, evil does *not* conquer, the state has *not* been toppled, and the present generation will both survive and reproduce itself.

The revolutionary funeral, by contrast, is a gesture of defiance against the established powers. It proclaims that even though a valued warrior has been struck down, his comrades are not demoralised by the loss. On the contrary, they take inspiration from his martyrdom. For every flower that is trampled down ten fresh ones will spring up in its place. The martyr-hero is even more powerful in death than he was in life. An examination of each of these four funerals in turn will shed further light on the political use of public ritual in the mid-seventeenth century, and should thereby enlarge our understanding of the English Revolution.

I

John Pym was one of the leaders of the parliamentary cause in the House of Commons in the early 1640s. The Member for Tavistock, he had through his eloquence, organisational talent and tireless determination or 'unweariableness', contributed to holding together the quarrelsome parliamentary coalition against the king for three years from the summoning of the Long Parliament in November 1640. The chief drafter of the Grand Remonstrance, he was also the 'dominating presence at the Committee of Safety' which directed the parliamentary war effort. Recent assessments of his career have called into question J. H. Hexter's judgement that he was the master strategist who created the financial and military structures which allowed parliament to win the Civil War. Neither ubiquitous nor omnicompetent, he was a parliamentary man of business, a front-man, who was frequently used by others – in both Lords and Commons – to fly kites and publicise positions taken up by colleagues and friends. Indeed a libellous royalist lampoon of 1643 portrayed him, not entirely unfairly, as a go-between and a drudge. None the less, this 'drudge' spoke on at least 900 occasions in the House of Commons, and at least eleven of his speeches are known to have been printed. Moreover, he was accorded the grandest funeral ever given to a commoner in the early modern period, and the Lords took the day off in order to attend it.[5]

When Pym died, on 8 December 1643, parliament's military fortunes were at a perilously low ebb. Over the previous nine months royalist commanders had won an almost uninterrupted string of victories against their parliamentary counterparts. The very real danger of royalist triumph had led to the portentous decision to forge an alliance with the Scots – 20 000 Scots troops in return for a guarantee that parliament would adopt the Presbyterian form of church government in England. For those three years Pym had worked around the clock, apparently surviving on three hours sleep a night.[6] The autopsy carried out shortly after his death found that he had died of bowel cancer.[7]

Royalists, of course, rejoiced that Pym was dead, throwing parties and lighting bonfires in honour of the occasion. They then set about to blacken his reputation, first by questioning the nature of his death, suggesting that he had either been poisoned or that he had succumbed to a loathsome disease such as phtheriasis, or that, like Herod, he had been eaten by worms. It was also alleged 'that hee dyed raving, crying out against that cause wherein he had been so great an instrument . . .'. In order to scotch these damaging rumours parliament published a pamphlet informing the public that during his illness Pym had been attended by three physicians, one of whom was the President of the College of Physicians, that four more physicians, two surgeons and an apothecary were present at the dissection of his body, and that a thousand more people had viewed his body, and proved for themselves that his skin was smooth and intact, and that there was no 'lousie disease', as was reported.[8]

In an effort to impress upon the public the strength and unity of their cause, the House of Commons ordered a full state funeral for its fallen leader.[9] All Members of the lower house were instructed to join the funeral procession from Derby House in the City to the Abbey, where a monument was to be erected in his memory. The funeral was celebrated on 13 December, five days after his death. For someone of Pym's political stature the interval between death and burial was very short. Most people in the seventeenth century were buried within seventy-two hours of their death in order to avoid the expense of embalming. Normally only individuals of considerable wealth or social status would be subjected to this process, which involved evisceration, filling the fleshy parts of the body with preservative herbs, wrapping the corpse in waxed or tarred sheets and double-coffining. Since Pym's death occurred in one of the coldest months of the year, it may be presumed that even though the interval between death was longer than normal, he did not undergo embalming.[10] His coffin was borne by ten of the most distinguished MPs, and followed by Members of both Lords and Commons, of whom 'a great part' wore mourning dress. Following them were one hundred or so members of the Assembly of Divines and 'many other Gentlemen of quality, with two heralds of armes before the corpse bearing his crest'.[11] In all, the procession numbered approximately five hundred.

At the Abbey Stephen Marshall, a leading parliamentarian preacher, delivered a three-hour sermon. He took his text from the Old Testament book of the prophet Micah, chapter 7: 'The good man is perished out of the earth', using it to elaborate on a favourite puritan theme: the idea of the faithful remnant, the beleaguered godly minority; 'the small number of the good, and the great multitude of evill men in the dayes wherein he lived'. Why, Marshall asked, did God so often permit his servants to be carried off in the midst of their work? Why in particular did he allow this calamity at a time when parliament was in so vulnerable a condition: ' ... our Parliament ... weakned, our Armies wasted, our treasure ... exhausted, our enemies increased ...'? It was partly in order to humble and shame the parliamentarians, but, more importantly, to demonstrate that God's cause did not depend on human agency but on God alone.[12] After Marshall's sermon Pym's body was interred in the chapel of King Henry VII among the kings and princes of England, and the sermon was ordered to be published.[13]

The grandeur of Pym's funeral, as well as his interment alongside royalty, was a deliberate attempt to bolster the sagging morale of parliament's supporters. The funeral, three years later, of Robert Devereux, third earl of Essex, had a different purpose, and was incomparably grander. No malicious rumours attended Essex's death: he was the victim of a stroke on 14 September 1646, which he had suffered four days earlier while out hunting.[14] In order to allow ample time for the preparation of a full Heraldic funeral, it was necessary to embalm the corpse. It was first disembowelled, steeped in oils, wrapped in a sere cloth, and then encased in a close-fitting lead coffin. The actual funeral did not take place until 22 October, almost six weeks after the earl's death. The outside of the coffin was adorned with his motto, his coat of arms, and his various titles.

Essex was easily the most socially prestigious leader on the parliamentary side. Early in the Civil War King Charles I had characterised him as 'the cheefe Rebell', and as such the only one with whom it would not be beneath the king's dignity to negotiate.[15] Fittingly, parliament had named him Lord General of all its forces in 1642, a post in which he had continued until he was removed, along with all the other aristocratic commanders, by the Self-Denying Ordinance in 1645. His removal had been part of a successful political manoeuvre by the Independent faction to replace Presbyterian military leadership with Independent or win-the-war leadership.[16]

By the time of his death a year-and-a-half later, Essex was a spent force politically. The battlefield victories of the New Model Army had thrown into stark relief his own indifferent military record and further sapped the political power of the Presbyterians in both houses of parliament. With the king completely defeated and taken prisoner the parliamentary majority were beginning to see themselves as the rulers of England. Nevertheless, his death furnished parliament with an opportunity to remind the nation that their first commander-in-chief had been a man of almost royal stature. It is no surprise, then, that they exploited the occasion by ordering obsequies of princely lavishness. £5000 was voted 'towards the discharging of his debts and defraying the expenses of his funeral',[17] a sum that was augmented by a large provision

from the Essex estate. Bearing in mind that from the 1580s onwards a major heraldic aristocratic funeral cost in the neighbourhood of £1000, while only £5 or £6 on average were spent on the
funerals of the Kentish gentry, the amount budgeted for Essex
was truly monumental.[18] Normally the two chief items in a funeral budget were black cloth for hangings and for the dress of
the mourners, and the funeral feast.

Essex's funeral was in fact modelled on that of James I's son
and heir, Prince Henry.[19] After the prince's death on 6 November 1612 at the age of eighteen, his body had lain a month at St
James's Palace, after which time it was borne to Westminster Abbey.
The members of the funeral procession, exceeding 2000 in number,
were led by 200 poor men dressed in mourning. This was still a
custom of continuing vitality, handed down from the Middle Ages,
reflecting the conviction that the prayers of the poor were especially powerful with Christ. Their reward was normally a funeral
dole of a few pence, and the gown in which they processed. A
great many trumpets played in Prince Henry's procession, ' . . .
and by the sound of their funeral march, most beautifully played,
they drew tears from the eyes of all who heard'. Another observer also noted the sorrow of the spectators, ' . . . whose streaming
eyes made knowen how much inwardly their hurts did bleed'.
Their sorrow was natural. Henry had died in his teens, a young
man full of promise: cultured, religious and warlike, he had already been regarded as England's ideal future monarch.[20]

Remarkably few of the funerals of the great in early seventeenth-century England were marked by any genuine expressions
of grief. The obsequies of the murdered duke of Buckingham in
1628, for example, were in stark contrast to those of Prince Henry.
Held at night by torchlight so as to avoid public displays of
hostility and contempt, the coffin was guarded along its route to
Westminster Abbey by the London trained bands, who kept up a
loud tattoo on their drums. Its purpose was evidently to drown
out the expressions of joy which the Venetian ambassador claimed
to have heard from the crowd lining the streets. As an extra precaution the soldiers also carried their arms on their shoulders, instead
of trailing them, as was customary at funerals.[21] Similarly, in 1641,
the earl of Strafford, easily the most hated man in England at the
time, could not have been buried in London, owing to fear of the
populace. Instead, after being embalmed in preparation for a long
journey, his body was quietly transported to Yorkshire, on the

pretext of burying it with those of his ancestors.[22] The most detested cleric in England, Archbishop William Laud, was buried
quietly the day after his execution in 1645, at All Hallows Bark-
ing near the Tower.[23]

As Clare Gittings has noted of funerals such as the one organised for the earl of Essex, 'a heraldic funeral was a tremendous
display of the power of the aristocracy'. The organisation of its
finer points was the responsibility of the College of Arms, who
followed, in great detail, established regulations and precedents.
They had to ensure that both the church and the rooms in which
the body lay in state were suitably adorned in black cloth. They
also had to supervise the erection of the hearse.[24] Finally they
had to organise the funeral-day procession. The strictest protocol
was observed, with everyone's position being determined by his
social status. Since the rule was strictly enforced that all mourners
had to be of the same sex as the deceased, there were no women
in Essex's procession.[25] Given that Essex's first wife had divorced
him for impotence, while his second wife had run off with
a lover, and that he died without issue, the rule in this case
would not have occasioned much resentment. According to Gittings,
again,

> The whole ritual of the heraldic funeral revolved around the
> legitimate transfer of titles and power; the private persona
> counted for ... little ... Once the titles and honour had been
> passed on to the successor, attention passed to him and away
> from the body, which now held little significance in the politi-
> cal show. Whatever private sorrow he may have felt at the loss
> of his father, the heir could not stay to see him interred, but
> had to return in the procession, so as to demonstrate publicly
> that the ranks of the aristocracy were once again restored to
> their full complement. The political purposes of the heraldic
> funeral overrode all private emotions and the participants, despite
> their feelings, were required to comply with the regulations.[26]

In accordance with heraldic protocol, Essex House was draped
in mourning black cloth bearing the earl's escutcheons. A great
hearse was erected, covered in black velvet, and bearing his coat
of arms and banners. On it was laid an effigy of Essex dressed as
he had been at Edgehill in white boots, scarlet breeches and buff
coat. He also wore his parliamentary robes, sword and coronet.

The house was opened to the public, and visited by many supporters during the weeks after his death.[27]

In preparation for the burial a second hearse was raised on
four pillars in Westminster Abbey. It, too, was hung with black
velvet, edged with gold and bearing his coat of arm, escutcheons,
banners and motto. At the top was a large coronet, implying that
more than an earl, he was a person of the blood royal. A smaller
coronet was also set at each corner of the hearse. Tacitly parliament was claiming to match the royalists in the social prestige
of its leadership.

On the day of the funeral the route from Essex House to Westminster Abbey was lined with five regiments of trained bands
from the metropolis: three from the City, one from Tower Hamlets and another from Southwark, in addition to 'the major part
of a regiment of horse'. If the regiments were at full strength,
there were over 5000 soldiers guarding the route. In advance of
the main procession the marshall of the City of London rode on
horseback with twenty men 'all suited in black cassocks and hose
trimmed with ribbons'. At 2 o'clock in the afternoon[28] the procession got under way, led by sixty-eight poor men in double
file – about a third as many as had led Prince Henry's procession. Next came a company of servants to the gentry, also in
double file. Then there marched four regiments of trained bands,
two of which had been with Essex at the expedition to Gloucester and the first battle of Newbury. The pikemen trailed their
pikes, while the musketeers bore their arms 'in a funeral posture'. The other two were the ' . . . eldest regiments within the
line', one from Westminster, the other from the City. In their rear
came ninety-five field officers and 267 captains, very few of whom
were presently in active service in the New Model Army.

The officers included many who would publicly identify them-
selves with the Presbyterian cause by dint of supporting parlia-
ment against the New Model Army in the crisis of 1647: Sir William
Waller, Sir Thomas Essex, Sir Samuel Luke, Major-General Richard
Browne, Colonels Richard Fortescue, Charles D'oilie [or Doyle],
Edmund Harvey, Thomas Sheffield, John Dalbier and Richard
Graves; Lieutenant-Colonels James Gray [or Grey] and Richard
Kempson; Major George Sedascue; Captains Henry Langham, Fulke
Musket, William Jackson, John Middleton, and others. No more
than a dozen or so of the 362 officers were in active service in
the New Model Army in the autumn of 1646: Colonels Richard

Ingoldsby, John Barkstead, John Okey and Robert Hammond; Major
Adrian Scrope, and Captains Christopher Mercer, [Ralph or Robert?]
Cobbett, [Henry?] Lilburne, Tobias Bridge, [William?] Covell,
[Henry or Thomas?] Disney and Waldive Legoe.[29]

They all marched from Covent Garden to Essex House, where
the main procession began. There they were joined by fifemen,
drummers and trumpeters with banners of the arms of Devereux.
Next came five chaplains, then more musicians, then the guidon
borne by Colonel Francis Thompson, and 'a horse led by a groom
covered with a black cloth, adorned and garnished with plumes,
shafferons, and escocheons of his Lordships arms'. Then more
gentry in double file, then more musicians 'with banners of the
arms of Lovayne', then more officers from the trained bands, then
about ninety auxiliary commanders 'bearing swords, wearing black
cloaks and black feathers in their hats'.

Then came more musicians with banners of the arms of Bourchier
(another of Essex's titles) and a riderless horse 'led by a groom
covered with black cloth, adorned and garnished with shafferons
and escocheons of the arms of Bourchier'. It was followed by
about fifty colonels and field officers ' . . . which had served under his Lordship's immediate command'. After them came more
musicians with banners of the arms of Ferrers. Behind them were
knights, baronets, younger sons of noblemen, and three officers
of the Essex household with white staves. Finally came six trumpeters with banners of Essex's quartered coats. The great banner
on which were displayed the arms of Devereux, Bourchier, Louvain
and Ferrers, surmounted by a princely coronet, was borne by Sir
Henry Cholmley and Lancelot Lake, esquire. This was followed
by the preacher of the funeral sermon, the Presbyterian Richard
Vines.

The effigy of the earl, with his coronet upon his head, was
borne in an open chariot of black velvet drawn by six horses
covered with black velvet to the ground, 'adorned and garnished
with plumes, shafferons, escocheons, and compartements of his
lordships armes'. The pall itself was carried by six youngish men,
all of impeccable Presbyterian credentials. On the right side were
Henry Howard, second son of the late earl of Suffolk, Denzil Holles,
second son of the late earl of Clare, and George Montagu, second son of the late earl of Manchester. On the left the pall was
supported by Charles Rich, second son of the earl of Warwick,
Colonel Algernon Sydney, second son of the earl of Leicester,

and Thomas Sheffield, son of the late earl of Mulgrave. Almost as great an honour was bearing Essex's armour and bannerolls. Again, the men thus honoured constituted a roll-call of prominent Presbyterians or men sympathetic to them: Sir William Balfour, Sir Philip Stapilton, Colonel James Sheffield, Colonel Davies, Sir John Meyrick, Major-General Philip Skippon, Major-General Richard Browne, Colonel Richard Graves, Leicester and Walter Devereux, sons of viscount Hereford, Sir Anthony St John, baronet, Sir John Botiller, Nicholas Leake, esquire, Sir Thomas Essex, baronet, Sir William Lewis, baronet, and Colonel Robert Hammond.[30]

Next, walking by himself, came viscount Hereford, the chief mourner. His eight assistants included some of the greatest noblemen of England: the earls of Northumberland, Pembroke, Suffolk, Warwick and Holland, as well as lord Lisle, Sir Robert Sherley, and Oliver St John. Men like Northumberland and St John had not been political allies of Essex for some time; doubtless they owed their positions of honour to the fact that the earl had named them executors of his will on the eve of the battle of Edgehill in October 1642.[31]

After the chief mourner and his assistants came the members of the House of Lords, the House of Commons, the Recorder and Aldermen of the City of London, the London Militia Committee, the Assembly of Divines, and, finally, a party of 50 to 60 cavalry.

So crowded was the Abbey with all the official members of the procession, that the House of Lords had issued an order '... to keepe out the multitude, and all women of any quality whatsoever'. Apart from the difficulty of accommodating all the members of the procession, who numbered over 1000, in addition to the nearly 10 000 soldiers and officers (the 5000 lining the route, and nearly that number marching in the procession) there was, as we have seen, the consideration that this was a heraldic funeral of a man, and so all the mourners had to be male.

Once the mourners had been seated and the hearse and other paraphernalia placed in the chancel 'where the Communion Table stood',[32] Richard Vines delivered a sermon of at least three hours in length. We need not assume that its duration would have tried the patience of the listeners, for Vines was one of the most eloquent preachers in a period when people were habituated to long sermons.

He chose as his text a provocative verse from the Second Book of Samuel, chapter 3: 'Know yee not that there is a Prince, and a great man fallen this day in Israel?' Essex, he said, was such a man, for his project had been nothing less than 'the defence of the liberty and property of the subjects of England'. Vaunting the grandeur of the funeral, Vines proclaimed that all of England was represented there. He compared Essex to Moses, a great man whom God had carried off before his goal had been reached. Why had God done this? In order to show that he did not depend on any human agent to realise his plan for mankind. The lesson of Essex's untimely death was to 'get death into your minds, and it will put life into your actions'. For all Vines's eloquence, and his liberal use of classical and biblical allusions, he could not make a great deal of Essex's slender military accomplishments. The best he could come up with was that Essex had been careful not to waste the lives of his infantry. If Essex was Moses, then Sir Thomas Fairfax, the Commander-in-Chief of the New Model Army, was Joshua, an incomparably more impressive military leader. 'Neither doth Joshua eclipse the worth of Moses, nor he the worth of Joshua.' The comparison, however, was inapt, since it would have been difficult to imagine what qualities in Essex might have made up for his military mediocrity.[33]

Once Vines had finished his oratorical *tour de force*, the listeners processed back to Essex House for the funeral banquet. They would not have stayed to witness the burial, since the disposal of the corpse was not what the ceremony had principally been about. Later Essex was laid to rest in a vault next to Lord Hunsdon, the cousin of Queen Elizabeth, in the Chapel of St John the Baptist. When the coffin had been lowered into the vault another important ritual of the heraldic funeral took place.[34] Three officers of the Essex household broke their white staves, the symbols of their offices, and threw them into the grave. Thus they signified that with the death of their master their employment was at an end, unless the heir chose to re-hire them.

Following the funeral proper came parliament's military salute. At 7 o'clock, five hours after the procession had begun, the great bell at St Margaret's Church next to the Abbey was tolled twice, which gave the signal to a gentleman of the Ordnance to raise a red ensign and a great lantern containing three lights. This in turn gave the signal to the Stone Fort in Southwark, across the Thames, to fire a great cannon. This signified to the next fort, at Vauxhall, that it should fire its greatest cannon, and so on around the eleven-mile perimeter of the Lines of Communication that had been erected to protect London against the royalist forces. The ritual was performed three times, and at the end of each time, the regiments of foot and horse fired volleys from their pistols and muskets. The effigy which had been drawn on the hearse in the funeral procession was erected over the tomb. Little over a month later a disgruntled royalist attempted to destroy it. When it was repaired it was placed in a glass case, where it remained until the Restoration.[35]

The funeral of Colonel Thomas Rainborowe was a much less grand affair. The son of a sea-captain from Wapping who had prospered under Charles I, Rainborowe had gained notoriety by 1648 as one of the king's most outspoken antagonists. Personal conflict with Oliver Cromwell over whether he should be promoted Vice-Admiral of the navy had encouraged his radical bent, so that by the autumn of 1647 he had emerged as a compelling spokesman for the Leveller Agreement of the People. His killing, at the hands of royalist agents at Doncaster in October 1648, inflamed radical opinion in London.[36] He was rapidly transformed into a martyr for the Leveller cause, and from the time of his funeral his personal colours, green and black, were adopted as the badge of the Leveller movement. His body was brought to London two weeks after his death. Entering the City by way of Islington, the funeral procession wound its way through Smithfield, past St Paul's Cathedral, along Cheapside, and out through the East End to Wapping Chapel, where he was buried beside his father. The procession consisted of women in fifty or sixty coaches, and men on horseback, impressively numbering nearly 3000 in all. Yet the turn-out was not so large as the one that would attend the body of the other slain Leveller hero, Robert Lockyer, half a year later.

The one note of official approval for Rainborowe came in the form of a cannon salute from the Tower of London while he was being interred.[37] The interment was, as expected, preceded by a funeral sermon from a Thomas Brooks, who spoke for about two hours. His theme was how God's saints who have been treacherously murdered here below will be glorified in heaven. The lesson to derive from Rainborowe's loss was that God can rescue any cause, no matter how hopeless it appears: '... though the work be too hard for the arme of flesh, too hard for an Army, or Parliament, 'tis not too hard for God'.[38] Brooks prefaced the printed version of the sermon with an apology for printing it, apparently without official authority. It was not his wish to publish, he alleged, but he was overpowered by people who insisted on it.

Rainborowe's funeral also prompted an outpouring of elegies in bad verse. Their inferior quality did not prevent them from being widely printed and circulated, however.[39] The controversy surrounding Rainborowe was mirrored in the derisive comments from the royalist press. The acid-tongued editor of *Mercurius Pragmaticus*, Marchamont Nedham, commented, 'the carkasse of Rainsborough was attended through London by a regiment of horse, and all the tag-rags of the faction that were able to hire horses, and entered at Wapping among his fellow-swabbers and skippers'.[40] The editor of *Mercurius Elencticus* joined exuberantly in the campaign, mocking Leveller pretensions that their tribune was a man supported by the respected classes of society. On the day of Rainborowe's funeral he wrote that the corpse was ' . . . met and attended on by a great number of the well affected of all professions, Will the weaver, Tom the tapster, Kit the cobler, Dick the door sweeper, and many more eminent apron-youths of the City, who trudg'd very devoutly both before and behind this glorious saint, with about 100 of the she-votresses crowded up in coaches, and some 500 more of the better sort of brethren mounted on hackney beasts'.[41]

It is curious that the private trooper Robert Lockyer, whose funeral seems to have been better attended than Rainborowe's, was much less a target of royalist satire than the Leveller colonel. The least socially significant of the four men we are examining, Lockyer was a member of Colonel Edward Whalley's horse regiment. In April 1649 he led the men of Captain John Savage's troop in a mutiny over pay. The mutiny was quickly put down, but its circumstances and timing gave the army grandees such a fright that they determined to make an example of its ringleader, whom they condemned to death.

The civilian leaders of the Leveller party had been labouring to stir up a revolt within the army since February of that year. At the moment of Lockyer's action all four of them were languishing in the Tower of London, whence they continued to pour forth maledictions against the shaky infant republican regime. It happened that Whalley's regiment was stationed in the heart of the City, with the sixty mutinous troopers barricading themselves in the Bull Inn near Bishopsgate, a well-known radical meeting place

A crowd quickly gathered in the courtyard of the inn and the adjacent street. Collaboration between an unruly crowd and a group of radically-inspired, mutinous soldiers represented the kind of nightmare scenario that the senior officers feared the most. So, led by Fairfax and Cromwell in person, they moved in with over-whelming force, stamped out the uprising, tried and condemned six of the ringleaders to death, and then reprieved all but one. Robert Lockyer was that one, not only because he was the chief ringleader, but also because he was a well-known Leveller acti-vist. A hastily published letter from John Lilburne and Richard Overton threatening popular insurrection if the army executed Lockyer only stiffened Fairfax's resolve.[42]

Like many public executions, Lockyer's constituted a memor-able piece of street theatre. The venue was the churchyard of St Paul's Cathedral. As he stood before the musketeers who would despatch him, Lockyer proclaimed to the crowd his sorrow that he should lose his life in a dispute over pay, rather than for the freedom of the nation for which he had fought during the pre-vious seven years. Disdaining the blindfold normally offered to those who were publicly shot to death, he stared his execution-ers in the face and entreated them to disobey the order to fire. He then knelt in prayer, and after a few moments gave the ap-pointed signal by raising both arms. Seconds afterwards he crum-pled beneath a rain of bullets from all six musketeers.

Lockyer's funeral bore out Oliver Cromwell's fear that the public shooting of a popular soldier who was also a native Londoner might screw the political tension another notch higher. More than the other three, its contours remind us of the use of mourning as a vehicle of political protest. The burial procession on 27 April 1649 was one of the most impressive that people could remem-ber. Starting from Smithfield in the afternoon, it trailed slowly through the heart of the City, and then back to Moorfields for the interment in the adjacent New Churchyard, which had been created eighty years before to alleviate the crowding of parish graveyards. The intention had not been to create a burial ground for outcasts, but by the mid-seventeenth century it had become a preferred destination for the funerals of the poor and of religious nonconformists.[43]

While contemporary crowd estimates must always be treated with caution, it appears that Lockyer's funeral may have attracted significantly more participants and onlookers than Rainborowe's or Pym's. Led by six trumpeters – a conscious imitation of the heraldic funeral – the corpse was accompanied by 4000 people. Lockyer's horse, clothed in black, was given a place of honour. It was led by a footman, ' . . . a funeral honor equal to a chief commander'.[44] Many wore black and sea-green ribbons, which were now recognised as Leveller colours. Others carried sprigs of rosemary for remembrance. Some dipped the sprigs in blood and placed them on the coffin. More alarming to the authorities than the size of the cortège was the fact that several hundred soldiers – some discharged men, but many others troopers currently in the army – joined the procession. A company of women brought up the rear, testimony to the active female involvement in the Leveller movement.[45] In addition to the mourners who walked behind the coffin, there were many thousand spectators who stationed themselves on the street or in overlooking windows.

When the procession arrived in Moorfields it was joined by a large contingent 'of the highest sort' who had not wished to be seen walking through the City. In the New Churchyard there were eulogies, but no sermon, and then the crowd dispersed. The eulogies, however, had tended to become politically pointed. The speakers expatiated on the anti-militarism of the Levellers, doing their best to discomfit the army grandees and their unpopular military dictatorship.[46] A few onlookers had derided the mourners as Levellers, while others regarded the procession itself as 'a high affront' to parliament and the army, and professed amazement that the City authorities had permitted it to pass through the gates. The general reaction, however, seems to have been sympathetic, even among royalist journalists. Some commentators thought Lockyer had more mourners than King Charles.[47]

II

Vanessa Harding has pointed out that for several generations after the Reformation Londoners continued to attach great importance to funerals, marshalling large processions, summoning colleagues and dependants, and commanding the attention of the community through the pealing of bells and other devices. The poor were still enlisted, to swell the procession, demonstrate the generosity of the deceased, and to manifest the unity of rich and poor in the face of life's most fundamental challenge. Many medieval practices associated with burial flourished for generations after the Reformation. Early modern Londoners still craved elaborate and traditional funerals, and yearned for immortality through commemoration.[48]

The four parliamentary funerals that we have examined exemplify much of this attachment to tradition. Traditionalism is seen most strikingly in Essex's funeral, which adhered rigidly to the requirements of the Heraldic rite, but it is also found in the most revolutionary ceremony of the four, Lockyer's, in the use of trumpeters, the separation of the sexes, the riderless horse, and so forth. Each funeral was typical, too, in the way it strove to exalt the achievements and social status of the deceased.

Where these funerals departed from tradition was in the conscious effort to use them for the purpose of political propaganda. In the case of Pym and Essex the propaganda message was the continuing strength and solidity of the parliamentary regime despite the disaster incurred through the loss of a prominent leader. Pym's funeral may have exaggerated his importance in the parliamentary cause, while Essex's was shot through with ambiguity and irony. The first general of the parliamentary army, Essex had been in military and political disgrace since his ejection following the creation of the New Model. By the autumn of 1646, however, the Presbyterians had regained the upper hand in the House of Commons, and were able to furnish obsequies for their fallen leader more magnificent than the capital had seen for thirty-four years. Dominating the funeral procession were the earl's political friends – Denzil Holles, Philip Stapilton, Sir William Lewis and others – while the Independents kept a low profile or stayed away altogether. In the case of Rainborowe and Lockyer the message was one of defiance against the enemies of radicalism, together with an attempt to embarrass the moderate representatives of parliamentarianism, who were held responsible for the deaths of these radical martyrs. The exploitation of religious ritual for political ends was thus no invention of the twentieth century.

Notes

1. R. Finlay and B. Shearer, 'Population growth and suburban expansion' in A. L. Beier and R. Finlay (eds), *London 1500–1700: The making of the metropolis* (London, 1986), pp. 48–9.

2. R. M. Smuts, *Court Culture and the Origins of a Royalist Tradition in Early Stuart England* (Philadelphia, 1987), pp. 54–65.

3. D. M. Bergeron, *English Civic Pageantry 1558–1642* (London, 1971), pp. 3–5. R. M. Smuts, 'Public ceremony and royal charisma: the English royal entry in London, 1485–1642', in A. L. Beier, D. Cannadine and J. M. Rosenheim (eds), *The First Modern Society* (Cambridge, 1989), pp. 67–8.

4. Smuts, 'Public ceremony', p. 80. The following two paragraphs are largely based on this excellent essay.

5. J. H. Hexter, *The Reign of King Pym* (Cambridge, Mass., 1941). A. Fletcher, *The Outbreak of the English Civil War* (London, 1981), pp. 134–52. S. Lambert, 'The opening of the Long Parliament', *Historical Journal*, xxvii (1984), 285. C. Russell, *The Fall of the British Monarchies* (Oxford, 1991), pp. 149–51, 438, 470. *LJ*, vi, p. 340. I am grateful to John Morrill for letting me read his unpublished paper, 'The unweariableness of Mr Pym: influence and eloquence in the Long Parliament'.

6. BL, Thomason Tracts, E80(1) Stephen Marshall, *The Churches Lamentation for the Good Man his losse* (1644), p. 36.

7. BL, Thomason Tracts, E78(11) *A Narrative of the Disease and Death of that Noble Gentleman John Pym Esquire* (1643), p. 3.

8. *Narrative of the Disease and Death of . . . John Pym*, pp. 2, 5. Marshall, *The Churches Lamentation*, p. 37.

9. *CJ*, iii, p. 336.

10. S. Porter, 'Death and burial in a London parish: St. Mary Woolnoth 1653–99', *The London Journal*, viii (1982), 77; Idem, 'From death to burial in seventeenth century England', *The Local Historian*, xxiii (1993), 201, 203.

11. BL, Thomason Tracts, E252(11) *A Perfect Diurnall*, 11–18 Dec. 1643, p. 165. The ten MPs who bore Pym's coffin were Denzil Holles, Sir Arthur Hesilrige, William Strode, Sir Gilbert Gerrard, Sir John Clotworthy, Sir Henry Vane junior, Sir Nevil Poole, Sir John Wray, Oliver St John, and Richard Knightley.

12. Marshall, *The Churches Lamentation*, pp. 2, 8, 12, 20, 24.

13. BL, Thomason Tracts, E252(11) *Perfect Diurnall*, 11–18 Dec. 1643, p. 165. *CJ*, iii, p. 341.

14. Dr Williams's Library, MS 24.50 (Diary of Thomas Juxon), f. 79v. I am grateful to John Adamson for this reference.

15. BL, Add. MS 62083 (Pythouse Papers), f. 4v. J. S. A. Adamson, 'The baronial context of the English Civil War', *Trans. of the Royal Historical Soc.*, 5th series, 40 (1990), 101, 103–8.

16. I. Gentles, *The New Model Army in England, Ireland and Scotland, 1645–1653* (Oxford, 1992), pp. 5–25.

17. *CJ*, iv, p. 679. *LJ*, viii, p. 508.

18. C. Gittings, *Death, Burial and the Individual in Early Modern England* (1984), p. 181. Porter, 'From death to burial', 201. It is noteworthy that the funeral of the marquess of Worcester, which occurred in the same year as that of Essex, cost only £464 14s. (Ibid.).

19. V. Snow, *Essex the Rebel* (Lincoln, Nebraska, 1970), pp. 488–95. G.

Parry, *The Golden Age Restor'd* (Manchester, 1981), p. 255. I am indebted to Graham Parry for conversation and help on the Essex funeral. See also, J. S. A. Adamson, 'Chivalry and political culture in Caroline England', in K. Sharpe and P. Lake (eds), *Culture and Politics in Early Stuart England* (London, 1994), pp. 191–3.

20. *CSPVen*, 1610–13, pp. 467–9. R. Strong, *Henry Prince of Wales and England's Lost Renaissance* (London, 1986), pp. 7–8. It is interesting that none of the men buried during the 1640s attracted such an outpouring of grief at his funeral procession. For the significance of the poor at funeral processions see, I. W. Archer, *The Pursuit of Stability: Social Relations in Elizabethan London* (Cambridge, 1991), p. 54; E. Duffy, *The Stripping of the Altars: Traditional Religion in England, 1400–1580* (New Haven, 1992), p. 360; S. Brigden, *London and the Reformation* (Oxford, 1989), pp. 32–3, 341.

21. R. Lockyer, *Buckingham: the Life and Career of George Villiers, First Duke of Buckingham 1592–1628* (London, 1981), pp. 457–8.

22. S. R., *A Briefe and Perfect Relation of the Answers and Replies of Thomas Earle of Strafford . . .* (1647), p. 98.

23. H. R. Trevor–Roper, *Archbishop William Laud* (2nd edn, London, 1962), p. 428.

24. Gittings, *Death*, pp. 168, 171.

25. Gittings, *Death*, p. 175.

26. Gittings, *Death*, pp. 178–9.

27. Except where otherwise noted, details about Essex's funeral are taken from, BL, Thomason Tracts, E360(1) *The True Mannor and Forme of the Proceeding to the Funerall of the Right Honourable Robert Earle of Essex and Ewe . . .* , (1646).

28. BL, Thomason Tracts, E358(16), *A Perfect Relation of the . . . Funerall of the . . . Earle of Essex* (1646), unpaged [p. 4].

29. For these identifications see the indexes of Gentles, *New Model Army*, and C. H. Firth and G. Davies, *Regimental History of Cromwell's Army* (2 vols, Oxford, 1940), and the references cited therein.

30. It is true that from 1647 onwards Skippon would throw in his lot with the New Model Army in its struggle with the Presbyterian-dominated House of Commons, but before that time he was regarded as a political moderate or Presbyterian. Robert Hammond, although he was Oliver Cromwell's cousin, was regarded as too moderate and hence politically unreliable by the revolutionary Independents. In November 1648 they took the precaution of removing the king from Hammond's custody on the Isle of Wight.

31. Dr Williams's Library, MS 24.50, f. 79v. John Hampden, who had died in 1643, was also named one of Essex's executors.

32. BL, Thomason Tracts, E358(16) *A Perfect Relation of the . . . Funerall of the . . . Earle of Essex* (1646), unpaged [p. 3].

33. Richard Vines, *The Hearse of the Renowned, the Right Honourable Robert Earle of Essex* (1646).

34. *A Perfect Relation of the . . . Funerall of the . . . Earle of Essex*, unpaged [pp. 4–5].

35. Snow, *Essex the Rebel*, pp. 493–5.

36. For an account of Rainborowe's life and death see, Gentles, *The New Model Army*, pp. 270–2 and *passim*.
37. BL, Thomason Tracts, E473(9) *Mercurius Elencticus*, 15–22 Nov. 1648, p. 504.
38. BL, Thomason Tracts, E474(7) Thomas Brooks, *The Glorious Day of the Saints Appearance* (1648), pp. 1, 20 and *passim*.
39. For samples see, *In Memoriam Thomae Rainsbrough ... Chiliarchae Fortissimi; An Elegie upon the Honourable Colonel Thomas Rainsbrough; A New Elegy; Colonell Rainsborowes Ghost; An Elegie upon the Death of that Renowned Heroe Coll. Rainsborrow*, all published between 12 and 20 Nov. 1648, and BL, Thomason Tracts, E473(8) *Mercurius Militaris* 14–21 Nov. 1648.
40. BL, Thomason Tracts, E473(7) *Mercurius Pragmaticus*, 14–21 Nov. 1648, unpaged.
41. BL, Thomason Tracts, E473(9) *Mercurius Elencticus*, 15–22 Nov. 1648, pp. 503–4.
42. Gentles, *New Model Army*, pp. 326–9.
43. V. Harding, '"And one more may be laid there": the location of burials in early modern London', *London Journal*, XIV (1982), 114, 119. I am grateful to Dr Harding for conversations about funerals in early-modern London, and for permitting me to read her unpublished papers, 'Death in early-modern London' and 'Burial of the plague dead in early-modern London'.
44. BL, Thomason Tracts, E552(21) *Kingdomes Weekly Intelligencer*, 24 April–1 May 1649, p. 1334.
45. BL, Thomason Tracts, E553(1*) *A Modest Narrative of Intelligence*, 29 April–5 May 1649, p. 35.
46. BL, Thomason Tracts, E529(29) *The Impartial Intelligencer*, 25 April–2 May 1649, pp. 68–9; E529(31) *The Kingdomes Faithfull and Impartiall Scout*, 27 April–4 May 1649, pp. 105–6; E552(12) *Mercurius Pragmaticus*, 23–30 April 1649, unpaged; E529(32) *Every Daies Journall*, 27 April–3 May 1649, p. 1006; E552(20) *The Moderate*, 24 April–1 May 1649, p. 483; E552(15), *Mercurius Pragmaticus (for King Charles II)*, 24 April–1 May 1649, p. 15; E552(21) *Kingdomes Weekly Intelligencer*, 24 April–1 May 1649, p. 1334.
47. BL, Thomason Tracts, E529(34) *Perfect Diurnall*, 30 April–7 May 1649, p. 2469.
48. Harding, 'Death in early-modern London', pp. 5, 7, 20.

Index